To: Libby —
I hope you love your return to Green Hills!
Love & hugs,
Ashli

IN THE TRENCHES

BOOK 2

VIRGINIA'DELE SMITH

BOOKS ARE UBIQUITOUS

Book 2: In the Trenches Copyright © 2022 by Virginia'dele Smith

All rights reserved. No part of this publication may be reproduced, distributed or transmitted in any form or by any means, including photocopying, recording, or other electronic or mechanical methods, without the prior written permission of the publisher, except in the case of brief quotations embodied in critical reviews and certain other noncommercial uses permitted by copyright law.

BOOKS ARE UBIQUITOUS

Published by Books are Ubiquitous, Inc.
Tulsa, Oklahoma in the United States of America
www.booksareubiquitous.com
contact@booksareubiquitous.com
Books are Ubiquitous is a federally registered trademark.

This book is a work of fiction.

Names, characters, places, and incidents either are the product of the author's imagination or are used fictitiously. Any resemblance to actual persons, living or dead, business establishments, events, or locales is entirely coincidental.

ISBN: 978-1-957036-08-3

Titles by Virginia'dele Smith

Book 1: Grocery Girl

Book 2: In the Trenches

To the best man I know.

*PJ, to write this book,
I borrowed your capacity to care,
your devotion, your patience,
your favorite movies, your love of football,
and even your three flaws.*

Now everyone will know what I already do:

I'm the luckiest girl in the whole wide world!

1

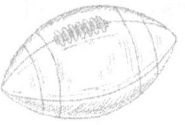

*What if everything you see is more than what you see—
the person next to you is a warrior
and the space that appears empty is a secret door to
another world?
What if something appears that shouldn't?
You either dismiss it,
or you accept that there is much more to the world than
you think.
Perhaps it is really a doorway,
and if you choose to go inside,
you'll find many unexpected things.
Shigeru Miyamoto*

Max Davenport was running.
Away from the press.
Away from social media.
Away from Mary Beth.
Max Davenport was running home.

The drive from Kansas City usually took five hours; today he'd made it in just over four. Four hours and fourteen minutes to be precise.

Usually, Max took his time to enjoy the trip. He appreciated the gorgeous route along the western edge of the Ozarks, down into Tulsa's green country, and finally into the thick, lush terrain that gave Green Hills, Oklahoma, its name.

Today, however, he simply wanted to get there. To a place of peace and tranquility, where photographers didn't chase him, and where he could enjoy the slow pace of a small town and an empty house.

He loved his life in Kansas City — he really did.

From as far back as he could remember, he'd fantasized about playing professional football. Now he got to live the dream. He'd earned the spot as the starting tight end for one of the most successful teams in the NFL. They'd won two of the last three Super Bowls, had a talented team with great camaraderie, and had managed to retain a fabulous coaching staff through the boom.

It was fun, and it was fast-paced. It was also hard work, long hours, and very intense.

On top of football practices, strength and conditioning workouts, mobility and yoga sessions, film study, game prep, and meetings, there were community service projects, media engagements, and more interviews than he could keep up with.

And there was Mary Beth, a renowned restauranteur in Kansas City.

Both being rather famous in Kansas City, and both being rather active in the local social scene, Max and Mary Beth had each been aware of the other, but they'd never been introduced before. In fact, they'd never even spoken in passing.

The night they'd first officially met, Max had been asked to represent the Chiefs' organization by appearing at a fundraiser. The event took place at one of Mary Beth's incredibly popular restaurants.

Truth be told, "restaurant" was a bit of a misnomer for this particular establishment. Josephine's was a Prohibition-style supper club that featured jazz and big band music, singing, dancing, and phenomenal American cuisine. A lively, happening lounge with a rich, soulful ambiance, it had great energy.

Max and Mary Beth had been seated side by side at the head table. They'd spent the evening talking and laughing throughout an amazing seven-course meal. He was one of the best-known bachelors in town. She was young, successful, and stunningly beautiful. People noticed.

With a plethora of photographers, journalists, and gossipmongers present, several photos were taken — both posed and candid. Whispers and speculations were running amuck by the time coffee and desserts were served.

The final piece of the night's program was a celebrity date auction.

Max avoided these things like the plague, but tonight's event focused on raising money and increasing education to end Alzheimer's disease, a cause near and dear to his family. Their beloved friend and pseudo-grandmother, Sadie Jones, had been widowed by the fatal disease, and Janie Lyn, one of the boarders at her home, the Marshall Mansion, had made it her mission in life to serve families living with ALZ. Max's sister, Maree, and Janie Lyn spent a lot of time together over the past year and had grown quite close. When he'd told them about this opportunity, they'd begged him to do it. Of course, he'd agreed.

The celebrities were being auctioned off for an evening of dinner and dancing at Josephine's. Max was one of a group of candidates — professional athletes, a few local news anchors, the two most popular local radio deejays, one famous author, and a half-dozen A-list actors and singers who lived in Missouri and Kansas, all eager to see to whom they would go.

The whispers about Max and Mary Beth became roars when he stepped on stage and the bidding began. With a calculating look in her eye, Mary Beth clearly intended to win. A few other ladies in the crowd jumped into the fray, raising their bidding cards for one thousand, two thousand, four thousand dollars. Then, seemingly tired of playing the game, Mary Beth stood, raised her card high in the air, and announced, "Twenty-five thousand dollars."

The room went silent. A statement had been made.

Max clapped and cheered, all the while fighting an urge to tug on his collar.

"Wow," he said, sitting back down at their table. "You've already done so much to make tonight a huge success — that was a very gracious donation."

"All for a good cause," she responded. "Besides, I feel certain you're worth it."

Again, his fingers itched to loosen his tie. He needed air.

One of the administrators from the local Alzheimer's Association came to congratulate Max and thank Mary Beth. With her busy in conversation, Max had an easy escape from the table. He circulated around the room, visiting with teammates and friends, dancing with a few of the players' and coaches' wives, and smiling for lots of pictures.

When the band announced their final set, Max scanned the room, looking for Mary Beth. No reason to put off the inevitable. Honestly, why all the effort to resist?

Mary Beth was amazing. Tall, lean, and lithe, she still looked like the college track star she'd been at Kansas State. Her eyes were the deepest, darkest brown, and her skin resembled caramel velvet. Tonight, she had her hair out, and it was something to behold. With her shoulders back confidently and her smile dazzling the room, she resembled a royal African princess adored by all her subjects.

He could admit that while he felt a little intimidated, he also felt a little smitten. She was smart, accomplished, and kind. The auction date would be fun; in fact, he knew the auction results could have turned out *much* worse.

They'd gone on their date that same week and had a wonderful time.

The food was again fantastic, the Duke Ellington tribute band playing that evening had been incredible, and their conversation flowed easily and naturally. He'd been worried for no reason at all.

Mary Beth wasn't looking for anything more than Max was wanting out of a new friendship. And that's all it needed to be: a friendship.

When he'd taken her home after their "date," there hadn't been an awkward moment. Mary Beth, relaxed as always, reached out to give him a brief hug and brushed a slight kiss on his cheek, thanking him for a fun date. He'd genuinely enjoyed himself and had offered to meet her for lunch whenever she had a day off. She'd said that sounded good, and he'd said, "Good night."

Max had felt like he was on top of the world.

He'd driven to his town house, changed out of his suit, and let his dog, Hank, out in the back courtyard to do his thing. Everything was great.

Until he'd opened his phone.

It lit up like the Fourth of July. He'd been tagged in numerous posts, tweets, and photos of his evening with Mary Beth. They were being touted as a "power couple" and "the face of new love."

What?

Max's stomach churned.

He'd been so careful throughout the years, making *absolutely* sure that he didn't — even accidentally — lead on the girls he dated. He wasn't looking for a long-term relationship. He didn't want to be half of a couple; nor did he want to be the face of any kind of love. He wanted to play football, spend time with his dog, and hang out with his family.

But the internet wasn't having any part of that.

Within a couple of days, more photos from the fundraiser surfaced. One photo gave the impression Max whispered sweet nothings into Mary Beth's ear, when in reality, he'd turned his head around to answer a question from the waiter standing behind them. Another zoomed in on his hand on her lower back, *above* the low V of her open-back dress, while he guided her to the table after the auction. The caption read, "A lover's touch, as soft as silk."

With each new "report," Max felt more and more hunted, exposed for something imagined and unreal.

When he and Mary Beth met for lunch, Max hoped they could nip this thing in the bud. Instead, his hopes were dashed when Mary

Beth confessed that she agreed with the paparazzi. She thought they were great as a couple, had fun together, and should give it a shot.

He sat dumbfounded as she chattered on about attending a tennis match together on Saturday morning, another fundraiser they should be seen at Saturday night, and brunch at Josephine's on Sunday.

"We've never even had a real date," he stammered.

"Oh, Max, we fit like a glove," she said, waving away his objection.

She enjoyed being caught up in the limelight, whereas he couldn't breathe.

He had to get out of there.

He had to go home.

"*I never should have done that auction,*" he repeated to himself over and over as he sped toward Green Hills.

But that had not been an option. Maree might have been disappointed, and he definitely couldn't let Janie Lyn down. His sister liked and respected Janie Lyn very much, though she didn't know where she'd come from, or even how old she was — her deep Southern accent was Maree's only clue.

Through her volunteer work at the local memory care facility, Janie Lyn had proven herself to be a champion of those who could no longer speak for themselves. She might look eighteen years old in her braids and thrift-shop overalls, but she had a keen mind for logistics. She'd organized several Alzheimer's awareness events in Green Hills, helped Maree with a quilt collection for fundraising, and started hosting support group meetings for community members faced with the struggles of caregiving.

Not only had she made a huge impact in their town, she'd also been integral to the completion of the remodel of Max's house there. A 1930s Craftsman-style home, it had three bedrooms, three full baths, a huge wraparound porch, a brick *porte cochere*, and a carriage house that would someday be turned into a detached garage with an apartment over it.

When Max found it a few years ago, the entire property had been in bad shape. The floors required refinishing, the masonry needed new mortar, all the appliances were inoperable, and the wall coverings were atrocious. Worst of all, the hand-carved trim throughout the house — the intricate designs formed by hours and hours of skilled labor — was covered in coat after coat of thick paint, which muted its beauty and the craftsmanship that made the structure so unique.

Max did as much of the work as he could during the off-season. He loved researching a technique and learning about how the house would have originally been built. He wanted to preserve the warm, welcome feeling of home that he'd sensed the first time he walked into it. So far, Max was pleased with the progress. He liked how he'd paired the best of the home's history with modern amenities that fit the look, feel, and theme of the property and his neighborhood.

After stepping in to assist Maree once when painters needed access to the house, Janie Lyn had essentially become his project manager. No one had given her that title; they'd never even discussed that she'd take over the scheduling and tracking of contractors. It had happened organically, and Max no longer knew how he'd managed without her help.

No, he hadn't had an option when it came to that fundraising event. He owed Janie Lyn way too much to disappoint her by declining an opportunity to support the cause she cared so much about. He'd had no choice, but now things were totally out of control.

Hence the reason he ran.

Max pulled into the drive, parked, turned off the ignition, and let out a deep exhale. *Ah, to be home.*

He grabbed his bag from the back seat, unlocked the side door of the house, and opened the fridge, looking for something to drink. His day improved another notch when he saw that someone had been at the house and left an almost-full pitcher of sweet tea. He grabbed an insulated cup, filled it with ice, and poured tea to the rim. He took a long, deep drink, then refilled the tumbler and set the lid in place.

He planned to hop through the shower, grab swim trunks, and hit his new pool. He'd helped design it last winter, but he'd not yet seen the project finished. Janie Lyn had a landscape architect finishing the green spaces, but the pool was ready. Max could not wait to jump in.

Refreshed from his shower, he put on the shorts, grabbed his tea and his sunglasses, and walked toward the wall of glass windows and doors overlooking the backyard from the living room.

Max was shocked to find someone already out there. Not just some*one*, but some woman!

She stood on the edge of the pool with her back to the house. Her one-piece swimsuit was a deep shade of orange. The shade reminded Max of the poppies planted in the front flower beds, and the style looked like something straight out of an Esther Williams movie. A treasured memory of watching those with his mom, many years ago, flashed through his mind, but the vision in front of him quickly replaced it. Strapless and gathered, the swimsuit showed off a pair of strong legs, muscular shoulders, and a perfect tan. Thick dark hair hung in cascading waves down her back.

When she dove in, Max slid open the door and walked toward the pool, stunned but curious. Very curious.

She swam to the back wall and performed a precise kick turn without breaking stride. She swam to her starting point, reached for the edge of the rock coping, and hoisted herself up to the deck in one smooth motion.

"Janie Lyn?" Max asked, astonished. This was *not* the young girl who wore nothing but old t-shirts, overalls, and Chuck Taylor Converse. She was voluptuous. Grown-up. And gorgeous.

"Oh!" Her head snapped up in surprise. "Maxwell," she breathed his full name. "You're home."

2

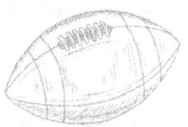

I make little account of victory.
Nothing is so stupid as to vanquish;
the real glory is to convince.
***Les Misérables* by Victor Hugo**

*J*anie Lyn swiped her hair back from her face, gathering it into one hand, twisting it at her shoulder to wring it out, and dropping the length of it to rest on her collarbone and trail toward her waist. Max had seen her do the habitual motion dozens of times before...when she studied a project, analyzed a problem, or talked on the phone. This time, however, doing it sluiced water down her body, literally from head to toe. There were even droplets on her eyelashes, thick eyelashes that framed innocently bright green eyes.

Max froze in a stupor. She definitely did not look anything like the version of Janie Lyn he'd become accustomed to. Suddenly, and seeing her in a whole new light, he couldn't stop staring.

"I'm so sorry." Janie Lyn jumped into motion. She stumbled over herself, grabbing a towel to cover up and scooping up her belongings like the Tasmanian Devil on Saturday morning cartoons. "I had no idea you planned to be here this weekend. I—"

"Hey, slow down." Max snapped out of his trance and reached out to stop her whirlwind. She stilled the moment his hands touched her shoulders, her chin tucked to keep her gaze on the patio floor. "No one knew I was coming; I didn't even call ahead to warn Maree. Honestly, I hadn't planned on it myself. I just had to get out of Kansas City," he explained, bending down to force her to look at him.

Had he noticed her small stature? Not fragile. No, she reflected strength, a force to be reckoned with when supervising contractors and dealing with suppliers and inspectors. He had seen that first-hand. *Petite*, he decided; that word seemed to fit her better. But not short. No, just perfect.

And her eyes. Hidden behind the thick tortoise-shell glasses she always wore, he'd never seen them clearly. Janie Lyn's green eyes were mesmerizing, so pale that Max thought they were almost translucent.

"It'll only take a few minutes to pack up my things. I'll be out of your way. I'm s—"

"You're not in my way," he interjected. After dreaming of isolation and solitude, suddenly he didn't want her to leave. "And I hope you already know that you're welcome to enjoy the pool anytime you want. It wouldn't even be here without you!"

"Actually, I've been staying here," she confessed. "I thought Maree had spoken with you to make sure you wouldn't mind. I'm so sorry!"

"I *don't* mind," he reassured her. "And please, stop apologizing."

She considered for a moment and then gave a slight nod of agreement.

"I've been staying here the past couple of weeks to create more space at Miss Sadie's. She opened Marshall Mansion — the entire house — to the Jensen family. They lost their home in a fire. Luckily, no one was injured, but they lost everything. Between the husband and wife, their four young kids, and his mom who lives with them, the boarding house was the best place for them to land.

I offered to stay at the lodge out on the lake, but Maree wouldn't hear of it and set me up here instead. I feel terrible that no one asked you first."

"I'm glad Maree strong-armed you. I would have said the exact same thing if I'd known what was happening. Come on now; sit down. Please," he added, taking all the stuff out of her arms, setting it at the foot of the chaise lounge, and pulling a second one a little closer to sit on himself. A sigh of relief lightened his chest when she did as he asked. "It's a gorgeous day. Let's enjoy it by the pool. Please, tell me you'll stay?"

"Well—"

She continued to deliberate, so Max shifted gears, hoping to stall her decision, if nothing else. "The front yard looks just how we envisioned it. I can see they're making good strides back here. How's it been going?"

He congratulated himself on his clever tactic when she turned to point out the landscape work taking place. She still hugged the towel to her chest and lap, but the worry lines between her eyebrows relaxed. Her eyes shone with excitement as she described her vision in both aesthetics and function. She painted pictures in his mind of how the finished backyard would be. Together, they seemed to be creating quite a showpiece.

She explained the process the masons would use to complete the outdoor kitchen and described the magnificent bluestone boulders on order. They would be cut into huge, natural pavers to create a walking path through the yard and gardens. Then the leftovers would be crushed into pebbles to pack under the custom wooden benches around the outdoor fireplace.

It was the most he'd ever heard her say in one conversation, and he enjoyed seeing the project from her perspective. She tended to blend into the background, never drawing attention to herself, never moving too quickly or saying too much. He really liked this new energetic side of her quiet personality.

"It's going to be fabulous," he agreed. "It would have taken me a decade of off-seasons to create what you've done in a few months. Thank you, Janie Lyn," he added with admiration.

He saw the veil of shyness settle over her. She seemed unsure what to do with his compliment and gratitude.

"I need a refill on my sweet tea; what can I get you?" Max rose to head for the house.

"I really should go so you can have your house to yourself," she said, bypassing his question.

"Nope. You're stuck with me," he countered. "Now read your book, and I'll be right back."

3

I am not what you see.
I am what time and effort
and interaction slowly unveil.
Slaying Dragons by Richelle E. Goodrich

Resigned, Janie Lyn did as Maxwell instructed. It was hard to say no to him. Especially for her. She'd had a crush on him since the moment she arrived in Green Hills.

Staying safe meant keeping her identity a secret, so she did her level best to be invisible. Janie Lyn dressed like a teenager, spoke softly, and never made eye contact. She was easy to overlook, easy to forget.

Ignoring her silent pleas for anonymity, his loved ones had pulled her into their fold with open arms. Even though they considered her part of the family now, she'd been able to maintain a secure distance from Max and all the cameras that went wherever he did.

Janie Lyn worked behind the scenes to help with his remodel project. She'd overseen the pool construction, working only with local contractors, and she'd built a life for herself that was both feasible and fulfilling. Janie Lyn might never live *in* a bubble of love, but she could support the people she loved. She could be close to them, help them, and experience joy through their accomplishments. It was enough. It had to be.

And yet, suddenly, her day felt different. Better. Full.

Maxwell Davenport. He was the reason.

Max had always been friendly and kind to her. He called regularly to talk to her, to make decisions for the house. He stayed in touch to check on Maree and her boyfriend Rhys, Miss Sadie, and the rest of their extended group.

This time, however, they were talking *with* one another. He could have — and *should* have — let her leave when he arrived. He didn't have to give up his peace and quiet for her. But he'd been adamant about convincing her to stay, and he seemed glad that she had.

Janie Lyn couldn't help but smile. This kind of different felt good.

"If I'd been paying any attention when I poured my tea the first time, I'd have known without a doubt that someone much more cultured than I was living here!" Max set a large acrylic tray on the small table between their lounge chairs. The tray was stacked with fresh fruit, a bowl of salted crisps, a variety of cheeses, a knife, and two paper towels neatly folded in thirds. "I'm not sure what all we have, but it looked great, so I brought it out. I also opened a bottle of wine to let it breathe inside for a minute. Wait, you are old enough to drink wine, aren't you?"

"Maxwell, how old do you think I am?" She was intrigued to hear his answer.

"I honestly do not know," he said with wonder.

"Hmm," she responded. "Well, I'm old enough to enjoy a glass of wine."

"That's it? You can't give me any more to go on?" He was teasing her. Maxwell Davenport was teasing — no, flirting — with *her*.

"Sorry, I was told to read my book, so that is what I must do." She smiled, picking up a clump of crisp green grapes and opening her book to ignore him.

"Will music bother you?" His voice revealed a sense of peace when he asked the question. He sounded happy.

"Not at all," Janie Lyn assured him, without looking up from her page. "Just make sure it's something good," she teased.

She could hear him chuckling as he walked back to the house to turn on the outdoor sound system. His laughter was a pleasant sound. Deep and rich, but still light and playful. She knew he'd had a rough childhood, losing both parents in a fatal car accident when he was only ten years old. Since then, he'd assumed the role of provider and protector for his two younger sisters. He'd shouldered a heavy burden his entire adolescent and adult life, yet he still had an open happiness about him. Janie Lyn could appreciate that; it wasn't easy to preserve that approach to life after heartbreak altered one's path.

He'd selected a Texas Red Dirt station, the songs a little country and a little outlaw. She liked his rough, raw edges just as much as his affable, go-with-the-flow demeanor. In all honesty, she liked everything about Maxwell Davenport. Everything *except* his job.

Not his job, *per se* — she enjoyed the game of football just fine — but rather, the celebrity that came with Maxwell doing his job at such a high level. He was a star, an actual all-star, invited to multiple all-star games. At one, he'd been named the MVP of *all* the all-stars playing that day. Like a beacon of light to the world around him, people noticed Maxwell Davenport, and they were drawn to him.

He not only lit up a room, he filled the space. Janie Lyn had noticed moods lift and spirits lighten whenever he walked in. Wherever he went, people flocked to be in his presence. Everyone wanted to be close to Maxwell Davenport.

It wasn't simply his athletic celebrity. Max was the life of the party because he was a good man. He was outgoing, yet he never monopolized the conversation. He was a skilled listener, and because he paid such attention to the person speaking to him, that person felt appreciated and important. Max made everyone feel comfortable, like they were his best friend. So, everyone loved to be around him.

Including Janie Lyn. She wasn't immune to his charms. Like

everyone else, her mood lifted and her spirits rose in his presence. Since she'd faded into the background after settling in Green Hills, it had been both easy and fun to watch Max interact with the world without being noticed herself.

He was very observant, seeing nuances and connections that others seemed to miss. He was also patient, giving people all the time they needed to tell their tale or find their way. When Maree and Rhys had been falling in love last year, Max had been watching out for his baby sister while also being supportive and understanding of Rhys's fears. In addition to being a good man, Maxwell had a good heart. He was kind.

He was also diligent; Max worked hard at everything he did. Whether mowing the lawn, remodeling the house, or preparing for football, he got after the task at hand. He never hesitated to jump into whatever needed doing, and she'd noticed he never quit until the job was done right.

On the other hand, Max wasn't perfect. A protective big brother, his sister M'Kenzee described him as overbearing and nosy. He could be a picky eater, especially if meat and potatoes were missing from a meal. And he was more than a little hardheaded; in other words, he liked to get his way. Max didn't "put his foot down" often, but when he had an opinion or a preference, he expected it to be heard and heeded.

No, Maxwell Davenport was not perfect, but Janie Lyn found him quite impressive.

And no wonder, really. Compared to the men in Janie Lyn's family, Maxwell Davenport was, as Miss Sadie would say, the bee's knees.

"Your wine." Max interrupted Janie Lyn's thoughts. She'd been daydreaming — about Max — and had not turned a single page in her book. She set it facedown across her legs and reached out to take the acrylic glass.

"Thank you, Maxwell. This looks wonderful," she said.

He loved the way Janie Lyn used his full name. She was the only person who did that. Somehow, it made him feel as though she saw him differently than anyone else. As though she saw all of him, not *just* a big brother, or *just* a professional athlete, or *just* a bachelor to be chased.

"Yeah, I didn't realize how hungry I was until I saw all the groceries in the fridge. You must like to cook."

"I do. Bake, actually. I love to bake," she replied.

Max waited, hoping she would keep talking, hoping to learn more about the person she hid from the rest of the world. When she remained silent, he gently prodded, "What is your favorite thing to bake?"

"Oh, goodness," she said on an exhale. "I guess breads are my favorite. Baking bread is a process. It takes time to make the end result really memorable. I like working the dough, rolling it, kneading it, watching it rise."

"Is it true that you have to punch it? I saw that in a movie one time and have thought on several occasions that I needed a big ball of dough when I had the urge to pummel something. Or someone," he admitted with guilt.

"Oh, yes," she answered. "Although, I like to be a little kinder to the dough, pressing it down rather than punching it with force, gently working it with my hands."

Max's body warmed with the image her words formed in his mind, a picture of Janie Lyn's hands massaging…anything.

"Let's make some." His voice croaked, making her look at him in question.

"What?"

"Let's make some bread," he said after clearing his throat, thankful that his voice went back to normal.

"Now?" Her accent gave it two syllables, making it sound like *nay-ow* and causing Max to feel flushed again. It also made him realize he sounded ridiculous.

"No," he said with a laugh, "not now. Later. This evening. How long does it take? I'll run to the Get'n'Go to get us a couple of steaks and baked potatoes for dinner. We can make bread to go with it, *after* we've enjoyed the pool. Will it be done in time if we do that?"

"Maxwell, you don't have to do that." Her Southern drawl was like catnip to Max, luring him in with every syllable. "I don't want to crash your weekend. I'll go stay with Maree. She won't mind me borrowing her couch."

"When I asked you to stay, I didn't mean just for the afternoon." Max looked her straight in the eye and spoke with clarity and intention. "Now, can we make homemade bread for dinner? Do we have enough time?"

For someone who rarely looked up from the ground, Janie Lyn impressed Max. Her eyes met his without hesitation. She didn't shy away, which was refreshing. He'd found that most women cowered or played coy around him. Mary Beth hadn't, which had been one reason why he'd enjoyed her company so much. There was nothing meek about Mary Beth. And while Janie Lyn gave off the impression she was docile, he knew that was not the case — not even close.

I guess I have a type, Max marveled to himself. *I like strong women.*

Max figured that while he was having an epiphany of self-discovery, Janie Lyn was weighing her options, or maybe his sincerity. When she finally gave him a nod, tangible joy spread through his chest.

"Sure. I know a great recipe that doesn't take too long to rise and bake. We should probably allow a few hours to make it, start to finish," she said, still looking directly into his eyes. He experienced a surge of relief at her agreement to stay, at least through dinner, and had no intention of letting her leave after it.

Max felt more relaxed and more at home after one hour with Janie Lyn than he'd felt since meeting Mary Beth. On top of that, Janie Lyn had been living in his house to help Miss Sadie and those staying at Marshall Mansion. This was essentially Janie Lyn's home — at least for the time being. There was no way he was letting her leave this weekend. And he wasn't above charming, begging, or negotiating to get his way.

"Perfect," he said. "Enjoy your book — I might lie back here and close my eyes for a minute — and we can start the bread in a couple of hours. Maybe around four o'clock?"

"Sure, that will work. I can get cleaned up and run to the grocery store while the dough is rising. And then you can punch it down before we bake it." She was teasing him. And smiling. Those both had to be good signs.

Max was thrilled. So happy that he didn't have words. He just smiled and nodded in agreement, reclined the top of his lounge chair, slid on his sunglasses, and laid back to relax. He loved the way she wove a fun, teasing thread under words that could've been as plain as day. He loved that she couldn't convince herself to leave, that she acquiesced in good nature. He loved that she was staying.

Wait— *Loved?*

4

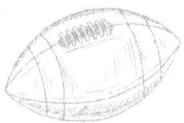

*The ache for home lives in all of us,
the safe place where we can go as we are
and not be questioned.*
Maya Angelou

What are you doing? Janie Lyn questioned her sanity. *What are you thinking?*

Looking over at Maxwell as he dozed on the chaise, she shook her head. He was larger than life. And she couldn't live large. She'd imagined spending time with him, thought a lot about him since meeting him when she'd arrived in Green Hills. To an outsider, she supposed it would look like a schoolgirl crush on the popular football player. But to Janie Lyn, it went much deeper than that. She couldn't be part of his life, but she could love him from afar. That much she'd known from the moment she'd laid eyes on him...

Janie Lyn had been riding a bus as far as she could get from home, planning to go all the way to the West Coast. But when the bus stopped in Tulsa, Oklahoma, along Route 66, she'd felt called to take a break from running.

She'd walked downtown from the bus station, discovering a

thread of hope and a sense of foundation she hadn't expected to find anywhere. Even though it was just past noon, Janie Lyn was craving breakfast and had just ordered a sandwich that was best described as brunch — a fried egg with lettuce, tomato, avocado, and bacon on a croissant — and a cinnamon roll for dessert when the two ladies in the booth behind her started talking about a quilting retreat they were excited to attend that weekend. They talked about a lakeside resort in a town called Green Hills. The two women painted an image in her mind of a magical place where the people were caring and kind and where the pace of life allowed one to breathe. Their descriptions of the thick green trees and the sparkling water on the lake sounded like a dream. Their plan to sit on the dock in old wooden rocking chairs, watching the sun set each night as they sipped a glass of wine and listened to the cicadas was the final straw. Janie Lyn had to see this mystical town and its purported beauty.

She was lost in their conversation when her food arrived. "Here you go," the waiter said, breaking through her trance as he set the plate in front of her.

"Oh my! That looks amazing," one woman said, prompting Janie Lyn to twist around in the booth to smile in response. She guessed the ladies to be in their midforties, both wearing University of Tulsa t-shirts with a *Homecoming 2019* logo on the front. Like the people they'd described from Green Hills, they looked caring and kind. It was something in their body language, something intangible that Janie Lyn sensed was genuine.

"And here's the rest...hot out of the oven and just iced," a second waiter said, setting a huge cinnamon roll on Janie Lyn's table. It looked ooey and gooey and smelled like heaven.

"Oh my is right! There's no way I can eat all of this," Janie Lyn announced. "Would you mind taking it to the kitchen to cut it into thirds?" She asked the waiter. "Ladies, I have to confess that I overheard you talking and was so taken with your descriptions that I became caught up in your conversation. I've been sitting here eavesdropping. I'm so sorry — let me clear my conscience by sharing this mind-blowing cinnamon bun. Please?"

The women exchanged glances. And then smiles. Then they grabbed their purses, their plates, and their sweet tea glasses and slid into Janie Lyn's booth. Sitting across from them, Janie Lyn felt their appraisal. They deserved to check her out after she'd so rudely listened in on their lunch date. She couldn't help but wonder what they saw. Did they see the fine fabric of her sweater and blazer? Or did they only see the wrinkled, rumpled creases caused by sleeping on the bus the past few nights? From their viewpoint, was she a young woman with rich brown waves of thick hair, or merely a ragamuffin who needed a brush and some makeup? Did she appear to be someone grabbing lunch in the middle of a normal day? Or someone running for her life, escaping everything — and everyone — she'd ever known?

"We'd love to!" One woman reached across the table to shake hands as she introduced herself. "I'm Rachel, and this is Suzanne. It's nice to meet you." Her expression was welcoming.

How odd. They don't even know me, yet they are so open and accepting.

"I'm Eliz—Jane—ie. Janie." She paused, figuring it out for herself. "I'm Janie. Lyn. It's nice to meet you, too." She smiled, albeit a shy smile, and tried to look convincing. If they noticed her stumbling over her own name, Suzanne and Rachel were too polite to comment on it.

"Well, with that luscious accent, you can't be from Oklahoma. I'm guessing Mississippi?" Rachel had a gleam in her eyes as she cocked her head to the side and studied Janie Lyn a little more.

Grasping hold of the lie, Janie Lyn simply nodded in agreement. *It's not a sin if you don't say the lie out loud.* That was the code she and her friends had used as children, to justify sneaking around and living out grand adventures no one would have allowed if the grown-ups had paid any attention to what they were doing. How had life come so far off the track? When had the train derailed? And why hadn't she felt the impact in that moment?

"I like your t-shirts. What a clever design," Janie Lyn said, hoping she could get Suzanne and Rachel to talk about themselves, rather than ask her questions she couldn't answer.

"Aren't they fun?" Rachel responded. Janie Lyn could tell she was the bubblier, more effusive of the two ladies. Janie Lyn nodded around a bite of her sandwich.

"We might spend too much time together," Suzanne started, "but we haven't dressed like twins in a very long time." She raised an eyebrow at Rachel; obviously, they had been close friends for a long time. "We came from a planning meeting, and the whole homecoming committee wore these for a photo. I swear, it took longer to get the blasted photo done than it has taken to plan the entire three-day event. If only they'd done what I—"

"We've been there, done that. I'm just glad I lived to tell the story," Rachel interrupted. Suzanne waved a hand at her to shoo away the sentiment. "Don't let her fool you — we've dressed the same a million times, and she loved every single occasion. Suzanne is my big. We met in college, and now we work together, so she's stuck with me for life." Rachel beamed at her friend.

"Your *big*?" Janie Lyn was lost at first. "Ah, your big sister." The lightbulb in her mind came on; one couldn't grow up in genteel Southern society and not know the definition of *bigs* and *littles*.

"Yes, my big sis in our sorority," Rachel said, confirming Janie Lyn's guess. "She's a year older than I am. When I went through rush and pledged her chapter, she chose *me* to be her little." Rachel was beaming again.

"Actually, she was selected for me. I tried to tell them she was too silly and boisterous and obnoxious, but the new member chair liked to prove she was in charge — particularly where I was concerned — and made me take Rachel." Janie Lyn had set down her sandwich to listen to Suzanne's side of the story. These ladies were so honest! Janie Lyn worried a little about Rachel's feelings.

"It was the best gift I ever received — besides my husband and kids, of course," Suzanne admitted. "A little sister *and* a best friend for life. I thank God every day that He didn't let me talk my way out of getting Rachel as my little." Rachel put her arm around Suzanne and forced her into a sideways hug. Suzanne relented cheerfully.

"We were both in the nursing school, which the university is famous for, but it's also very tough." Rachel took over the narration. "Suzanne being a year ahead of me was integral in getting me through. I have dyslexia, so I struggled to put the information I knew on paper. I'd never have made it through without her." Rachel's eyes glistened, and Janie Lyn blinked back the warmth of tears in her own eyes.

"Oh, phooey," Suzanne said with dismissal. "Rachel is brilliant, can hear instruction one time and never forget it. She has a photographic memory, and her mind crunches numbers like a calculator. If you ask me, academia puts too much emphasis on assessment and not enough value on comprehension and capability." She was rather indignant on Rachel's behalf.

"Yes," Rachel said in a teasing tone, "I'm sure Janie Lyn can tell I'm the smart one, and you're just riding my coattails." That got all three of them giggling, reassuring Janie Lyn that Rachel's feelings were far from hurt. It was evident the two friends shared admiration and a deep respect for one another.

"So y'all stayed here in Tulsa after college?" Janie Lyn resumed work on her sandwich and the homemade sweet potato chips served on the side.

"Oh yes, I married my college sweetheart and started my nursing career the summer after graduation," Rachel answered first. "Tommy is an attorney in town and works with domestic violence victims. I'm so proud of him and all he does to help those in need. We have two babies, a boy who's four and a girl who's about to turn two. They are the axis my world revolves around. I am a lucky and blessed girl." Janie Lyn envisioned the happiness and fullness of Rachel's life through her words and tone. Rachel obviously cherished her family and the life she'd built. Janie Lyn recognized that as a gift she had most likely sacrificed by running away.

"I actually left for a few years," Suzanne said. Rachel lightly bumped Suzanne's shoulder in support. "I followed the wrong man to the wrong place for the wrong reasons."

"But you're here now. You've wrangled the most wonderful man to be your husband, along with his three fabulous kiddos to love as their bonus mom. And we are headed to a quilting retreat for the weekend," Rachel said, redirecting the conversation from what Janie Lyn guessed must be a painful experience for Suzanne to rehash.

"It sounded amazing from what I overheard." Janie Lyn tried to look chagrined for her rude behavior, but she couldn't be too sorry since her rudeness had led to sharing time with these women and getting to hear their stories.

"Oh, it is!" Rachel lit up as she spoke. "Everything about this weekend is wonderful. We—"

"You should come with us," Suzanne exclaimed. Both Rachel and Janie Lyn looked at her in surprise. Janie Lyn hadn't known the woman for more than thirty minutes, but she sensed that inviting a stranger on a weekend away was out of character for the no-nonsense nurse. "She should," Suzanne reiterated, turning to look directly at Rachel. "You know Sadie has plenty of room at the mansion, and if Janie Lyn doesn't have other plans for the next few days, she should join us." The emphatic tone in her voice brooked no argument.

"But I don't know how to quilt," Janie Lyn said, letting them off the hook of Suzanne's impromptu invitation.

"Well, that doesn't matter as there aren't any spots left at the resort center," Suzanne admitted. "Every bed and workspace is taken. But there is room at Marshall Mansion, a bed-and-breakfast just outside of town you'll absolutely love. Take the weekend, relax; enjoy Green Hills for what it is: an indulgent escape from the pressures of life. If you don't mind squeezing in the back seat with sewing machines, suitcases, and tubs of fabric, you can ride with us. When we're finished quilting Sunday afternoon, we'll stop by to see Miss Sadie for a cup of tea and pick you up to drive back to Tulsa. It'll work out perfectly!"

"Wow," Rachel responded. She looked dumbfounded, but not necessarily *against* the idea. No, she was definitely *for* the idea. She just seemed impressed — and a little miffed — that it had come from Suzanne and not herself.

"Wow!" Janie Lyn echoed. "I feel compelled to say *no*; that's the polite thing to do. But my manners seem to have gone missing in action today. I really want to say *yes*." Where had all this "do what you want" strength come from all of a sudden? Talk about out of character!

"Then say *yes*," Suzanne encouraged.

"Come with us," Rachel chimed in.

"When are you leaving?"

"We hit the road first thing in the morning. Do you have a place to stay tonight?" Suzanne asked.

Janie Lyn's suspension of manners and good upbringing could only go so far. She would not let them shuffle her home with either of them tonight.

Besides that, Janie Lyn couldn't help but wonder: how could Suzanne tell she wasn't from Tulsa? How did she know Janie Lyn was essentially homeless now? Was it that plain to see?

"Yes, I have a hotel room, just down the street," Janie Lyn lied smoothly.

"Perfect. We will give you our cell phone numbers. You send us the hotel address, and we will text when we are on our way in the morning."

"No!" Janie Lyn spoke so forcefully that both women looked up, Rachel from her last bite of cinnamon roll and Suzanne from rummaging in her purse. "I mean, I will probably come back here to the diner for breakfast — the food is great — so we could meet here in the morning. If that's okay with y'all?"

Rachel and Suzanne shared another knowing glance. Then they nodded, and that was settled.

The next day, as they were delivering her to Miss Sadie at Marshall Mansion, Janie Lyn met Maxwell Davenport.

Sharing that cinnamon roll with Rachel and Suzanne altered the trajectory of her life. Miss Sadie called things like that "God's work." Janie Lyn didn't know about all that — she'd done a lot of praying in the past with very few answered prayers to show for it — but she did know something in her universe had shifted that day. She was pretty certain Maxwell Davenport had been at least part of the catalyst for that shift.

Since then, she'd cherished her time with him, treasured the opportunities to get to know him. She looked forward to their phone calls and fondly remembered everything he'd shared with her: every story about his family and teammates, every idea for the house, and every hope for his future. She'd spent an embarrassing amount of time creating full conversations with him in her head, rehearsing all the things she longed to say.

Janie Lyn liked everything about Maxwell. To her, he was a dream come true. And the hour they'd just spent together talking — and flirting — by the pool proved that while she'd built him up to grand heights, she still had not given him enough credit in her dreams. *He's so much more in real life.*

5

*Where there is love
there is life.
Mahatma Gandhi*

"Knock, knock? Janie Lyn? Are you home?" Poking her head around the front door to announce her arrival, Maree called out to the empty space after using her key to Max's house to let herself in. She was balancing a large shipping box on one hip while removing her key from the lock and then giving the door a gentle kick to close it. "Hello? Anyone?"

"Hi, Maree," Janie Lyn greeted her, walking around the corner from the kitchen. "Oh my, here, let me help you with that!" She rushed over to Maree and took one end of the cumbersome box.

"Thanks! Guess what just arrived at the shop?"

"Something heavy would be my first guess. Something old and something precious would be my second and third." Maree heard the anticipation and giddiness in Janie Lyn's answer.

"You would be right with all three!"

"Let's set it on the breakfast table. I was just washing vegetables to make a salad," Janie Lyn said.

"Is Max here?" Maree asked. "I saw his truck in the drive."

"Yes— I can't believe you never asked him if I could stay here!" Janie Lyn accused, her tone incredulous.

"I meant to. I was going to. I just never got around to it," Maree confessed. "I'm sorry. But it wouldn't have mattered. He would have said *yes* if I had remembered to ask."

Janie Lyn responded with one raised eyebrow as they set the heavy box on the table. She moved to grab a pair of scissors from the gadget drawer to very carefully cut the packing tape. "I felt terrible when he showed up to find a stranger in his house. Not just *in* his house, but swimming in his pool and sleeping in his guest room. I was mortified."

"Don't be silly. You're not a stranger, and I know he didn't mind a bit." Maree started unpacking the box. Janie Lyn's silence made her nervous. Max had a huge heart. He was kind to everyone, all the time. No way he'd been anything but polite when he arrived to find Janie Lyn borrowing his home. "Did he?"

Janie Lyn didn't answer. Maree shifted to look past the bundle in her hands, only to find Janie Lyn mesmerized by the quilt they took out of the box. Maree couldn't help but smile. She shook out the quilt a little so Janie Lyn could get a better look. That prompted Janie Lyn to reach out to lift the heavy fabric draping on the floor; her eyes never left the quilt top. Maree loved seeing the rapture on Janie Lyn's face. And Maree had to agree, the quilt was sensational.

"Janie Lyn?" Max called, walking through the door from the backyard. "Oh," he exclaimed, switching gears when he entered the kitchen to find his little sister. "Well, there she is," he said to Maree, obviously surprised to see her.

"Yes, here she is," Maree answered, not sure if she was playing along in their routine greeting to one another, or if she was pointing out that he'd found what— no, make that *whom*, he was looking for: Janie Lyn. "But why are *you* here? You said you couldn't make it back to Green Hills over your open week. And where's Hank?"

"We had a great practice yesterday, and we don't play until a week from Sunday, so they cut us loose. After dropping Hank off last week, he is officially in residence at the Willow Creek Retrieval

Academy in Baxter Springs, Kansas, learning to be a loyal yet manageable guard dog. He's only been gone a few days, and I miss him like crazy… It's going to be a rough three months," Max explained as he gave her a hug and kissed the top of her head. "On a whim, I decided that a few days at home were needed, threw some stuff in a bag, and hit the road. When I got here, Janie Lyn was enjoying the pool. She— It— Looked— The water— *The pool* looked really good…"— a man known for not dropping the ball sure seemed to be fumbling —"…so I joined her. I guess I fell asleep for a minute."

Maree narrowed her eyes at Max. She cocked her head to one side, waiting out his bumbling commentary and surveying the situation. She was intrigued. Particularly because Max's eyes never left Janie Lyn.

"Hm," was all Maree said for a second. "Well, I'm glad you're here! I came by to drop off a package for Janie Lyn that was sent to the studio and to invite her to Rhys's house for dinner tonight. Now you can join us, too." Maree smiled.

"We, uh, kinda already have plans," Max stammered.

"Do you now?" Maree asked.

"Yeah… Janie Lyn was going to teach me how to make homemade bread. Then we were going to run over to the Get'n'Go for a couple of steaks to throw on the grill."

"You were going to bake bread. And then go grocery shopping?" Maree spoke very slowly. Her disbelieving tone got Max's attention.

"Yes," he replied. The look he turned on her was one of her favorite big brother glares. It screamed "don't go there" which meant she must razz him a tad bit more.

"That's perfect!" Maree exclaimed. "You bring salad — since Janie Lyn already has it started — and the fresh bread that I can't wait to try. I'll stop to pick up two more steaks on my way home."

"*Home?*" Max picked up on that word in a flash. "Your home or Rhys's home?"

"Ever the protective big brother," Maree said sweetly as she winked at Janie Lyn, who'd not said a word since Max had entered the conversation. That was par for the course; Janie Lyn was coming out of her shell around their group — their beautifully pieced family — but she still said very little and often tried to sink into the background.

That was one reason Maree had stopped by to invite — and force, if necessary — Janie Lyn to dinner. They'd been spending a lot of time together the past several months. Ever since Maree's knee replacement after a devastating car accident, Janie Lyn had been a wonderful friend and a huge blessing to Maree. Janie Lyn had taken over the coordination efforts on Max's house remodel, she'd handled all the business transactions that couldn't be postponed at Maree's company, Main Street Design, and she'd kept Maree company for countless hours.

That last part had been the most helpful. Janie Lyn had brought food and meds like clockwork, which had allowed Maree to remain hooked into a continuous motion contraption that her surgeon had sent home with her. The CPM machine had moved Maree's surgery leg for her, bending and straightening her knee joint for eight to ten hours a day. Her doctor attributed her outstanding range of motion and wonderful joint function to getting so much passive exercise. For Maree, that time had been her best rest. She'd been miserable trying to sleep in bed, in a recliner, or on the couch. She'd never been a back sleeper, so the inability to turn over frustrated her. During the nights when she should've been sleeping, she'd ended up watching TV…cooking shows and competitions, a full twenty-three-episode season of her favorite drama, and too many romantic movies to count. Then she'd spent all day sleeping with the motion of the CPM. Every time she needed a bathroom break, a bite to eat, or another round of pain pills, Janie Lyn had been right there to help her.

Maree's memory was foggy from those weeks. She'd had a terrible time with the narcotics necessary to manage her extreme pain levels. She couldn't remember everything she'd seen on the television or even the specific meals Janie Lyn had served, but she did remember Janie Lyn had stayed right by her side every moment Rhys had been at work.

Rhys's boss, Fire Chief Everett, had granted Rhys time off for the entire first month of Maree's recuperation. But a week into that time, a string of fires had disrupted their quaint and quiet town. Green Hills, Oklahoma, was a community of friends and neighbors who supported and encouraged one another, but over the past year, a serial arsonist had emerged. It was unfathomable that a local resident was responsible, but it was true nonetheless. Someone had started by setting fire to a couple of abandoned buildings. After a dilapidated barn, a few hunting blinds, and an empty warehouse had burned down, the Green Hills Fire Department announced that all the recent fires had been the work of one person.

Just before Maree's knee replacement surgery, the firebug had stepped up his game by trying to start a fire in town. He'd placed multiple tinderboxes in the alley behind a row of shops that faced the square downtown. One of those shops was Maree's two-story studio and apartment, where she designed and sold quilting fabric in the storefront downstairs and lived upstairs. Luckily, a neighbor had noticed a strange man loitering and digging through the dumpster. She'd called Maree, who'd called 911 in time for the fire department to arrive and put out the starter fires before the buildings had caught fire, too.

No one was hurt, and no damage had been done that day. But only two weeks later, the fires had started up again. This time in the city park and empty fields outside of town, but they had the same signature. Green Hills was still on the lookout for a criminal set on burning their beautiful town.

Rhys had refused to leave Maree at home alone so soon after her surgery. Maree had insisted he go back to work. She'd spent most of her day sleeping, and they needed him at the station. In the end, he'd agreed only when Janie Lyn had offered to stay with Maree during his shifts at the fire station.

Janie Lyn had been a godsend. More than that, she'd become a very dear friend.

One who deserved a strong, charming, handsome, funny, warm, and loving man. A man just like Maree's big brother.

Liking where her thoughts were heading, Maree beamed her signature smile at Max and Janie Lyn.

"Janie Lyn, your new, old quilt is fabulous! I've never seen an antique quilt in such pristine condition. I'm leaving it with you and heading to the Get'n'Go." Maree plopped her half of the heavy quilt into Max's hands as she spoke. "We'll have the steaks ready at seven thirty, but y'all come over whenever you — and that fresh bread — are ready. Rhys can even open another jar of my strawberry jam to celebrate... If I don't ration him, he goes through it faster than I'm able to make it!"

"What are we celebrating?" Max asked, sounding a little shell-shocked by Maree's exuberance and the whirlwind of motion she'd created.

"Why, family, friends, and love, of course," Maree answered with a quick hug for both Max and Janie Lyn, and then she was out the front door, humming a tune as she climbed into her seat, buckled her seat belt, and turned on the ignition. She gave her phone a moment to connect to her car — a new full-size SUV with all the latest safety bells and whistles as demanded by both her brother and her boyfriend after the accident.

She was happy to be driving again! The surgery, the rehab, the physical therapy, and especially weaning off the pain pills had been so much more than anyone could have explained or she could have imagined. When people asked her about the entire ordeal, her best description was simply that it was *more*. More difficult, more challenging, more painful, more everything. Her surgeon had explained that a knee replacement was one of the most difficult surgeries to undergo, and the procedure was considerably harder for young people than the traditional knee replacement candidate in their sixties or seventies. Younger bones were denser, and nerve bundles were more intact, making them worse to cut through. He told her that because of practicing yoga, Maree was more in tune with her body than his typical patient, more aware of the trauma her body was going through. Therefore, she felt more of the pain. *More, more, more.*

There had been days she'd wondered if she could do it, if she could stand the pain, the constant discomfort, the cloudy mind that refused to clear. She had wondered several times if that feeling of confusion was similar to what someone living with dementia felt every single day. It was terrifying.

For weeks after she quit using the narcotic pain medications, she'd doubted she'd make it through the withdrawal symptoms. What textbooks predicted would last for ten to fourteen days had lasted a full nine weeks. The temperature shifts were debilitating. She'd been beyond miserable, going from sweating with a fever to shaking with chills. The jittery sensations like she was coming out of her skin were unlike anything she'd ever known. For the first time in her life, Maree sensed what someone fighting addiction or dependency must go through. She felt firsthand how tremendously difficult it must be to survive, much less succeed, when fighting those demons.

Again, the whole experience was just so much *more* than she'd expected.

And yet, she had done it. Maree had managed the pain and the withdrawal symptoms. She'd done the hourly exercises, trudged through the months of physical therapy. She'd rehabbed her new knee to the very best it could be. Her surgeon called it a "top one percent of all prosthetic knees in the world," which made her very proud. Maree was back to walking up and down stairs, back to practicing yoga, and back to driving.

But she'd not done it alone. Maree's support network — Rhys, Miss Sadie, her sweet friend Landry Stark who also lived with Miss Sadie, Max, and especially Janie Lyn — had been vital to her achieving her postsurgical goals. She was absolutely certain that without them, without their love and support and encouragement, she'd have failed miserably.

She treasured and cherished each one of them. She wanted their lives to be as rich and full as hers. They'd helped her build a beautiful life here in Green Hills, and she wanted to give them that same gift.

Maree hit the button on her console to make a call before putting the vehicle into reverse to ease out of Max's drive.

"Hello?"

"Are you still going to be here in time for dinner?" Maree greeted her sister with a question.

"Yes," her sister, M'Kenzee, replied on the other end.

"Oh good! Guess what I just saw?"

6

> *I was made and meant to look for you*
> *and wait for you*
> *and become yours forever.*
> *Robert Browning*

"I think a tornado just swept through here," Max said, shaking his head to clear it after his sister's whirlwind visit.

No response.

"I mean, I'm incredibly grateful she's doing so well! She seems completely healed and back to her usual self," he added.

Still no response.

"But wow — she was rolling!" He waited for Janie Lyn to say something.

Anything.

Max was still holding up the quilt in front of her, so he couldn't see her face. When she remained silent for another long minute, he dropped his hands to bring the quilt below his eyes. Doing so unveiled a sight that had his heart lurching.

Tears streamed down Janie Lyn's face, yet her eyes still hadn't left the quilt.

"Janie Lyn? What is it? Are you upset about having to go to Rhys's for dinner? I know Maree just barreled through like a steamroller; I'll call her right now to say we aren't coming. You— We don't have to go."

That broke her trance. She looked up into his face with a weak smile, her eyes full of anguish.

Max didn't know what was wrong, but her raw sadness was killing him.

He gathered the quilt and set the heap onto the table so he could step closer to her, one hand reaching out to hold hers, the other lifting to her cheek. He wiped away her tears.

"Hey, whatever you're feeling, it's okay," he soothed. Then he folded her into his arms, hugging her against his chest.

She wasn't as short as Maree, probably even taller than average. But next to Max's six-foot, four-inch frame, she was just the right height to nestle perfectly under his chin. Her shoulders shuddered as she tried to stop crying. He held her tighter, telling her without words that she could let it all out.

Max had essentially raised his two younger sisters. They'd been orphaned when he was ten years old; M'Kenzee had been seven, and Maree only five. Over the past twenty years, he'd learned that sometimes a hug was all one needed, that sometimes words were not helpful or even necessary. He was a fixer by nature, so it was tough to stand still, remain silent, and simply listen to Janie Lyn work through her emotions. But he didn't mind. He wanted to be there for her, as she had been there for him so many times over the past months with house projects and Maree's ordeals. Janie Lyn was a good friend to their family. Max wanted to be the same for her.

His body didn't seem to agree. At least not on the "be a friend" part.

She felt really good in his arms.

She'd looked so gorgeous rising out of the pool when he arrived.

And she was fun to be with, quiet yet engaging. She was kind.

And funny. She liked to tease him in an understated way, a way no one else did. And she was smart — brilliant.

Max had always found uncompromising, clever women attractive. He attributed that to his sisters as well. M'Kenzee and Maree had very different personalities, but both were intelligent, savvy, and quite capable. Without a doubt, Max considered all three ladies a force to be reckoned with if someone was dumb enough to go against them.

Yes, Janie Lyn was a lot like his sisters in several ways.

Again, his body didn't seem to agree. The way it felt was decidedly *un*brotherly.

Dragging his thoughts away from the softness of her skin, the silkiness of her hair, and the heat emanating from her body into his, he realized she'd stopped crying and gone still. Max loosened his arms and eased back to look down at her.

He didn't want to overstep, but he couldn't stop himself from wiping her tears away, tracing his thumbs across her cheeks, and then lifting her face to catch her gaze.

Emotions still roiled through her eyes, through her jagged breaths. But a sense of peace seemed to settle over her like a soft sheet shaken out in the breeze now drifting back down to earth.

"Better?" Max needed to drop his hands from the sides of her face. He meant to do just that, but the velvety softness of her skin was like a magnet to his fingers. They continued to trace her cheekbones and to dry stray tears that escaped.

Janie Lyn nodded and even managed a small smile. She was utterly gorgeous.

"You know, Maree would be very irritated to see that you are what she calls a comely crier. When we watch movies, she is forever moaning in envy about how pretty some actresses are when they cry. She claims it's not fair that some people can look lovely when they are an emotional wreck while she resembles Rudolph the Red-Nosed Reindeer." Max was happy his story made her small smile grow a little larger.

"I can hear her saying that," Janie Lyn said. They were her first words since Maree had left over twenty minutes ago. "That girl and her movies; she loves them."

Max was relieved Janie Lyn sounded more like herself, soft-spoken yet strong.

"It might be a family trait," Max confessed, shrugging as he dropped his hands and took another step back to give her some space.

"Do you watch the same ones over and over? Maree is the worst! I've known her less than two years, and I already know she is incapable of turning the channel past *Pretty Woman, 9 to 5, My Fair Lady,* or anything in *The Fast and the Furious* series."

"What??" Max teased. "No one in their right mind clicks over *The Fast and the Furious!*"

Bad English began crooning "When I See You Smile" in his head. Should he further confess that in addition to being a movie junkie, he was a sucker for classic rock, in particular '80s hair bands? There was just something about her — her quiet grace, her competent strength . . . her smile. Being around Janie Lyn brought him joy.

"Is that so?" She moved to the table and began to fold the quilt. Max grabbed two of the corners to help. "What other movies cannot be, as you put it, *clicked over?*"

Now this was a topic he could expound upon.

"Oh, where to begin . . . *Road House, Top Gun, Point Break,* and *White Christmas.* Almost any sports movie, but definitely *The Natural, For Love of the Game,* and *Remember the Titans.* Every *Rocky* movie! There's *Hitch, Ocean's Eleven, The Thomas Crown Affair* — either version because both Steve McQueen and Pierce Brosnan are great — *The Italian Job, Days of Thunder,* and *The Matrix.* Oh, and *Gladiator*! I would never ignore *Gladiator.*" Her eyes grew to the size of saucers. A look of wonder had replaced her sadness. He would list movies to infinity and beyond to keep that expression on her face. "More recent releases include *King Arthur: Legend of the Sword* — you know, you kinda remind me of Mage — and *Ford v Ferrari.*"

"Wow!" Janie Lyn looked adorable in her astonishment.

"Oh, that's not all. Of course, there's *Tombstone, Lonesome Dove*—"

He broke off in a gasp of near pain. "There are just too many westerns to whittle it down to a mere list."

"A mere list," she repeated with emphasis. "Oh, my. I do believe you are even worse off than your sister." Janie Lyn was shaking her head, a look of amazement on her face. "Did I hear *White Christmas* in there?"

She took the folded quilt out of his hands and set it back into the shipping box.

Now empty, both of his hands flew to his chest, stacked over his heart.

"Mmm." His eyes closed for a moment to savor the image in his mind. "The Haynes sisters fluttering those huge feather things around, singing in the inn while Bob and Phil don't have a clue what's hit them. It's a classic. Our parents loved it." His voice changed when he mentioned his parents. His volume dropped softer, his words came out raw. "Every single year we popped popcorn and made hot chocolate, both on the stove, the old-fashioned way. Then all five of us squeezed onto the couch to watch. No one could talk — or even run to the bathroom — once the show began." It had been a wonderful life. Now it served as a treasured memory, a memory he hadn't thought to share with anyone else even though he, M'Kenzee, and Maree made it a point to continue the tradition, albeit with microwave popcorn and instant hot chocolate, no matter where they were for the holidays.

"So this is a hereditary affliction," Janie Lyn said, shaking Max from his reverie.

"Oh, yeah," Max agreed with fondness. "We get it from Dad. He was a tireless worker, so when he allowed himself some downtime, he loved to be entertained by movies and television shows. And he wanted us there with him, especially Momma. He never cared if the dishes were washed after dinner or if the laundry had been folded and hung up. He just wanted her nestled next to him on the couch. She had this one quilt that her grandmother gave them when they were married — Maree will have to tell you the story behind that quilt . . . it's a good one! Anyway, that quilt only left the living room to be washed, dried, and put right back on the sofa.

Momma was always tucked under that blanket, snuggling up to Dad's side. They were so in love. That's where Maree got her capacity to love, to believe that love conquers all. She was still a preschooler when they died, but she'd already absorbed that lesson from Momma and Dad, and she's never grown out of it."

"A love of movies might not be the only thing your parents passed down to all three of you," Janie Lyn said with a kind smile that Max took as a good sign. "I'm sorry for the crying jag. It was ridiculous, but hearing you talk about your mom and dad cozied up together makes me think that perhaps you'll appreciate the story of this quilt."

"Janie Lyn, you don't have to explain, and you don't have any reason to apologize."

"Well, I'm sure when you left Kansas City this was not what you hoped to find: a stranger living in your house, swimming in your pool, and bawling in your kitchen." Despite his assurances, her tone was still self-deprecating, tinged with a trace of embarrassment.

"You're a welcome surprise — crying, swimming, and all," he replied. "I promise," he added with certainty. He didn't want her to feel bad. Just the opposite, he wanted to do whatever it took to keep her smiling and talking. This was a new side of her he hadn't seen before. And he wasn't lying to placate her; he was glad to find her at his house, to notice her in a new light, and for this time to get to know her better.

Who was he kidding?

More than glad to find her here, he kept tripping over himself to impress her. He wasn't sure where the need to keep her close came from, but it was there, strong and steady. Without any effort, he could see this need for her developing into more, into something significant.

Many of the guys he knew would be running scared from this feeling. But Max had seen his parents together, watched how one of them lit up when the other entered the room. He'd listened to them talk to one another with genuine interest and respect. Even as a little boy, he'd felt their love for one another, for each of their kids, and for their family as a whole.

He wasn't afraid.

Max had been playing football his entire life and figured he'd taken a million tackles between practices, scrimmages, and games. He'd never enjoyed the impact of a hit more than the gut punch he'd experienced when he recognized it was Janie Lyn ascending out of his pool. He'd known from childhood what love looked like, known what kind of relationship he wanted for the long haul.

More than anything, Max was ready and willing to go after it — willing to fight for it if that was what it took. Love was worth it. Janie Lyn was worth it, too.

7

Without bread all is misery.
William Cobbett

Janie Lyn absorbed his kind words as she finished tucking the quilt back into the box and securing the flaps. "Thank you, Maxwell," she said, lifting the box into her arms.

"Where to?" he asked, taking it from her.

"Oh, I can put it in my room— your room— I mean, the guest room where I've been staying," she protested, embarrassed to be the one tripping over her words now.

"I've got it," he said with a wink as he turned to walk out of the kitchen.

"Thank yo—"

"Stop thanking me," he hollered over his shoulder.

Janie Lyn moved to the sink to finish washing the salad vegetables she'd just gathered when Maree had burst in. Janie Lyn meant to keep her eyes on the task at hand, mindless as it was, but his footsteps coming down the hall made her heartbeat race, and she couldn't stop herself from looking up when he returned. In addition to making her heart rate spike, his presence caused an unexplainable warmth to spread just beneath her skin. She knew her cheeks were glowing, or blushing, or both. *Good grief.* The smile on his face was truly happy; it reached his eyes, making them shine a crystalline shade of baby blue, and caused smile lines to appear at the corners. That big grin should have been reassuring, but somehow it made her more nervous. It made her long for things that could never be.

"How can I help?"

Maxwell stood hip-to-hip with her at the sink, reaching across her to squirt soap into his hands, and then working the soap into a lather that he rubbed through his fingers, around both wrists, and a good six inches up his forearms. It was riveting. She couldn't drag her eyes away.

"Well?" He reached across her again to snatch the tea towel she'd set on the counter. Her eyes followed the motion until he dried his hands, bent at the elbows, so that her eyes also caught the fine form of his chest under the plain white shirt he still wore with his swim trunks.

When she finally forced her eyes up to his face, his smile deepened to yet another degree. She froze in place, utterly speechless.

Until he winked. Knowing she was making a fool of herself, and knowing he knew it as well snapped Janie Lyn's attention from the hypnotic effect he had over her. She snatched the towel from his hands — which only made him chuckle — and turned back to her vegetables, the cutting board, and a sharp chef's knife.

"I'll chop these if you want to pull the ingredients to start the bread." *Surely, I can think rationally enough to remember the recipe.*

But of course she could. She'd made this a thousand times, maybe a million. She could bake this bread in her sleep . . . which was a little how she felt. The entire afternoon had been a dream, one she hoped never to awaken from, so it never had to end.

"Let me guess — flour, sugar, and eggs?" Maxwell moved toward the refrigerator.

"You're on the right track: flour, sugar, three eggs, salt, oil, and one packet of dry yeast," she said as he brought the egg carton back to the countertop. "It's in that cabinet next to the spices." She pointed across him to the upper cabinet by the cooktop and huge copper vent hood. As she pointed and turned in his direction, he turned in hers. Mere inches separated them. She held her breath, not in the least bit sure what she wanted to happen next. Her eyes fell to his lips, which were full and inviting and probably perfect for kissing. They were also turned up a little on one side; he was flirting with her and not hiding the fact that he was enjoying every second.

Her eyes darted back up to his, determined to prove herself immune to his charms, knowing good and well that she absolutely was *not*.

Again Maxwell chuckled. But he continued to gather the ingredients as well as measuring cups and spoons. Janie Lyn used the cover of chopping carrots, tomatoes, cucumbers, and yellow squash to reset her equilibrium and regain a clear head.

"We also need two mixing bowls — a small one and a large one — and a few sprigs of rosemary from the plum-colored pot on the back patio." He didn't say anything as he followed her instructions and collected everything she listed. She appreciated the space to take a full, deep breath when he stepped outside. He really did fill up a room.

"Is this enough?" He proudly showed her the two stems of herb he'd broken from the plant when he came back inside.

"Perfect," she replied. "Now plug in the stand mixer over there and grab the dough hook from the drawer beneath it."

"I didn't know I owned one of these," Maxwell mused before studying the mixer to clip on the attachment.

"Well, now you do," she confirmed. "Use that bowl to mix two and a half cups of flour, one tablespoon of sugar, three-fourths teaspoon of salt, and the yeast. You can let the dough hook do the work. Just turn it on low for a minute."

"How do you do that?" he asked with wonderment in his tone.

"You just flip the switch on the right side of the mixer."

"I can figure out how to turn the machine on," he grumbled. "How do you recite a complicated bread recipe to me while chopping vegetables like it's nothing?"

"Well, first of all, it's not a complicated bread recipe. It's just about the easiest bread recipe I've ever made. And secondly, I've been making it from memory since I was six years old. I don't think I could ever forget it, even if I tried." Her voice held a tired resignation that she hoped Maxwell didn't notice.

"I'm still impressed," he replied.

"Don't be," she responded, grabbing a small pan and filling it with a bit of water from the faucet and a short pour of oil. "Here, put this on the smallest burner over medium heat."

"How do you know how much water and oil to put in?"

"I just know."

"What if it's the wrong amount?"

"It's not." He was testing her for fun, and she couldn't help but enjoy their exchange.

"We'll see," he challenged.

"Yes, we'll see," she agreed. "Add two eggs to the mixing bowl and turn it on medium speed. As soon as the water starts to radiate heat, it's ready to be added to the mixing bowl, too."

"Should it make bubbles first?" She liked that Maxwell was taking their baking to heart, trying to learn and do a good job. She couldn't say why, but that meant a lot to her.

"No, water boils at 212 degrees Fahrenheit, and we only want the mixture to reach about 130 degrees, so you can set your hand above the water to see when it's warm. If you can feel heat coming off it, that is a good indicator it's ready." She finished tossing the chopped veggies with the lettuce she'd already put in a silver serving bowl and sprinkled dried cranberries on top before sealing the salad with plastic wrap.

"I think it's ready," Max said as she set the salad bowl in the fridge.

Janie Lyn joined him at the stove, held her hand over the water with his, and nodded in agreement.

Maxwell turned the burner off and slowly poured the hot mixture into the mixing bowl.

"Now switch the dough hook back to medium for a few minutes," she told him, heading back to the sink to wash up the cutting board and knife.

"That's a nice salad bowl," he said, picking up the tea towel to dry the two pieces she was washing.

"Yes, you splurged on that one"— she smiled up at him —"but Maree said you just had to have it." She emphasized the *had* for good measure.

"I bet I did," Maxwell agreed while nodding slowly, one eyebrow lifted in disbelief. The way he went along with the baby sister he loved so much endeared him to Janie Lyn even more. She found his good nature and kindness captivating.

The day she and Maree had seen the hand-hammered pewter palazzo bowl at the farmer's market, Janie Lyn had oohed and ahhed over it, commenting how perfect it would look on Maxwell's dining room table with its custom top made from an incomparable four-inch-thick reclaimed wood plank. Maree had immediately said they should get it for him, despite the enormous price tag. Janie Lyn had suggested they send him a photo and see what he thought. Maree would have none of it. She was determined that if Janie Lyn thought it needed a new home at Max's house, then that was where it belonged. Janie Lyn stood outside the market booth shaking her head as Maree paid for it with Max's credit card — the one they kept for remodeling projects and house purchases. On a whim, Maree had bought him the beautiful piece of culinary art while simultaneously making the artist's entire month with one sale. And now that he knew, he didn't seem to mind one bit. Janie Lyn didn't doubt he'd do anything in his power to make his sisters happy. And Miss Sadie. Indeed, he'd do anything in his power to make all his loved ones happy. That type of devotion was a priceless gift.

Janie Lyn checked the mixer to find their dough was ready.

"Sprinkle a little flour here on the island, and drizzle a little oil in the large bowl that you got out earlier," she instructed. "Now set the dough onto the flour and knead it back and forth, side to side."

"Like this?" Maxwell turned the dough hesitantly. He looked afraid to be too rough with it. Janie Lyn placed her hands over his and guided them to push the dough with more confidence. The warmth of their hands merged with the heat from the dough. The more they kneaded it, the smoother it became. Lost in the timeless motion of something she'd done so often throughout her life, she forgot to step back and let Maxwell knead the bread by himself.

"Sorry." She grabbed the towel, needing something else to hold. She was twisting and wringing it when he pulled it out of her grasp to set it back on the island.

"I'm not." His voice dropped, low and husky. Time slowed. Her breath caught. Their gazes held. She could drown in those pools of blue. It would be a satisfying way to go.

"It's ready."

"What?" Maxwell choked.

"Set the dough in the bowl and stir it around a bit to coat it with the oil; it's ready to rise," Janie Lyn explained.

He expelled a deep sigh. Had he been holding it in anticipation? Did the simple act of breathing become more difficult for him as it did for her when they stood this close? All the more heartbreaking if it did, since nothing could be done about it. No space existed for these feelings to grow.

"Now put a clean tea towel over it, set it there on the countertop where it's in the sun, and we'll check it in about an hour and a half," she added, determined to get her mind back on track. "In the meantime, I'm going to go get ready for dinner. Thank you for the help." A little distance couldn't hurt, either.

"Thank you for teaching me." She'd moved to walk away. The uncertain inflection in his voice had her turning back. "But when do I get to punch it?"

In all the heated and cozy moments she'd felt with him in the kitchen, she'd forgotten about his request to pummel something. Apparently, he had not.

"That's coming," she said with a laugh. The humor — which she knew he'd added on purpose — helped her relax. "It needs to rise to double in size. Then you get to add the rosemary and punch it down to get rid of air bubbles in the dough. After that we will divide it into pieces, roll the pieces into fat ropes, braid the ropes together, add an egg wash on top, and bake our bread. I'll be back in ninety minutes to help you," she promised and left for her guest suite down the hall.

8

***If you do what you love,
you'll never work a day in your life.
Author unknown***

*S**he has no idea.*
      Max shook his head in disbelief as he watched her turn into her bedroom and connecting bath. He needed to go shower and get ready for their dinner with Maree and Rhys, too, yet he was stuck in the middle of his kitchen. Watching bread rise.

Janie Lyn was the most beautiful, genuine, engaging woman he'd ever met. And she had no idea, which was positively remarkable. Perhaps that was the exact reason she was so classy and attractive to him.

One thing she must know: he *was* attracted to her. Like metal to a magnet. And he'd not bothered to hide it all afternoon. He wanted her to feel his gaze, to notice his pulse race when she stood in his arms, and to understand that he saw her now — truly saw her — not the version of herself that she presented to the world behind baggy clothes, obviously unnecessary glasses, and a little girl's braids.

Just the thought of how she fit perfectly into his hug, how her cheeks flushed anytime he stood next to her, and how she seemed to get lost in the moment when their gazes locked, had him wishing they were still standing in the room together. He simply wanted to share space with her, to be close to her. Shaking his head once more, he headed down the hall to his own master suite.

A cold shower it is.

Twenty minutes later and feeling refreshed, Max sat on the couch in the family room. He grabbed a yellow legal pad of notes and turned on the TV to study video from their last practice. It sometimes amazed him that after twenty years — starting with flag football at ten, two junior high teams during seventh and eighth grades, four years on the high school varsity team, three years of college ball, and the past eight years in the league — it never got old. He absolutely loved this game. He loved the challenge, the chess match that took place between the offense and the defense through sets and routes, blocking schemes, and tendencies. He loved scouting personnel, taking away their advantages and exposing their weaknesses. He loved the speed and the strength of the sport. He loved the locker room, the camaraderie, the coaches, the families, every bit of it. He felt blessed to be doing this game he loved as a profession.

His only regret was that his parents, particularly his dad, had never watched him play. The spring of his third-grade year, they'd signed him up for flag football, which would begin in the fall when school started back up after summer vacation. He remembered that day so clearly...

It was a Saturday morning, and they'd wanted to be first in line because he'd also had a baseball game later that afternoon. He'd woken up to the smell of bacon frying, one of his favorite smells in all the world. His dad was standing over the skillet when Max walked into the kitchen, his mom whisking eggs to scramble. Maree was laying out biscuits on a cookie sheet. M'Kenzee was setting the table and systematically presenting her arguments for why she needed — not merely wanted — her own camera, one that had a memory card instead of film, so of course she would *need* a computer and photo printer, too.

"Hey, Sport," Dad called out over a shoulder when Max shuffled in, hair still mussed and eyes still sleepy. "After breakfast we're headed straight to the gym to get you registered. Are you excited?" He already knew the answer, they all did. Max had talked of nothing but football for the past two weeks. But Max was also a bit nervous, so all he managed in response was a subdued nod.

Momma saw right through him, as always, and ruffled his thick, wavy sun-kissed hair. "It's going to be great, Maxwell. All you have to do is work hard, try your best, be a good listener, and have fun," she promised with a kiss on the top of his head.

"What if I'm not good at any of the positions?"

"What if you are good at several of them?" she countered.

"But, what if I can't remember the plays?"

"Then you'll ask your coaches to help you learn them," Dad replied.

"And what if I drop the ball?"

"You will definitely do that," Momma promised, to Max's horror.

"Everyone does, and more than once if you play for very long, Sport," Dad reassured. "That's just part of the learning curve. And for those who don't give up, the positions get easier, the plays become second nature. The ball becomes an extension of their arm, so they drop it less and less until they rarely ever drop it at all."

"So as long as I don't quit, I'll be okay?"

"That's right, son. Whatever you feel called to do, do it with a joyful heart, working hard and trying your best, just like your momma said, and you'll be better than okay. You'll be extraordinary."

"But why?" Maree asked in her tiny but scrutinizing way.

"Well, Angel Girl, the Lord puts a calling in our hearts—"

"Like my camera," M'Kenzee interjected to make her own point.

"Yes, like M'Kenzee's yearning to take pictures," Momma said with grace and patience. "God put that in her heart, and then it became part of her. It's the Lord's way of guiding us along the plan He made for each of us before we were even born. And if we follow His lead, by listening to our hearts and working hard on the calling He's placed there, then we will always be better than okay..." Momma spoke slowly to Maree, helping her to understand a concept billions of adults struggled with every day. When she locked eyes with Max and M'Kenzee in turn, holding one's gaze for a full blink before moving to the other, both knew her message was meant for them, too. They might've been young, but they knew their cue.

"We'll be extraordinary," all three children repeated together.

That summer before fourth grade, Momma took Maxwell to the sporting goods store to buy his first pair of football pants, and Dad taught him how to put the pads in the hips and knees. Then he showed him how to heat a new mouthguard in a warm glass of water to soften it before biting halfway down on it to shape it perfectly to Max's mouth. Momma showed him how to swipe on eye black to keep the sun from blinding him, even though Max insisted it was *not* like her makeup.

Dad spent hours and hours throwing the football to Max in the front yard, teaching him how to turn his palms out and watch the ball into his hands to finish the catch. All the while M'Kenzee took pictures of every flower, snail, and butterfly she could find with the camera she'd claimed God had put in her heart and Maree practiced riding her bike around the cul-de-sac. Those evenings after Dad got home from work and before the sun went down were the best moments of Max's life, before he'd ever played a down of football, and before he and his sisters were orphaned by a drunk driver, just days before his first game.

Devastated and traumatized by losing his parents so suddenly, Max had folded his football gear — the pads and pants, the helmet and mouthpiece, the jersey and the eye black — in a box and hidden it under his bed. On the day of the funerals, Max slid the box out to hold each item, remembering Momma and Dad helping him with each piece of equipment. He felt their love and excitement for him in a tangible way by touching that gear.

"Praying, are ye?" asked a booming voice that blended a Scottish brogue and a Texas twang in a unique way, a way that could only belong to one person. His best friend's dad, Mr. Stewart, had found him kneeling next to his bed with the box.

"No, sir," Max admitted. "Just looking at this stuff one last time."

"One last time, y'say?"

"Yes, sir. I've got to take care of the girls now. And there's no one to take me to the practices or games. I was supposed to do football with my dad. He volunteered to help coach. Momma was going to be our team mom. Without them, I don't really want to play anymore." Max's voice caught with brokenness and tears.

"Well, y'know, lad, your da and I signed up to coach you boys together, so I know he was right excited to see y'play," Mr. Stewart agreed. "Perhaps we give it a go — you, me, and Brennigan? I think your da would enjoy looking down upon that from way up thar in h'ven."

August had marked twenty years since the fatal car accident, and he was still at it, following the calling in his heart. And working hard meant studying, running, lifting, and catching even during an off week, so he'd asked the video director to upload a variety of practice and game footage onto his laptop to review over the long weekend.

"Which one are you?" Janie Lyn asked from behind the couch.

"Eighty-seven," Max answered, pausing the video so she could find him on the tape. "See the center, number fifty-six? He's right in front of the quarterback and has one hand on the ball. I'm three to the right."

"I see you," she said, coming around to sit on the couch next to him. He glanced up and saw her, too. She was back in baggy overalls — rolled up a few times at the ankle — and her worn-out canvas tennis shoes. The only concession to style was a long-sleeve, form-fitting forest green waffle tee under the overalls, one that hugged her curves and defined her toned shoulders and arms just right. The camouflage didn't work on him anymore — this time he saw the real Janie Lyn right through her facade.

"You can hit play," she said with a nod toward the television.

He ran the play at regular speed, then backed it up again. Next, he ran the play at half-speed.

"Well, what do you think?" He was intrigued to hear her answer.

"Can you play it once more, slow again?" So he did. "You were open by the sideline. Why didn't he throw it to you?"

"I was running a quick-out to the flats. Campbell was open on the corner route. That was the quarterback's first read."

"But he didn't score," she pointed out.

"That's true"— he grinned —"but we did get a first down."

"I bet you would've scored," she said, standing up from the couch and heading into the kitchen. She was arguing for him against the fastest receiver in the National Football League, and he liked it.

Max filed that fact away for later, turned off the TV, closed his laptop, and set it on the coffee table.

"Time to punch the bread?" He followed her to the sink to wash his hands again. This time she washed hers briskly and quickly, laid the towel across his shoulder, and moved to the island before he could even turn the warm water on. She'd effectively turned her back on him. He was getting to her, and he liked that, too.

"It's time." Janie Lyn uncovered the dough by gently lifting the tea towel over it. She looked up, gauging his reaction.

"It's huge," Max responded with a big smile and animated eyes.

"Which is why you may now punch it down." She slid the bowl toward him.

"In the bowl?"

"Yes, in the bowl. But before you do, let's add some of the fresh rosemary." She grabbed the two sprigs, handing one to Max. "Grab the end and slide your fingers down the stem to break off the needles." She did hers first, and Max copied her. "Toss your needles onto the dough."

After he did, she nodded and continued. "Make a fist and press it down into the center of the dough. You can feel the air bubbles deflating."

Max did as she'd instructed, amazed that they'd waited an hour and a half for the bread to rise just so they could push it back down.

"Now pull the edges of the dough back to the center where your fist was to shape the dough into a ball," she said, helping him and tossing in most of the rosemary needles in her hand before wiping her hands together, allowing the remaining bits of rosemary to fall to the floor. Max looked at her in wonder. She'd been meticulous all afternoon, washing every bowl and utensil the second they were finished with it.

"What? It's good luck," she protested.

"Really?" He'd never heard that before.

"Really," Janie Lyn assured him. "You can place a sprig beneath your pillow to ward off bad dreams, and you can place a sprig on the floor to ward off evil spirits. You can wear a crown of rosemary to ensure happiness, and you can give it to someone you fancy as a love charm—"

"*That's* good to know," Max interrupted.

"You can use it to cure both baldness and bad breath — neither of which you currently suffer from. It smells piney and fresh, and it symbolizes memories, love, and death, but that is my least favorite part of my favorite herb...its figurative connection to dementia." A sad shadow passed over her.

Max reached out to clasp one of Janie Lyn's hands to offer comfort. He knew how passionate she was about advocating for treatment and a cure to end Alzheimer's disease. She gave him a slight smile in return.

"Can we circle back to the part about making a love charm?" Max asked, lifting her hand to his lips and nose. "Mmm, lovely," he said as he brushed his lips over her fingers and took a deep breath to inhale the scent of rosemary that lingered on her skin.

She nudged his arm with her shoulder and reclaimed her hand. "Grab the flour container and dust a little flour here on the island; it's the best place to roll out the dough."

Max dumped a scoop of flour on the surface and tried to spread it evenly with a swipe of his hand. "Is that enough?"

"That's perfect," she affirmed. Her praise made Max want to pull back his shoulders and puff out his chest, so he did, which made her laugh. He was a big fan of that soft giggle. She didn't share it often, so hearing it was all the more impactful. "We need about one-third of the dough for the first braid; do you know how to braid?"

"Are you kidding?" Max paused to look down at her. Janie Lyn's lifted eyebrows continued to question him. "I raised two little sisters. When I'm too old and rickety to play football, I'm going to become a professional braider...pigtails, French braids, Dutch braids, fish-tails, ropes...I can do them all."

"Oh, wow!" Janie Lyn laughed even harder. The sound went straight to his heart, his chest feeling the impact like a block right to the numbers on his jersey. "I had no idea, but I'm relieved to know our bread is in safe hands," she teased.

He followed her lead to roll out three long strips of dough, Janie Lyn working with two-thirds of the original dough ball, and Max working with the remaining one-third. "Do I need to brush up on my technique with a six-strand braid?"

"No, silly." Max smiled.

When was the last time he'd felt relaxed enough to simply be silly? When had someone been uninhibited enough around him to call him out for it? These days it felt like everyone — besides his family and closest friends — walked on eggshells around him. He took his job seriously, and playing in the NFL created intense pressure. His buddies and teammates in Kansas City were fun and liked to unwind outside of work, but they were never silly together. Women were either throwing themselves at him or trying too hard to impress him; rarely did they let their natural personality show around him. Silly was a refreshing change. "I'm going to make a thick braid with this section, and you're going to make a skinnier braid with that section. Then we will stack them and let it rise for another thirty or forty minutes. The loaf will be gorgeous once it bakes with an egg wash on top."

"How long will it take to bake?" Max figured they had about an hour and a half before they needed to leave for Rhys's house.

"Twenty-five to thirty minutes. I'll set the timer for twenty to be safe. We might need to cover it with foil the last little bit if it's getting too dark on top. If we leave right after it's finished baking, the bread will still be warm when we get there. I'll clean up in here if you need to watch more football film," she offered.

"That's okay. I'm happy to help," he said, grabbing the glass bowl the dough had been in to rise and taking it to the sink.

"Maree says you're a tight end. And that you love it," Janie Lyn said as she reached across the sink and grabbed the sponge. She began wiping down the island, which was still dusted with flour.

He watched her move with practiced efficiency. Janie Lyn knew her way around a kitchen, and she was very comfortable in there. When she walked back to the sink, he grabbed the dish soap and held out his hand for the sponge. She gripped the sponge tighter and mimicked his gesture for him to hand over the bowl. "She's right. And you're a lot like her: bossy in the kitchen." He it said with a playful smirk, but he handed the bowl over all the same and picked up the clean dish towel to dry after she washed. "When I was young, I wondered how people did the same job every day for thirty or forty or fifty years. I was a seasonal kid — football in the fall, basketball in the winter, track in the spring, baseball in the summer — so I couldn't imagine a life filled with only one activity. When I got to college, football became year-round, but it never felt old. It was still seasonal — games in the fall, off-season and strength work in the winter, practice in the spring, conditioning/game-planning/camp in the summer — so I never got bored or burnt out."

"Maree says you live football all day, then you come home and turn football on to watch at night, and that when you get on the phone with friends, all y'all talk about is more football," she informed him, her accent doing strange things to his equilibrium again. He was enjoying how they worked in tandem, comfortable together in the kitchen. Although, being so close to her had an electrifying effect on him.

"Miss Maree seems to have a lot to say," he teased. "Do you talk about me often?" Max questioned, fishing for compliments, and they both knew it.

"She talks — she adores you, you know? And I'm good at listening. She also says you saved her childhood, that without you, y'all would've been separated into different homes and foster programs. She says you stood up to every judge and every social worker who ever tried to take the girls away from you. She says you never backed down from a fight if it meant protecting your family."

Max felt a dark heaviness pervade the air. He normally used affable humor to diffuse tension, but he wanted to be real with Janie Lyn, wanted her to know she could be real with him, too. He waited until Janie Lyn had moved the bread from the countertop where it had been rising to the oven so it could bake. After she closed the door and set the timer, he answered.

"I'm not sure it was ever a conscious decision. I just knew that Momma and Dad would want us to be together, loving one another as they had loved us. And I guess Maree's right, when it comes to fight or flight, I've never felt the urge to run. My high school coach said that trait was going to make me a lot of money someday, my love of living in the trenches. Of course, that was after I'd pancaked a defensive lineman from a rival school who had the audacity to talk trash about M'Kenzee across the line."

"In the trenches? Pancaked? Across the line? Are you still speaking English?" Her drawl intensified when she teased him. *Oh, Lord.*

"To pancake someone is to lift them off their feet and slam them to the ground, legally and in the midst of a play. Like this..." Max moved in front of Janie Lyn, and she stepped back until her hips met the island. His hands came up between them, and he gently grasped her overall straps. As his body pressed into hers, she naturally lifted onto her tiptoes. He looked directly into her eyes, watching the pale green irises darken to resemble emerald crystals. "Then you finish the block." He spoke softly. "The defensive lineman lands flat on his back, like a pancake, and the running back has a huge hole to run through. It's devastating, and it's beautiful."

"But *not* legal," she said. Max lifted an eyebrow and shifted his chin. "I believe that's holding," she said looking down at his grip on her overalls. It came out as *Ah baleeve tha's holed'n.* The words resembled warm honey oozing over his senses.

"Only if I get caught," he whispered. His right hand lifted to roll a lock of her hair between his thumb and fingers. He studied the strands before brushing the thick silk behind her shoulder and moving his hand to her jaw, his thumb sweeping over her chin, then feeling the velvety softness of her lower lip. Her chest trembled when she took a breath. He was a goner the moment she bit her bottom lip and then released it from between her teeth. He lowered his head, intending to touch his lips to where hers now glistened.

Right then, the oven timer beeped louder than a church bell.

Max and Janie Lyn jumped apart, hearts thumping like staccato beats of a drum.

She slid past him and grabbed hot pads.

Max stood in place, taking one deep breath, and then another, willing his pulse to regulate his heart's rhythm. When he turned around, Janie Lyn faced him, the oven door open between them. Either the heat of the oven or the heat of their near kiss colored her cheeks. She lifted the baking sheet to show him the bread.

"It's perfect." He was shocked. "We made perfect bread."

"You sound so surprised. Did you doubt me?"

"Never. I've witnessed contractors, landscapers, and plumbers all succumb to your wishes. I know better than to doubt you in any way," he pledged. "I might have doubted myself, though. Maree will never believe that I had a hand in making something that looks like *that*."

"Well, let's go test your theory. I'll wrap this in a flour sack, get the salad from the fridge, and grab my things. Give me just a minute, and I'll be ready to go." She whisked around the kitchen and dashed off down the hall.

He waited for her by the back door to the *porte cochere*, answering an email on his phone. When she emerged from her room, he slid his phone into his pocket and looked at her, head to toe and back again. He leaned against the door, crossing his arms to watch her walk toward him. She'd tied an oversized sweatshirt around her waist, put on her glasses, braided her hair into two plaits, and added a frayed and washed-out camo ball cap that had seen better days. The transformation was complete.

"Nice hat," Max murmured on a sigh of defeat.

9

> ***Friendship is certainly the finest balm***
> ***for the pangs of disappointed love.***
> ***Northanger Abbey by Jane Austen***

*M*ax pulled up to Rhys's house and immediately noticed touches of Maree. He could admit the midcentury modern ranch-style home was one of his favorites in this neighborhood. His dog, Hank, especially loved its location on the last street of the subdivision, backed up to woods that Hank happily explored for hours at a time without getting bored or tired. The gray paint and dark stained wood trim fit the setting perfectly. They lent the structure a sense of strength and foundation, rooted in the ground. The poppy-red door gave the property a burst of energy and enthusiasm — the exact shade of Janie Lyn's swimsuit earlier that afternoon. The homemade quilt and pillows on the porch bench and the numerous terra cotta and ceramic pots filled with vibrant fall flowers were all Maree.

Hmph.

"I'm sorry?" Janie Lyn inquired of his grunt. He hadn't spoken on the way over, hoping she was enjoying the ride and not sensing the plunge in his mood. They'd spent all day together, talking and sharing and being themselves. Then she'd retreated right back into her disguise. It rubbed him the wrong way.

"Did I say that out loud?"

"Well, you didn't say a *word*, but you definitely made a sound." She had a hint of sassiness about her, particularly when he was wound a smidge too tight. He appreciated that, liked that she didn't demur when he showed an emotion besides that of the easygoing, dumb jock next door. Very few people aside from his two sisters and his best friend were interested in him beyond the glossy image they saw in public.

"I was just noticing the flowers and the decorations. And the quilt on the ben—"

"It's fabulous!" Janie Lyn, eyes alight with enthusiasm, began talking a mile a minute. "I was researching vintage quilts online, looking for the one Maree brought over this afternoon, when I found this one listed through Goodwill. It wasn't finished; they were selling the pieced topper — do you know what that is?" She paused just long enough for Max to lift his eyebrows, creasing his forehead. It wasn't a full nod, but it must've been enough confirmation because she plowed right ahead. "True, the blocks were tattered and torn. Maree had to recreate a few of them. And the original assembly was fraying, so Miss Sadie had to do some mending on it. But it was listed for only fifteen dollars! Can you imagine?" She emphasized the *mahdge* in imagine, and his heart fell for her a sizable fraction more. She was offended on behalf of a half-shredded piece of fabric.

"Someone put their time and their effort into picking those fabrics, cutting each piece, selecting just this pattern, and then handsewing it all together. And when they couldn't get it completely finished, it was tossed aside and forgotten. I couldn't stand it, so I showed it to Maree. She agreed, so we bought it and worked together to match the style and tone of the original work in the repairs, choosing a backing fabric, and quilting it in a traditional motif. Like I said, Maree and Miss Sadie did the bulk of the work on it, but they taught me how to bind a quilt, so even I had a hand in that finished product. It's a piece of art."

"And Maree leaves it on the front porch?" That didn't seem smart after all that quilt had been through to simply exist in this world.

"Not overnight or in bad weather." She shook her head. "She brings it out in the morning, curling up in it while drinking a cup of hot tea. Then she picks it up to take inside after she waters the plants in the evening."

"Does she now?" His lips pursed and lifted to one side, but Janie Lyn didn't respond. She was already stepping down from the truck, bread bundle in hand. Max reached in the back seat to grab the huge silver salad bowl.

Max smiled when he saw a small note that read *Come on through - we're in the back.* Maree had signed the bottom with a sloppy heart and taped the paper on the massive double front doors, which were completely unlocked. Only in Green Hills could that still be safe in America. An integral part of the community's magic, neighbors in Green Hills looked out for one another rather than trying to one-up one another. It remained a place where friends took the time to check in, to be there for others when they needed a hand. Maybe there was something in the water, a special mineral in the dirt? Kindness bloomed in Green Hills.

Janie Lyn led the way through the house. Again, Max noticed bits of Maree's influence scattered here and there: another quilt folded on the couch; next to it, a tea tin that housed her sewing stuff like binding clips, quilting needles, a thimble and thread; a sketchpad for doodling and a jelly jar filled with colored pencils, in the center of the kitchen table; and two rolled-up yoga mats leaning in the corner.

Janie Lyn didn't look around or even hesitate, so she must've been there enough to feel familiar with the space. Max was aware Maree had convalesced at Rhys's house for five or six months after her car accident and knee replacement surgery. Had she ever moved back to her own apartment above her fabric design studio? Max's life moved quickly during football season, making it hard to keep up with what was going on in everyone else's world. What else might he have missed in addition to not noticing the *real* Janie Lyn, the gorgeous, spirited woman hiding beneath her "young and frumpy, invisible girl" routine?

"You made it!" Maree threw her arms in the air. "Here, set the salad on our makeshift buffet." She half strode, half hopped over to Max. "Well, there she is," she mimicked his usual greeting to her. Every word dripped with unspoken meaning.

"Mmm-hmm. There she is," Max conceded on multiple fronts...because Janie Lyn had agreed to join the party, but also because evidence of Maree could be seen in every corner of Rhys's house. Being the big brother was rewarding, but it wasn't always peaceful.

Janie Lyn unwrapped the homemade bread, folding the tea towel underneath it. There was a serrated knife next to a tub of butter and a tall jar of Maree's strawberry jam. Janie Lyn was cutting a few slices when Maree exclaimed, "Where did y'all buy that?"

"We made it," Max said, joining them to admire his bread-making success.

"You did not!"

"He di—"

"*We* did." Max corrected Janie Lyn. "Together." He said it pointedly, making sure Janie Lyn understood that the afternoon spent with her was significant.

"Let the party begin," a booming voice erupted from the side gate. Daniel Davis — simply known as Davis — was Rhys's best friend and fellow firefighter, and definitely enjoyed being the center of attention. He held the gate open for Landry. And behind her, Max and Maree's sister, M'Kenzee.

"What?" Max lit up. "I didn't even know you were in Oklahoma!" He jogged down the porch steps and scooped her up in a bear hug, squeezing until she protested and begged for air.

"Well, I'm here. Maree called and said you'd surprised her, so I figured turnabout is fair play."

"She looks good, doesn't she?" Max gestured toward their baby sister with a slight jerk of his head. They'd been through a world of tragedy and challenges in their relatively short lives. Then they'd been scared out of their minds when Maree was T-boned in a terrible car accident the year before.

"Better than good. She looks radiant. No one could guess what she's been through, how hard she's worked at physical therapy. That knee is almost as good as new."

"There's more to it than that. She looks happy, jubilant even. She's in love. The forever kind." He nudged her shoulder with his elbow. M'Kenzee had not hidden her displeasure with Rhys last year. She'd been furious with his tendency to give Maree hope only to walk away from her on multiple occasions. She hadn't pulled any punches when telling Rhys that he'd hurt Maree and didn't deserve her.

"Yeah, maybe," she begrudged.

"I'm happy you're here." Max put an arm around her and planted a kiss on the top of her head.

He walked over to the grill where Rhys was flipping steaks.

"Rhys." Max sounded pompous even to himself.

"Max," Rhys replied without looking up from the steaks.

"Looks like Maree is pretty comfortable around here." Had he ever sounded more like a stuffy, judgmental big brother?

"I hope so." Rhys lifted his head to look at Max directly. "I want Maree to make herself at home here. Actually, I'd like to talk to you about that." The steady cadence and rock-solid tone of Rhys's voice made Max's heart beat faster. He caught M'Kenzee's gaze and called her over with a discreet flick of his head.

"Hey, Rhys," M'Kenzee allowed when she came to stand between the two men.

"Hey, M'Kenzee," Rhys replied, again without looking up from the steaks.

"What's up?" She'd asked it conversationally, innocently. But Max knew that Rhys knew that everybody knew *something* was up.

"I've been waiting to get you in the same room for a few months now, a chance to talk without Maree listening in," Rhys began. Whereas Max's pulse was beating out of his chest and M'Kenzee's scowl had created creases around her eyes and lips, Rhys was one hundred percent relaxed. Happy, even.

"Whatever for?" M'Kenzee questioned.

"I think we all know what for." Patient as ever, Rhys simply grinned at the frown plastered on M'Kenzee's face. "I want to marry Maree. I want to build a life with her, start a family with her. And I want your blessings before I ask her."

"What if we say no?" M'Kenzee asked in a haughty tone.

Rhys continued to smile at her. Max worried she might stomp her foot and stick her tongue out at Rhys if he didn't wipe that grin off his face, and soon.

"Well, if you say no, I'll ask her anyway. But I don't think you'll say no. I think, M'Kenzee, that you know how much she means to me, that we are meant to be together, to love and treasure one another for the rest of our lives. And I hope, Max, that you know those things, too. I've learned you can't make someone else safe. You can't say or do any specific thing to make them happy. I've also learned that life doesn't come with guarantees — no moment should be wasted. Maree brings tremendous joy into my world, and I think I do the same for her. I want to spend every possible minute I have left on this earth with her, and I'm going to start by making her my wife."

Max absorbed all that Rhys was saying while watching Maree talk to Janie Lyn and Landry across the yard. She pointed out new flowers and vegetables she'd planted to make a fall garden. She did look jubilant, like she'd been encased in a bubble of peace. Her limp was gone, she still had a slight tan from summer, and her eyes glowed. She looked at home here because she *was* home here. With Rhys.

"Of course you have our blessings, Rhys." M'Kenzee's eyes flew to Max's when he spoke on her behalf. He simply lifted a hand to cup her chin and give her a wink before pulling her under the canopy of his arm. "M'Kenzee and I both know you and Maree have a special love...the kind our parents had, the kind that never ends. Don't we, Kenz?"

She took a deep breath before answering, glaring up at her big brother before conceding. "Yeah, I guess so." Max chuckled — his little sisters were something else: brilliant, passionate, and strong. Both amazing. And where Maree was cheerful and exuberant, M'Kenzee was guarded and skeptical. She didn't trust easily, so when she deigned someone worthy of it, Max knew it meant something huge. "But if you screw up, Rhys, I'll be right here to make you pay." Deadpan silence. Not a flicker of humor.

"Fair enough, M'Kenzee," Rhys agreed.

"Fair enough," Max echoed. He removed his hand from M'Kenzee's shoulder, sneaking a glance at Maree to be sure she wasn't watching. "Congratulations," he offered to Rhys, but his voice caught. He swallowed hard as Rhys grasped the hand Max stuck out to him. In the end, a brotherly nod was the best Max could do. Life was changing, growing, just as he knew it should.

Dinner was spectacular. Max was grateful to be there, glad he'd run home instead of burrowing in his town house in Kansas City to avoid the public for the three days of the long weekend he had off of practice and meetings.

Rhys cooked the steaks to perfection; seared with a robust seasoning rub on the outside and pink throughout, each bite melted in Max's mouth. Maree had made his favorite corn pudding and her famous "smash" potatoes on the side. Janie Lyn's colorful salad was crisp and flavorful, served with a tangy honey mustard dressing. And of course, their homemade bread stole the show. Topped with butter and jam, it tasted divine.

After dinner, they pulled their chairs around the fire pit in the center of Rhys's backyard. The Oklahoma sunset painted a breathtaking masterpiece with burning shades of red and orange that faded into feathers of gold and pink extending the length of the horizon. When the day relinquished its hold, the clear night sky created a deep midnight-navy backdrop for a billion stars twinkling bright.

The only thing missing was Miss Sadie. Max had called to check on her that afternoon before working on his football films. She had sent a box of s'mores supplies for their dessert, but she'd said she didn't want to leave her boarders. They were a family of seven, reeling after the loss of their home and everything they owned. She had taken them in and gone into caregiving mode without hesitation.

Thinking of her — missing her, their precious and cherished self-assigned matriarch — turned Max's thoughts to the fires and the arsonist who had plagued Green Hills on and off for almost a year.

"What's going on with these fires around town?" Max's question halted the side conversations and focused everyone's attention on Rhys and Davis.

"The Jensen's house was the latest incident." Rhys spoke first, shifting in his chair to plant both feet on the ground and rest his elbows on his knees, hands clasped in front of him.

"And not a small incident," Davis added. "The worst one so far." He, too, sat up straight, bouncing one knee.

"Does the fire department have any leads on who's doing this?" Max knew from previous conversations with Rhys that this case had been on the top of Chief Everett's priorities since the first deer blind had been burned down months and months ago.

"Mrs. Dawsey, who owns the candy shop downtown, saw a man in a threadbare trench coat in the alley behind Main Street. She didn't get a good look at the man's face, but she did see him setting starter flames next to the building and under the dumpster. By what she was able to describe and taking into account that Mr. Armstrong has been missing since the warehouse fire last fall, we're afraid it's him." Rhys's voice was fraught with regret.

"Mr. Armstrong?" Maree asked with trepidation. "But he's such a sweet old man."

"He's a sweet old man who suffers from PTSD," Davis chimed in. "And that's just what we know. He could also struggle with delusions, anger management, and several other severe conditions. He's been living off the grid for decades. I remember as a kid our moms would prepare backpacks of food and have us ride our bikes into the woods as far as the trails went to drop the bags for him. He never met us in person to get them, but he did build a small shelter of sorts out of reclaimed wood and junk — kind of like those tiny libraries you see in neighborhoods around town for sharing books — so the food didn't get ruined in the rain. And he always left the empty backpacks for us to take back to our moms. It's hard to imagine him being our firebug." Sadness tinged Davis's words.

"PTSD is a bad deal," Max said when the silence stretched. "Bren had a time of it after his tour in the Navy. I don't know what he saw — or what he was tasked to do — but I know he was deployed to Libya, Afghanistan, Pakistan, and Somalia. Those are just the locations he's told me about, all some pretty bad places. There's no telling where else he went."

The air around them had turned oppressive.

"Who's Bren?" Janie Lyn asked as M'Kenzee rose and walked into the house.

"Brennigan Stewart," Maree filled in. "He's Max's best friend and our second big brother. When Momma and Dad died, his parents took us in. When the state refused to let us stay, they immediately signed up for foster parent training. They were never awarded custody of us, but they never quit trying, never stopped watching out for us. They're the best." Rhys gripped Maree's hand when her voice shook at the end.

"That was a tough time," Max admitted.

"But we made it through, and we never spent a night apart no matter how rough those nights and those foster placements were." Maree and M'Kenzee exchanged a glance as the older sister returned and sat back in her chair. Red rimmed M'Kenzee's eyes, but Max let it pass; she wouldn't let her guard down, wouldn't allow herself to release the emotions still festering under her skin.

"Well, I hope Mr. Armstrong is found safe and sound, and I hope that if he is the person starting the arson fires, he receives the help he needs." Janie Lyn's words were filled with hope.

"Me too," Maree said, looking at Rhys with love, devotion, and support in her gaze. Max thought a quick prayer of thanksgiving for the lucky man who would soon be family.

"Who's ready for dessert?" Maree asked. She hopped up to hand out skewers she'd brought from inside, prompting Landry to open Miss Sadie's basket and start passing around marshmallows.

"Pick your poison, friends," Landry challenged. "We've got both plain and cinnamon graham crackers; regular milk chocolate, chocolate with rice crisps in it, and caramels."

"I better grab some paper towels," Maree offered, standing.

"Might need the whole roll." Davis rubbed his hands together, gleeful with anticipation.

"I'll help," Rhys said with a slight nod to Max and a wink for M'Kenzee. *Here we go.*

Davis, Landry, and M'Kenzee chatted while spearing their marshmallows and debating the perfect way to roast them. Davis and M'Kenzee held theirs directly in the flame of the fire pit. Landry held hers just above it.

Max sat back in his chair. The floor-to-ceiling wall of glass along the back of Rhys's house made it easy to watch the couple in the kitchen.

"Everything all right?" Janie Lyn claimed the chair next to Max. He answered with a tilt of his head toward the house without taking his eyes off the window.

They watched as Rhys sat Maree down at the breakfast table. He kneeled before her. His arms lifted, buried his hands in the thick strawberry blond waves at the base of her head. Rhys touched his forehead to Maree's, then his lips to her mouth. Then he straightened, still kneeling on one knee. He took something out of the front pocket of his blue jeans. Maree's hands flew to her cheeks. She dropped to one knee — *not* the one that had been replaced — in front of him, throwing her arms around him. They clung to one another like their lives depended upon that connection.

Max felt a swift and sudden determination to find a love like what he'd just witnessed between Maree and Rhys.

"I think she said yes." Max turned his gaze to Janie Lyn.

As their eyes locked, something tangible clicked into place. He refrained from asking if she'd felt it, too. It was enough for him to acknowledge it, to embrace and welcome it.

Momma said when the Lord puts something in your heart, you just know it's right.

He'd never known his momma to be wrong.

10

...the spotlight can change everything.
Liya Kebede

The night had cast a spell. Times like that — the food, the fellowship, and the friends — were a gift Janie Lyn hadn't expected she'd ever enjoy after leaving home. Rhys's proposal had been an added bonus that infused the night with a joy so warm that they all seemed to be glowing when they'd said their goodbyes. As Maxwell drove them home, Janie Lyn felt as though she'd been infused with happiness. She likened the sensation to a potent shot of B12 that made the body awaken with an extra bit of energy.

"Maree's engaged," Maxwell mused aloud. He must have read Janie Lyn's mind.

"Yes," she answered, looking across the cab of the truck to watch a range of emotions pass through his expression. "How do you feel?"

"Engaged," he said again, not answering her question, although his voice expressed hints of being both awestruck and unsure. Lending moral support through patience and a smile, she waited for him to say more. He glanced over a few times, but he hadn't gathered his thoughts enough to share them until he was turning into Foxtail, Maxwell's historic and dignified neighborhood. "They're in love."

"Without a doubt," she agreed.

"They can't take their eyes off one another for a full minute at a time."

"That is true," she agreed again, this time with a chuckle at his understatement. "Each one lights up when the other enters the room."

"He adores her."

"And Maree cherishes Rhys," Janie Lyn pointed out.

Maxwell's chin lifted in a gentle nod as he pulled into the driveway. He parked and shut off the ignition. Then he turned his attention to Janie Lyn.

"He's going to take care of her," he said, half statement and half question. Who did he need to convince? Janie Lyn or himself?

"They're going to take care of each other, Maxwell." She rested a hand on top of his where it still gripped the steering wheel. "It's okay to share the responsibility you feel toward Maree. You can trust Rhys with her. They're going to be very happy together." She gave his hand a comforting squeeze, encouraging Maxwell to look directly into her eyes.

She saw him refocus on her, saw the blue depths of his eyes darken. Janie Lyn's heart did an odd flip-flop. Heat blossomed through her body like a flower opening to the sun.

Flustered, she pulled her hand back, but Maxwell was faster and turned his hand to catch her wrist. Ever so slowly, his grip slid down to her palm. Her heartbeat shifted from quick to erratic. Then he closed his fingers around hers, sliding his thumb side to side across the skin just above her knuckles.

His gaze shifted to her lips. She might have whispered a whimper. She hoped it was only in her own head, but she was pretty sure he'd heard it. He looked back up, into her face, and the corners of his mouth lifted into a slight smile. The predatory intensity she'd felt from him eased.

He lifted her hand to his lips. Her heart stopped beating entirely.

She held her breath to prevent any additional whimpers from escaping, but she couldn't stop herself from licking her bottom lip. Their eyes were locked together.

"Thank you." He breathed the words against her skin. The moist heat and his genuine gratitude shot arrows through her heart. Although thankful it was beating again, she still stayed stuck in place. Whatever this spell — either from the night with friends or Maxwell's hold over her — it had her absolutely entranced.

He brushed his lips over her knuckles once more, gave her a gorgeous grin, and released her.

As she took a moment to blink away the fog, Maxwell got out of the truck and walked around to her side.

When she opened her door, there he was, smiling down at her. Her heart responded. Again.

"Let me help," he said casually. *Casually!* Janie Lyn was falling all over herself, a bundle of nerves, and Maxwell was his normal, calm, cool, and collected self.

"I've got it." It came out harsher than she'd intended.

Maxwell didn't appear fazed, and he didn't cease his chivalrous assistance. Opening her door wider, he lifted the huge salad bowl from her lap and gave her a hand down. Janie Lyn tried to be appreciative, but she was a tiny bit miffed that his attentions turned her inside out and seemed to have no impact on him whatsoever. Plucking the bowl out of his hands might've been petty, but it made her feel marginally better.

She followed Maxwell around the truck and stood behind him while he unlocked the door. When he stepped back, opening the door for her to go first, she glowered at the ground but walked into the house as expected. *What is wrong with me?*

Janie Lyn refused to fall down the rabbit hole that answered that question, so she walked to the kitchen sink, set down the empty salad bowl, and switched on the hot water. She poured too much dish soap into the bowl, scrubbed it with more vigor than necessary. She scolded herself for pouting and being utterly ridiculous. When she felt Maxwell standing behind her, Janie Lyn froze.

He took off her ball cap and tossed it on the countertop.

"Tonight was fun, just hanging out with friends and family." His voice sounded husky.

She remained stock-still, but managed to nod and say, "Yes."

"I really am thrilled for Maree and Rhys," he confirmed. "They found what we're all looking for."

He tugged off the bands that held her braids.

She couldn't put words together coherently to reply.

"Having you there made it perfect," he said. No, he *pledged*. She didn't know what he was promising, but the vow was there in his voice all the same. Her eyes closed of their own volition when his fingers unplaited the strands.

Then he swept her hair over her left shoulder and leaned down to place a harmless kiss on the shoulder strap of her denim overalls. *Is anything about this man harmless?*

At the same moment, his cell phone began to ring.

Janie Lyn didn't move a muscle as he stayed right where he was to see who was calling.

"I have to grab this," he said, an apology in his tone. "But Janie Lyn, don't ever believe that I'm immune to you." He leaned down again, this time to set his lips on the tingling skin just below her earlobe, and spoke, soft and slow, emphasizing each word. "I see you."

No, not harmless.

Janie Lyn swished the soapy water to find the sponge. Her hands trembled. Her movements were jerky. After rinsing it, she dried the dish and put it away, intentionally constraining her thoughts to that task and *not* allowing her mind to stray to Maxwell, his touch, his gaze, his body, his energy, his baby blue eyes, his thick dark blond waves, his huge heart, his capacity to love his family, and definitely *not* his last three words.

Maxwell was still on the phone when Janie Lyn tiptoed past the living room. He was sitting on the couch, his phone on speaker, a football game on the television. He was sketching plays on his yellow legal notepad and talking through them with whoever was on the other end of the line. Janie Lyn justified her slinking by and not saying a word as being polite. She ducked into her room and closed the door silently in hopes that he didn't even notice her go by.

By the next morning, Janie Lyn had resolved to step back from Maxwell. The decision had come after a largely sleepless night of thinking about Maxwell, about how right it felt to be close to him, and about how being there could only end poorly. Very, very poorly. And Maxwell had quickly become too important for her to allow that end to come to fruition.

She was pulling a baking sheet of homemade granola out of the oven when he entered the kitchen.

"Good morning," he said, walking to the coffeepot with a jaunty bounce in his step.

"Hi," she said without looking his way. That felt safer. Looking at him could be dangerous. Making eye contact might be lethal.

"This looks great!" Maxwell stood in awe of the fresh fruit, yogurt, light and fluffy scrambled eggs, and sizzling bacon set out buffet-style on the breakfast table. "I'm a big fan of breakfast, but my eggs and bacon never look quite like this."

Janie Lyn transferred the granola into a bowl, then picked up a pot of syrup simmering on the cooktop and drizzled it over the oats, grains, raisins, and dried cranberries. She stirred the glaze into the granola, sprinkled sugar and cinnamon on top, and set it on the table with the yogurt.

"I hope you enjoy it." She added a cereal bowl to the single place setting at the table.

"This is all for me?" he asked.

"Of course." She was used to particular members in her family expecting her to have their meals prepared and served hot on demand. His humble gratitude was refreshing. And another magnetic force of his personality that she had to resist.

"You're not joining me?"

"No, I need to get to Memorial. I said I'd be there to help with Saturday morning games and crafts."

"That's the memory care facility close to downtown where Sam and Miss Sadie stayed toward the end of his battle with Alzheimer's disease?"

"Yes, I—" She started to say more but stopped herself. He was so easy to talk to that she had to catch herself to keep from sharing too much.

"Maree invited me to meet her at Daisy Lake for a yoga class this morning. I was hoping you'd come with us."

"Oh, no. Y'all go on ahead. You'll love the class — Audrie is the best instructor."

"So, you normally go to yoga with Maree?"

"Well, yes"— she hesitated —"but this morning I need to go help at Memorial."

"Is there only one yoga class offered on Saturdays?"

"Well, no," she demurred again.

"I'm sure Maree won't mind meeting us for a later class. That way I can go with you to lend a hand at the memory care facility." *Why must he be so accommodating? And agreeable? And adorable?*

"I'm sorry. That just won't work at all," she balked.

"It won't?" She must look like a lunatic from his vantage point.

"No, I know how excited Maree must be to have you in town unexpectedly." The argument was coming together as she spoke. It was quite convincing, if she did say so herself. "After last night, I also know she'll be eager to spend some time with you, to bask in the glow of that engagement ring. And to reassure you there is nothing for you to worry over concerning her, Rhys, and their future as husband and wife." Indeed, it was sound reasoning, even to her own ears. "You go enjoy your day with Maree. And M'Kenzee, if she hasn't already darted off to an assignment somewhere. There's a new restaurant at the marina where y'all can get lunch, and…" Her voice trailed off as she scooped up her backpack and sunglasses. "Maybe I'll see you later," she said with a polite smile as she tugged her go-to ball cap down on her head and darted out the door.

She was a coward. She knew it.

Perhaps Maxwell hadn't noticed.

11

***Open your mind and heart
to the possibility that you can attract
whatever you want in life.
What you receive is up to you.
Maya Mendoza***

"*Maybe I'll see you later?*" Max repeated.

"With your feet hip-width apart, rock back and forth to connect the four corners of each foot with the earth beneath your mat." The yoga instructor looked directly at Max.

"I mean, what is that all about?" he whispered loudly.

"It means she'll see you later," Maree actually whispered back. "Now hush."

"Wiggle your toes, lift your kneecaps, let your navel reach toward your spine," Audrie said from the front of the deck. It was a gorgeous setting with Daisy Lake as a stunning backdrop, the sun glistening off the water as smooth as glass on a perfect fall day. The air was still without a hint of a breeze, crisp but not too cool. The leaves were beginning to change, framing the beaches along the shoreline in brilliant reds, golds, and oranges.

Yet, until that moment, Max hadn't noticed a thing.

"Hmph," he growled under his breath. "Of course she'll see me later, we are living in the same house."

"Shhhh," Maree insisted.

"On a deep inhale, roll your shoulders forward. Continue lifting them to shrug your shoulders close to your ears. Hold onto that breath for a pause. As you exhale, push your shoulders back to squeeze the spot right between your shoulder blades. Then relax your shoulders to let them fall down your back as you lift your gaze — your *drishti* — to the sun, perhaps closing your eyes as you absorb balance and warmth." Audrie's voice was leading every class member into bliss. Except for Max.

"It was the strangest thing—"

Maree cut him off. "I refuse to speak another word to you until this class is completely finished."

"Thank you!" The appreciation was spoken in unison by several people practicing yoga on the mats around them. Maree gave him a telling look.

Max angled his head in a silent plea, but when she mouthed a stern *NO*, he settled into the yoga flow.

He wasn't new to yoga. Max had been introduced to yoga years ago when he was a freshman at the University of Tulsa, where the entire football team incorporated yoga into their recovery schedule on a weekly basis. In the beginning, Max was doubtful. He'd expected the guys to cut up and be silly, laughing at one another and making fun of their attempts to look graceful or be flexible. What he'd found had surprised him. The older players, especially those Max knew were projected to continue playing professional ball in the league, were totally engaged in the class. They shared aches, pains, bruises, and areas of tightness with their instructor. Max heard his teammates ask for specific postures and stretches to help heal their bodies. The players encouraged one another, albeit with a tease here and there.

Seeing their teammates take yoga practice seriously set the tone for the new kids, and by the end of that first summer, Max was a believer. He discovered the obvious benefits of yoga like better balance, increased flexibility, and injury prevention. He also realized that by controlling his breathing, he could extend his power and intensity. He discovered that mindfulness elevated the mental aspects of his game and unleashed a strength he'd never tapped into before.

Over the years, he'd become a big fan of yoga and even shared it with his little sisters. Maree immediately decided it was life-changing; M'Kenzee immediately decided it was too slow. Max practiced yoga at home and in Kansas City regularly, but he'd never taken a class at the Lakeside Yoga Studio outside of Green Hills. Janie Lyn was right; the owner, Audrie, was a gifted teacher.

The theme for the day was "Open to Possibilities." The class was centered around opening the hips, heart, shoulders, and mind. Audrie had shared an inspirational quote to help set intentions at the beginning of class. Max had been too scattered with his thoughts on Janie Lyn to hear the instructions.

Audrie shared the quote again at the end of class, after they'd enjoyed *Savasana* with a cold towel over their eyes and their bodies fully relaxed.

"I have a challenge for each of you." Audrie had Max's attention — he loved a challenge. "Set an intention to take with you, something that will serve as a reminder that in the changing season, the upcoming holidays, the hibernation of winter, the blooms of spring, the lazy heat of summer, and back around to next fall, there are opportunities all around you. Embrace chances to invite new people, new experiences, and new dreams into your life." Audrie paused with a peaceful smile on her face. She took the time to make eye contact with each person in class. "You only have to open your heart and your mind to that which you want to attract. And believe that whatever you want is possible. Thank you for sharing your practice with me today — *Namaste*."

As Audrie lowered her head in reverence to the class, Max's thoughts went straight to Janie Lyn.

They were not chaotic frustrations skittering over his brain this time. Now he was calm, rational. He was attracted to her. He wanted Janie Lyn. He wanted to spend time with her, to get to know her, to kiss and to hold her. He wanted to explore a relationship with her, a real relationship with real possibilities. Max wanted love — true love. The kind of love Maree and Rhys had found with one another. He was confident that Janie Lyn wanted the same thing. For some reason, though, her mind and her heart were not yet open to those possibilities.

"Tell me about her," he demanded. Maree glared up at him from where she was sitting on the wooden bench that lined the perimeter of the dock.

"No." She pursed her lips and shook her head as she threw her tote bag over her shoulder and pushed past him.

"Come on, Maree." Max followed so closely on her heels that when she suddenly stopped to say bye to Audrie and a group of friends, he stumbled over her. She glared again, sharper.

Max lifted his hands in resignation.

"Thank you, Audrie! Today's class was amazing," Maree said. She'd flipped a switch and become her usual sweet self.

"It was wonderful," Max complimented Audrie, following Maree's lead. "And exactly what I needed. Thank you."

"I'm glad you were here today," Audrie said to Max, and then turned to face Maree. "And we are always grateful to have this special gift with us." She moved closer to put an arm around his baby sister. Audrie's eyes glistened, and he had to swallow a lump in his throat. They'd come so close to losing Maree last year. Now she was back at yoga — with a few modifications here and there — and preparing to marry a man who Max truly believed deserved such a treasure.

"I have some news," Maree confided, leaning into Audrie's hug. "Rhys proposed last night," she said, lifting her left hand in front of them, "and I said yes." Pure, unadulterated joy bloomed across her cheeks, and tears filled her eyes. Her smile was tremendous.

"Oh, Maree," Audrie gushed. "I'm so happy for you both!"

"Thank you!" Maree hugged her friend once more.

"You know," Audrie continued, "a happy ending is actually a

beginning. I believe you and Rhys are going to enjoy a beautiful journey together."

Maree agreed with an energetic nod but seemed unable to speak.

"Go, enjoy your day with your big brother," Audrie told her with a nudge. "I'll see you next week."

Max had stepped back to give them space to talk, so he rejoined them, holding his hand out to Audrie. "It was nice to meet you," he said, meaning every word. It *was* nice — a relief, honestly — to see firsthand how entrenched Maree's life had become in Green Hills. She was a valued, important member of this community, loved and respected. It was what she had wanted more than anything: a home.

"And you as well," Audrie said, shaking his hand with a smile. "I've heard a lot — and I mean *a lot* — about you, so it's a treat to meet the legend."

"I have a long way to go to be considered a football legend," Max replied.

"Not a football legend," she said with a kind smile. "Something much more important." Max watched her walk away to visit with other class participants still milling around the dock. He was bewildered by her statement.

"Are you ready?" Maree asked.

"Yeah, sure." Max followed her to his truck. "Janie Lyn told me there's a new place to eat at the marina. Do you have time for lunch?"

"Absolutely! I'm hungry after yoga," Maree said as she climbed in and buckled her seat belt. "So, *Janie Lyn told you?*" She tossed a keen glance at Max. "What exactly has she said?"

"I know she's a strong swimmer and likes the water. She likes to read and finds it relaxing. She is a fabulous project manager and has astounding vision. She's soft-spoken yet formidable…strong and capable, and she has a knack for expressing her wishes to see a job completed exactly how she wants it done. She seems shy, yet she'll surprise you with a teasing comment when it's least expected. She's old enough to drink alcohol but prefers tea — both hot and cold. She can bake mouthwatering bread without a recipe, and she's generous in serving others. She cries over old quilts. She asked to watch practice tape with me and seemed to enjoy it. She is brilliant, asks great questions. She's a really good listener. She is stunning and downright gorgeous under those baggy clothes and baseball caps she wears all the time. She has the manners of a Southern belle, and the way she drawls out *Maxwell* instead of just calling me Max is bewitching."

"Wow." Maree was floored.

"I've learned all of that, and yet it occurred to me during yoga that I don't even know her last name."

Maree didn't reply as Max pulled into a parking slot, shifted the truck into park, and killed the engine. He looked at her for help. Her lips and shoulders lifted on one side in a compassionate shrug, as if to say, *Sorry, Bubba.* Then she opened her door to hop down from the truck.

They ordered at the walk-up window — a catfish basket for Max and a club salad for Maree — and filled their glasses at a metal-topped table that served as a drink stand with a cooler of ice and pitchers of fresh lemonade and iced tea. Their order was called quickly, and they sat at one of the colorfully painted wooden picnic tables set on the dock between the restaurant and the boat slips.

"I don't either," Maree said. Max looked up from his food midbite. Maree shrugged her shoulders and said it again. "I've known Janie Lyn since the day she arrived in Green Hills, and I don't know her last name, either."

Max set his catfish back in the plastic basket. "How can that be? I thought y'all had gotten pretty close since your accident and knee surgery."

"We have. We are. I consider her one of my *best* friends."

"Then how do you *not* know her name?" He pushed the basket away and rested his arms on the table.

"When she first introduced herself, I thought maybe Janie was her first name and Lyn was her last. But the more I heard her talk and the more people I saw her meet, I realized she simply goes by Janie Lyn." Maree mixed her salad and dressing with her fork; Max hoped she planned to say more. When she stabbed a chunk of chicken and lettuce and raised the fork to take a bite, he gave up.

"And did you ever ask her about it?" How could she chew and swallow so slowly?

"I wanted to," she admitted. "But Miss Sadie told me to let it be. She said it didn't matter, that Janie Lyn was the same person no matter what she chose to call herself." She took another perfectly curated bite of salad.

Max continued to watch, and wait, but he didn't say a word.

"I can't believe it's already getting cool in the middle of September. Thank the Lord for today's bright and beautiful sunshine!" Maree lifted her face to soak up the sun's rays. "I love it," she said, closing her eyes and worshiping the warmth.

"Maree, you were telling me about Janie Lyn."

Maree shook her head, laughing at his impatience. She picked up her fork and refocused on her food.

"It's not like she's been a fountain of information about anything since she rode into town with Rachel and Suzanne," Maree reminded him around bites. "Miss Sadie believes Janie Lyn will tell us what she's comfortable sharing, and the more she feels at home, the more she will open up with us."

"Rachel and Suzanne? I remember them; they were some of your nurses at the medical center?"

"Yes." Maree pointed her fork at his catfish and fries. "Eat!"

"How did Janie Lyn know them?" Max pulled his lunch tray closer and picked up the fried catfish strips less than enthusiastically.

"She didn't," she said, scooping the last tidbits of salad toppings onto her fork.

"Maree," he growled through teeth clenched not from chewing his meal but in irritation.

"I don't think I've ever seen you quite so worked up over a girl," she said, obviously unaffected by a grumpy big brother. "Stop glowering. You eat, and I'll tell you what I know."

"Thank you," Max grumbled with a head tilt of genuine gratitude.

"Rachel and Suzanne moved here after the hospital renovations were completed, just a few weeks before my car accident. As part of the bond package to pay for the construction and improvements at the hospital, the park and recreation department, and the school buildings, the chamber of commerce and city government partnered to offer relocation packages as incentives to attract medical professionals. Between the instruments, the technology, and the talented staff additions, I benefited greatly from those programs and all the upgrades that turned our rural hospital into what was just renamed the Green Country Medical Center. Imagine us having a state-of-the-art, Level I trauma unit right here in our tiny community." Maree's voice was filled with gracious awe. Her voice dropped to a more serious tone as she continued. "You know, if my accident had been a year earlier, I might not have been so lucky…in life, nor in love. Those incentives are what put Green Hills on Rhys's radar, too." Max softened at the peachy glow of her complexion and the shiny glint in her eyes. Yes, she was lucky. Life and love were gifts from above.

"Before moving here, Rachel and Suzanne lived in Tulsa. They're friends from college and were both living, working, and raising families there. Back then, they came to Green Hills as often as possible for vacations, girls' weekends, and quilting workshops, so they already loved the area. When the hospital reopened, they took advantage of the opportunity to make Green Hills their home. They met Janie Lyn February before last, the day before they drove here for the annual 'Longest Day at the Lake' quilt retreat."

Max had finished eating, wadded up his napkin, and set the basket and trash to the side of the table. He was leaning on his arms again, head tilted forward, listening to every word.

When Maree finished, Max reached for the trash, only to find it gone — presumably a worker had been by their table to pick it up — and his lemonade refilled. He hadn't noticed either; he'd been fully engaged in what Maree had to say.

"Momma would've said Janie Lyn has a huge servant's heart. She would've really liked her," Max said when Maree finished telling him about Janie Lyn's determination to help Miss Sadie with the bed-and-breakfast at Marshall Mansion, her endless energy volunteering at the dementia and Alzheimer's facility, and her willingness to spend time with Maree as she rehabbed after her knee replacement.

"You'll get no argument from me. Janie Lyn is a huge blessing to everyone around here, a real angel! And you're right, Momma would've loved her — we all do," Maree said with a knowing look.

Max didn't want to talk about how much "we all do" just yet.

"How did she get approved to volunteer at the memory care facility if she doesn't have a last name? Didn't they require a background check?"

"Max," she began, saying his name as if he were a small child who required the most basic explanation. "We might have a fancy teaching hospital, but it's still Green Hills, and Miss Sadie is still Sadie Marshall Jones. The first several times Janie Lyn went to help at Memorial Care, she was accompanying Miss Sadie, and no one in this entire town is going to question a guest of Miss Sadie's. By the time Janie Lyn started going on her own, I'm sure everyone there had already gotten to know her, so it never occurred to them to question who she is or where she came from." She made it sound like common sense. "Besides, she's made herself indispensable. They can't afford to run her off; they rely on her too much."

"How often is she there? Besides helping everyone with everything, does she work? You know, for a paycheck? Does she have an income? How—"

"She's there almost every day." Maree cut off his barrage of questions. "Beyond that, you now know what I know about her past. I agree with Miss Sadie, those things don't matter. I don't need to know who Janie Lyn is to know *who* she is: a kind, caring, smart, sensitive, hardworking, helpful, and loving friend."

Max sat back in his chair, crossing his arms with an exhale. He still wanted to know more. Why did she wear those awful clothes? Not awful, just not *her*. Why hadn't she shared her last name? Or told anyone anything about her family? Or where she'd lived before coming to Green Hills? Or why she'd landed in such a small out-of-the-way town as Green Hills in the first place? Why hadn't Janie Lyn gone with them when Rachel and Suzanne arrived to pick her up that Sunday afternoon on their way back to Tulsa? So many questions.

"I *can* tell you that the quilt she asked me to order for her online was not inexpensive," Maree said as an afterthought. "And she gave me cash to buy it...nine crisp one-hundred-dollar bills."

That piqued Max's interest.

He sat up in his chair, a myriad of additional thoughts popping into his mind.

Janie Lyn hardly says a word in public, but when she speaks, it's with authority and assurance. She doesn't seem to work, but she has a stash of money. She buys only secondhand clothes at the resale shop over by the train station, but she spends nine hundred dollars on an antique quilt.

The answers he'd asked for had only created more questions.

Max had listened to Maree and Miss Sadie talk for hours about quilts. He'd watched Maree's fabric designs take form after hours and hours of research. He'd seen M'Kenzee's photos bring fabric to life in pictures of Maree's new quilts as well as Miss Sadie's vintage quilts. On more than one occasion Max had heard each of them say that every quilt tells a story.

"Tell me more about that quilt," he requested, grabbing his lemonade and settling back into his chair.

12

> *From the fabrics pulled to the pattern selected,*
> *from the time it takes to cut shapes*
> *and piece them back together,*
> *from the joy of creating it*
> *to the pleasure of giving it,*
> *every quilt is a beautiful story.*
> **Ashli Montgomery**

"Janie Lyn?" Max called as he walked into the house, hoping she was home. He had questions.

"I'm in the kitchen," she replied.

"Something smells good," he commented, walking straight to the cooktop to see what was simmering. "Peaches?"

"Apricots." She was rolling pie crust into a huge rectangle on the island. "For mini fried pies."

"Those sound amazing! Do I get to sample one?"

"Oh, I imagine I can spare one or two." Her Southern accent made it sound like *Ah'magine Ihh can spayer whun'ah two*. He could listen to the way her words melted together all day long. They sounded even sweeter than the scent of the apricots cooking. He was especially pleased to be teased by her after their awkward parting that morning.

Maybe I'll see you later. It still rankled.

But there they were: indeed later, and definitely seeing one another.

"I'd be much ah'bliged," he teased right back with his own exaggerated accent. He was proud of his efforts when she laughed under her breath. He turned to get a glass from the cabinet. "Are these just for fun, and can I get you a glass of tea?" He paused, hand midair and waiting for her response. When she looked up through her thick dark eyelashes, his heart skittered.

"No," she answered, contemplating him with those gorgeous green eyes. "And yes. Please. A glass of iced tea sounds nice," she said with a slight smile. "How's Maree? Still glowing?"

"She is that. You should've heard her telling the yoga teacher about Rhys proposing; she was so happy showing off her ring." He'd been antsy to grill his little sister for information about Janie Lyn, but he hadn't missed Maree's exuberance.

"I'm sure Audrie was appropriately delighted. She's a sweetie."

"There was squealing, jumping, hugging, and even a few tears," Max confirmed.

"Ah, that's perfect," Janie Lyn said. Genuine happiness colored her voice and gleamed in her eyes. Janie Lyn cared for his little sister, was a good friend to her, and that meant the world to Max. "And how was Audrie's yoga class today?"

"Fantastic. She talked a lot about possibilities, about opening your mind and your heart. She said that when you do that, you can have whatever you want in life." He maintained eye contact with her the entire time he spoke. He hadn't meant to throw down a gauntlet, but there'd been a challenge in his voice all the same.

Max liked her. A lot. And he was quite certain she felt the same way about him.

"Audrie is a gifted instructor," she said as she resumed rolling the dough.

"It was good advice." He came up behind her and set down a glass of tea for her. She stiffened and held her breath until he moved past her to the sink. "Can I help?" he asked as he began washing his hands.

"Um. Uh, yes. Sure." Her voice quivered. He liked it. He liked ruffling her feathers. "You can stir the fruit in that pot on the stove."

"What's in here with the apricots?" he asked as he started to stir the mixture, knowing that food — talking about it, preparing it, sharing it — settled her. While he was relieved she felt the electrical charge between them, he didn't want to make her nervous or skittish.

"Apricots, raisins, dried cranberries, a little lemon juice, sugar, and butter." *Sugahh* and *butahh*. His heart flipped. "Let an apricot cool a bit on the spoon. Then you can test it to see if it's soft enough. And sweet enough." She was killing him.

Without waiting long enough for it to cool, he popped the apricot in his mouth. She giggled at him again. He must have looked like a mom-to-be breathing through labor, trying to blow out the heat and not have to spit out the burning fruit. The pain was worth the pleasure when she brought his tea glass to him, standing right in front of him, her light green eyes looking up into his. Her eyebrows lifted, and she shook her head to rebuke him, but she didn't say *I told you so*.

"Thank you." Max exhaled the words after a long drink. She was still standing inches away.

"How was it?" Janie Lyn's voice was quiet.

"Soft. Sweet," he whispered back. They looked at one another for a long moment before she turned away. "And delicious."

"Good," she said matter-of-factly. "Use a potholder to bring the saucepan over here, please." She'd walked back to her spot in front of the pie crust and was sprinkling cinnamon over it. "We also need the ice cream scooper from that drawer, if you don't mind grabbing it," she asked, pointing toward a drawer next to the oven. It seemed she knew his house and its contents much better than he — which was fine with Max.

"Ice cream scooper?"

"Yes," she confirmed, stirring the pie filling vigorously to mix the ingredients once more before taking the scoop from Max.

Janie Lyn set a scoop of fruit every few inches across half of the dough and sprinkled another dusting of cinnamon over the pies. Then she clapped her hands with flour like a gymnast does with chalk before working her fingers along the edge of the pie crust and sliding her hands underneath the half that wasn't covered in scoops of fruit. Deftly, she flipped that half over to sandwich the filling.

Next, she whisked an egg in a small bowl, the fork moving at warp speed. She poured the egg wash over the dough and ran the palms of her hands over it to spread it perfectly. At the same time Janie Lyn smoothed the egg wash over the dough, her fingertips pressed the two layers together around the mounds of fruit filling. Max watched, mesmerized by the efficient fluidity of her movements.

Janie Lyn washed her hands, drying them on a cup towel as she picked up a pizza cutter that had zigzags on the blade. "That looks like one of Maree's fancy fabric cutters. She once threatened to stab me in my sleep with the matching scissors if I ever touched them."

"Pinking shears and a pinking blade for her rotary cutter," she filled in for him. "Both murder-worthy. As is this pastry cutter, I assure you."

"Death threat noted," Max joked. "And there I didn't even know I had a pastry cutter."

"You didn't. You don't. It's mine," she said, caught up in their banter. Then she added much softer, "It was a gift from my grandmother." Without another word, she began slicing the dough to create the mini pies.

It was the first time she'd ever mentioned family. That meant something. The tear she wiped off her cheek with the back of her hand meant even more. Like trying to balance on a swinging bridge in a storm, he knew his next step was crucial.

Her hands flew over the pies. He reached out to still them.

"Let's not lose a finger," he said, gently taking the cutter from her hand and stepping beside her. His other hand rested on her lower back. He wanted to offer support, but he didn't want her to skitter off. "Like this?" Max ran the pastry cutter across the dough from side to side to finish cutting out each pie.

"Yes." Janie Lyn leaned into him just a little. Max didn't know if her shift was done subconsciously or intentionally. He guessed the former over the latter.

He took the opportunity to move even closer, sliding his left hand around her waist, nestling her into his body to feel her heat, hoping that his would lend her strength. There was much more to this woman than she wanted to let on to the world.

"Now what?" He set the blade on the island. "Do I get to fry them?"

She smiled. It was a check mark on his list of desired responses from her.

"Almost," she promised. "Just a little more cinnamon and sugar on top." She lifted a hand to pinch a little of each from their bowls and scattered them over the pies. Max rested his right hand on her waist to mirror his left and watched over her shoulder. Being tall had its advantages.

"Did she teach you how to do this? Your grandmother?" He made sure to keep his voice gentle, patient.

"Yes," she said after a brief pause. "She taught me everything that's good in my life." She swiped her hands to clean them and set them on the edge of the island.

"Like baking?"

"And cooking. How making meals for others is an act of love… that few things are more rewarding than seeing someone derive elation from your food. My happy place was always in the kitchen with Gram. Anytime I'm washing fruit, cutting vegetables, mixing ingredients, or stirring a batter, I feel close to her. Because of that, being in a kitchen is special, almost like a session of therapy. She was the glue that held not only my family but our entire community together."

"Like Miss Sadie," Max said when she paused.

"So much like Miss Sadie," Janie Lyn agreed. "She's such a gift!"

"So are you, Janie Lyn," Max said, turning her to face him, his hands coming to rest on the island behind her, one hand on each side so she was caught in the middle. "I don't know what brought you to Green Hills — I'd like to, but I don't need to — but I do know this town has been blessed by your being here. My family adores you, Miss Sadie loves you like her own grandchild, and I understand the memory care facility can't function without you. From what I've heard, everyone you've met is in awe of you." She shifted in the cage of his arms. "Including me," Max vowed, lifting her chin to look into her eyes, refusing to let her shy away.

"Thank you for telling me about your grandmother," he said. "She sounds awesome."

Tears glistened in her eyes; Max didn't want to push too far.

"Now," he said, straightening to his full height again, "can we fry something?" Punching dough yesterday. Frying it up today. Max was having a blast. Unexpected and out of his norm, but great fun all the same.

She answered with a quick nod but didn't speak.

Max moved both hands to either side of Janie Lyn's head and leaned down to lay an innocent kiss on her forehead. Then he walked over to the oven and slid the cast iron skillet onto a burner. She'd already filled it with grease, so he lit the burner. "How hot?"

"Medium-high heat," she answered. Her voice was back to normal, and the tears had dried without overflowing.

Over the next hour Max and Janie Lyn cooked the pies, set them on a plate covered in paper towels to cool, and cleaned the kitchen together. All the while, they talked about everything and nothing. She told him about the craft activity she'd led with her dementia patients and their visitors earlier that morning. He told her about the Dallas Cowboys, whom he'd be playing next after the bye week. Max described Kansas City and his favorite places there. Janie Lyn described a project she and Maree had started last year and were developing as an awareness campaign and fundraiser to help end Alzheimer's disease. Janie Lyn talked about a book series of cozy quilt mysteries by an author she'd recently discovered who also had a connection to Green Hills. She'd borrowed the books from the library on her way home from volunteering and looked forward to diving into them. Max commented on how fun it was to own a house in a town where people still used the public library on a daily basis.

"Of course, they do!" Janie Lyn feigned indignation on behalf of her fellow citizens.

"I'm sure it's a happening place," he said, throwing his hands up.

"I'll have you know that the Green Hills Public Library is *the* place to be, especially from 1 to 3 p.m., Tuesday through Friday, and every Saturday morning." *Thuhhh playce ta bay… From whun ta thray…*

Warmth filled Max's chest. He was falling hard.

"Tuesday afternoons are 'open sew' time for the Busy Bees' Quilt Guild — your sister and Miss Sadie are regulars," she elaborated. "Wednesdays are for reading groups, including the Book Belles which, again, Maree and Miss Sadie rarely miss. Thursdays are for mah jongg…Maree and I both sit at the beginner's table. Fridays are for playing bridge; some of those ladies have been playing every week for over forty years! And Saturday mornings are for the kids with circle time, story hour, writing workshops, illustration and art camps, read-a-thons, pajama parties, Donuts with Dad, and Muffins with Mom, just to name a few."

"Wow. Okay!" He tried not to laugh, at least not too hard. "I *am* amazed. And I'm obviously missing out." She laughed with him; he delighted in it. "I just have one question."

"All right, what is it?"

"When does my sister get any work done?" Their laughter rang out even louder.

"Hmmm," she contemplated, shifting her chin. "I see what you mean," she allowed, once their giggling began to subside.

"Well, I have to agree with you," Max said. "The kitchen *is* a wonderful place to be." She straightened her head and smiled — a no holds barred, light up the world smile — upon him. He felt the warmth of that smile from the top of his head to the tips of his toes. Absorbing it. Letting it fill the lonely corners of his heart. Then he smiled and conceded, "As well as the library, of course."

She swatted at him with the cup towel, and he let her. Both continued grinning from ear to ear.

13

***Success is stumbling from failure to failure
with no loss of enthusiasm.
Widely attributed to
Abraham Lincoln and then Winston Churchill***

Janie Lyn acknowledged to herself that Maxwell wasn't lying. Being in the kitchen — with him — was wonderful.

Janie Lyn couldn't remember a time she'd had so much fun, at least not since the last time she and Gram had baked together.

It was so easy to be with Maxwell. She'd felt it the day before, sitting by the pool, baking bread, riding in the truck, and today it became more evident. She really, *really* liked him. Too much. This was going to hurt.

"What are we doing with these apricot pies?" His question pulled her from her wool-gathering.

"I'm donating them to Earl at the Three-Toed Turtle."

"His customers will love them! Do you bake for him a lot?" Maxwell followed her lead to slide each pie into a clear cellophane bag. While he did that, Janie Lyn cut pieces of baker's twine and tied them shut.

"No, this is the first time. Maree set it up, and I agreed to do the baking."

"She can be rather persuasive in her persistence."

"I don't mind, really." She walked into the pantry to grab a large breadbasket. Once she'd placed a cup towel in the basket, Maxwell began setting the pies in place. "As I mentioned yesterday, I love to bake," she told him, "and Earl is doing a special boxed lunch event tomorrow as a kickoff to make people aware of the upcoming Alzheimer's walk."

"You find the most creative ways to promote that cause."

"You're sweet to say so." He gave her more credit than she deserved. Her work was a tiny drop in the bucket of what was needed to end the death sentence of Alzheimer's disease. "Sadly, it's not enough."

"I love Triple T's — Earl serves a great chicken-fried steak. Let's eat dinner while we're there."

"While we're there?" A chill overlaid her words.

"Don't we need to drop off the pies?"

"I can ask Maree to come pick them up. Like I said, she's the one who set it up." She took the basket and placed it on the entry table by the front door. She felt his questioning gaze follow her and looked for something else to fiddle with so she didn't have to go back to where he stood in the kitchen.

In the end, she took the coward's way out and ducked into her room and straight into the connecting bath. She sat on the edge of the tub, hating herself and her situation. Maxwell had said, "Don't we..." *We*. She couldn't be part of a *we* with Maxwell Davenport. Her chin dropped to her chest. Her eyes burned. She tried to slow her heartbeat and breathing.

Once she felt calmer, she leaned against the counter, standing in front of the sink. Her reflection in the mirror confirmed the sadness she was feeling.

This was silly. She'd indulged herself by reading too much into his flirtations. This was Maxwell Davenport, here for the weekend. Nothing more.

She splashed cool water on her face and patted it dry. She smoothed her hair. Then she added balm and a swipe of gloss on her lips. One more deep breath, and she opened the door.

He stood in the doorway between her room and the hallway, one shoulder resting against the door jam. He studied the quilt she'd put on her bed, the one she'd cried over after Maree left yesterday. "Will you tell me about this quilt?"

She felt the color drain from her face.

"Please?" Little more than a whisper, his soft voice exuded patience. And kindness. Par for the course where Maxwell was concerned, she found herself unable to say no. She bit her lip but moved to perch on the edge of the armless wicker chair in the corner of the room, just to give herself some space. Maxwell faced her, sitting on the wooden blanket chest at the end of the bed. He leaned his elbows on his knees, clasping his hands together. Janie Lyn had his undivided attention, the intensity of his focus both exhilarated and unnerved her.

"It's a *Rose of Sharon*—" Janie Lyn stopped herself midsentence. "Do you know what appliqué is?"

"I think so," Maxwell answered. "It's where you sew the fabric on top of other fabric instead of sewing pieces together, right?"

"Exactly. This quilt was finished in 1863, by a woman named Vashti Masterson. The appliqué pattern is called the *Rose of Sharon*."

Janie Lyn continued, "In those days, a girl began working on and sewing items for her future home long before she got engaged, even before she could be courted by a boy. And by her wedding day, the young bride would have created at least thirteen quilts to begin her marriage. Twelve were considered 'everyday' quilts, made for heavy use and functionality. One was special, often referred to as her 'great quilt.' This quilt covered her marriage bed. The *Rose of Sharon* was a very popular pattern for this show piece and is named after a verse in the Bible...Song of Solomon 2:1, which says, *I am a rose of Sharon, a lily of the valleys.*

"God blessed Solomon with great wisdom and keen understanding. In that verse, he describes the girl he is courting by comparing her to a beautiful flower that grows in a field famous for beauty and fertility. Every new bride prays to be both beautiful and fertile — well, at least back then they did. Making a *Rose of Sharon* quilt was more than a work of art for a bride's new home. This quilt was the result of a prayer, prayed in the hours and days and weeks it took to sew every stitch, a prayer for her new life."

"It's incredible. How did you learn all this?" Maxwell's eyes grew large; his eyebrows were raised as he asked the question.

"This quilt was my grandmother's. Gram's." Just saying Gram's name made her heart race out of her chest. She could barely speak. When he remained silent for a long moment, Janie Lyn thought perhaps her voice had been too quiet for Maxwell to hear her words.

"This exact quilt was your grandmother's?" His voice pitched high in awe.

"Technically, it was her great-great-*great*-grandmother's. It was passed from mother to daughter — or daughter-in-law — on the eve of each daughter's wedding for six generations. My dad didn't have any sisters, so he and my mom were the last to receive it when they married in 1993, one hundred and thirty years after Vashti Masterson made it."

"That's wild!"

"I've been searching for it online, calling museums, and emailing resale shops. A few weeks ago, I tracked it down to a vintage quilt dealer in Vermont. With Maree's help, aided by her influence and celebrity as a famous fabric designer and leader in the quilt industry, I purchased the quilt before it went to auction."

He walked to the side of the bed, closing the distance between them, but turned to look closer at the quilt. He bent his knees, coming to a crouch to inspect the binding and hand-quilted stitches. His head shook side to side. "Talk about a needle in a haystack," he said as he looked at her over his shoulder. He released the quilt and reached to wipe a tear from her cheek before she realized it had fallen.

"Sorry." Janie Lyn moved to dry her eyes, but Maxwell stopped her hands, holding them as he shifted to kneel in front of her chair.

"Don't apologize, Janie Lyn. No wonder you were overwhelmed when Maree brought it over yesterday. But, if this pattern has been so popular as a wedding quilt for over a hundred and fifty years, how can you be sure it's the right quilt?"

Janie Lyn stood. Maxwell dropped only one of her hands as he, too, stood and stepped back for her to walk to the bed. She liked that he continued to hold her fingers in his.

He followed her around the foot of the bed and the chest he'd sat on earlier. When she turned back the bottom corner of the quilt, there, stitched in elegant script, was her proof: a fancy *M*, exactly three inches tall, with two lines of text below it; the top line read "Edmond & Vashti" and the bottom read "June 7, 1863."

"My mother never appreciated how special a gift this quilt was, not the morning Gram gave it to her and certainly not the Sunday morning she left it in a collection box on our way into church. I begged her to let me have it instead of giving it away, but she just lectured me once more that putting too much value in material things was a sin. I couldn't let it go." Janie Lyn paused, trying to stop, trying to turn off the flood of memories. But once opened, she couldn't close the flood gates nor plug the hole caused by hurt and humiliation; the pain still flowed fifteen years after that horrible day. "I threw a terrible tantrum right in the middle of the church lobby. Mortified, my mother accused me of bringing the devil into sacred space. I got the spanking of my life as soon as we got home from church, and she punished me again when I arrived home from school every afternoon for two weeks."

Janie Lyn ran her fingers over the embroidered letters, back and forth, lost in the memory.

Then she looked up to Maxwell and attempted a smile.

"But that was a long time ago, and now I have it back," she said, dropping her gaze down to the quilt once more, this time feeling triumphant rather than sad. Seeing that embroidery — touching the stitches and threads — soothed her heart.

Maxwell reached an arm across her back and laid a hand on her shoulder. The weight and warmth lent her strength. She exhaled a cleansing breath, and his half hug tightened, encouraging her to lean into him. Before this weekend with Maxwell, she hadn't indulged in support in years. Janie Lyn tried to resist the luxury, but ultimately, she enjoyed the security of shelter.

Janie Lyn appreciated how Maxwell didn't interrupt or try to downplay the story to make her feel better.

"Do you go to church with Miss Sadie and Maree?"

"What?" His question surprised her.

She turned to face him. He didn't drop his hand as it slid across the top of her back, instead bringing the other up so that both his arms rested on her shoulders as he looked directly into her face.

"On Sundays, do you go with them?" he asked again. She couldn't read the expression on his face.

"Rarely." Her voice was clipped. Janie Lyn didn't want a lecture nor a sermon on the many ways she was failing God. She shifted to move away, but Maxwell didn't budge. She lifted her head in defiance. "Why do you ask?"

"I can't imagine a parent — especially my momma — using God to terrify or punish me or my sisters. I think it would turn me off religion and church entirely."

She continued to meet his gaze but didn't know how to answer.

"Janie Lyn, that's not how a relationship with the Lord should look or feel. I hope you know that, know that what your mom said and did is not a reflection of His love for you."

She tried to step back, to look down so he wouldn't see the glisten of tears forming in her eyes. Again, he didn't budge. Instead of letting her retreat, he lifted her chin, forcing her to see him.

"Loving your grandmother and holding on to your connection to her through this phenomenal quilt is not a sin." Maxwell's voice was strong yet soft, forgiving. A single tear dropped from her eye.

Maxwell caught it with a tender swipe of his thumb and pulled her into his chest, wrapping both arms around her and nestling her head under his chin.

When her body shook with sobs, he only held her closer.

And when the tears were cried out and her breathing steady, he smoothed a hand over her hair and ran it up and down her back. He was so good at giving comfort, at sharing his solid strength.

"I hope you never take this quilt off your bed. It really is incredible," he said, finally releasing her to stand on her own two feet. "Now, let's get those apricot pies to Earl."

She immediately thought to dissuade him from taking her to town, but he was down the hall before she got a word out. By the time she caught up, he'd grabbed the basket, a cap, and his keys and was opening the door for her to walk through first.

"I'll let you drive me to deliver them, but I can't stay to eat. After I give these to Earl, I'll run into the Get'n'Go for groceries, so I can make us something here at the house."

Janie Lyn would not, *could not*, go out to dinner with Maxwell. It sounded wonderful to sit across the table from him, talking about everything, and nothing — nothing important, but all the little things that people share over a casual meal. What she would give to simply relax while enjoying good food, a fun ambiance, and great company!

It sounded like a dream.

And a dream was all it could be.

14

What's in a name? That which we call a rose
By any other name would smell as sweet;
William Shakespeare,
Romeo and Juliet, Act II, Scene II

"We'll see," Max said once they were in the truck and headed to town.

"Hm?" Janie Lyn's eyes were filled with confusion, as though she'd drifted somewhere else for a moment.

"I said we'll see," he answered. Then he gave a slight laugh. "I guess we do turn into our parents. Momma used to say that all the time, but especially when she didn't want to tell me *no* outright. I'd say I wanted to do something that she wasn't going to agree to, like staying up after bedtime or eating brownies for breakfast, and she'd say *we'll see* as if she didn't want to argue but fully intended for things to go her way rather than mine. Now, here I am saying it, too."

"She wanted what was best for you, even when you didn't know what that was yourself." Janie Lyn's gaze was out her window. Her voice was almost haunted.

"I'm sure that's true. If it had been up to me back then, I would've had dessert first at every meal, played outside with my friends all day — every day — instead of going to school, and I would never have had to take a bath!"

She glanced at him with a kind smile but then turned her head back to the passing scenery.

They drove the rest of the way downtown in easy silence, a slow country song playing low on the radio. When they arrived, Max pulled into a parking spot right in front of the diner.

"I'll take them in," Janie Lyn announced, practically jumping out of the truck before he'd put the gearshift in park.

"Let me hel—"

"No," she interrupted. "I'll be right back."

Max sat dumbfounded. He'd figured she'd relent once they got inside, heard the music playing on the old-time jukebox, saw couples and families filling the restaurant, and smelled the food cooking. But it seemed she was quite adamant about not going anywhere with him, at least not in public.

She'd refused to go to yoga with him, although she'd admitted she often accompanied Maree. Now she wouldn't even walk into a diner with him. It wasn't his imagination. Janie Lyn worked to avoid being seen with him, and it hurt.

He contemplated that fact while he waited for her. His forehead tightened into a scowl, the muscles between his eyebrows scrunched. He filled his chest with a deep breath and exhaled slowly, trying to smooth away his frown before Janie Lyn returned. He wanted to growl, but bellowing wasn't his style, and he didn't want to scare her away.

When she opened her door, stepped up into the truck, and set the now-empty basket on the back seat, Max restarted the truck and asked, "Where to? Somewhere else for dinner? Then maybe a movie at the Majestic? I heard about a new coffee shop next door to the theater. I understand they stay open late to serve delicious desserts after the last movie showing on Friday and Saturday nights."

"That's okay, just stop by the grocery store. I'll pick up something to cook at the house." She was trying to sound nonchalant, but her words were clipped. The tension in the cab of the truck was palpable.

He pulled into the Get'n'Go parking lot, turned off the truck, and moved to open his door.

"I've got it, Maxwell. You don't have to go in with me." Again, she tried to sound helpful, but the words came out as a plea. And once again, she hopped out of the truck and jolted into the building in a flash.

She returned less than ten minutes later with a bag of groceries in each hand.

Max stepped out of the truck to take them from her. She rushed into the truck and sat low in the seat as he set the bags in the back seat.

They drove home in silence again, but this time there was a chill in the air rather than a companionable peace.

When they arrived, Max carried in the basket and the shopping bags. Janie Lyn moved to turn the oven on while he took frozen pizzas out of the bags and opened their boxes. She lined two cookie sheets with foil, spritzed the foil with cooking spray, and held each out for Max to set a pizza on. He opened the oven door, and she placed the cookie sheets on the racks to cook.

They worked in tandem, efficiently, like they'd been doing it for years. They moved as though they were a team, a team that naturally worked well together, that knew each other's next step without needing to be told. Like dancers moving in unison without needing choreography.

It was rare to find that kind of a team, a team that melded together and fit like a glove before they'd even tried, before they'd battled together, before they'd learned one another. Being part of a team like that was a gift. The kind that usually came around only once in a lifetime, if even then.

Thoughts whirled around his head. And every single one began and ended with Janie Lyn.

Meanwhile, she busied herself with dinner...making a salad, gathering dressings and toppings, checking to see if there was enough sweet tea in the fridge. She seemed to be doing anything she could think of to keep from having to stop and face him. He felt her avoidance even as they filled the space of his kitchen, together.

Max pulled paper plates from the pantry and tore off two paper towels from the holder under the sink.

"You good eating on the couch?" He grimaced at the grumble in his voice. "We could watch a movie while we eat," he added, intentionally softening his tone.

"That sounds great, Maxwell," she said, sounding pleased and finally looking up to meet his gaze. Was she happy to spend more time together, or simply happy she wouldn't have to talk to him for the next few hours?

He nodded, struggling to pull his eyes away from hers.

"You pick the movie," she offered. "We've already established that you're the expert, and I like anything." It couldn't have been any clearer that she worked extra hard to sound light and jovial.

He brought a huge wooden cutting board over to the coffee table, set the paper plates and makeshift napkins in front of it, and turned on the TV. Janie Lyn laid a pizza cutter on top of the cutting board. Their eyes met again as she straightened. How could they be so comfortable *and* walk on eggshells around one another at the same time? She wreaked havoc on his senses. He no longer knew which way was up. Or forward.

The oven timer broke their trance.

They both walked back into the kitchen. He filled two glasses with ice cubes and sweet tea. She pulled the hot pizzas from the oven. They carried everything into the living room. Max set the drinks on coasters, and Janie Lyn slid the pizzas onto the cutting board. He tried to focus on selecting something to watch while she leaned over to slice the pizzas, but the scent of her perfume drowned out the smell of the food and made him squeeze his eyes shut. *Lord, give me strength*, he prayed silently.

Janie Lyn took the pizza cutter to the sink and came back with the salad, dressings, and parmesan cheese. When she settled next to him on the sofa, she looked at Max and smiled, but then she quickly looked back down at the food. Max knew that if his outsides looked like how his insides felt, his expression was a twisted mix of lust and frustration.

"How about *King Arthur: Legend of the Sword?*" Max needed something fast-paced and action-packed, something to balance the intensity he couldn't seem to diffuse within himself.

"I remember it from your list," she teased, still trying so hard to be cheerful. *Bless her heart*, he thought on a cringe. He really was starting to sound like his momma. "But I've never seen it, so yes, that's perfect."

They filled their plates. Janie Lyn scooted back against the cushions, crossing her legs and pulling a quilt onto her lap before getting her plate and paper towel situated. Max sat toward the edge of the cushion, leaving his plate on the table and leaning forward to reach it.

"Ready?" He looked back over his shoulder as he asked. He was struck by her beauty. Talk about perfect. She belonged — right there on his couch, snuggled under a blanket, in his life. How could he have ever thought her plain? How could anyone not notice her?

Her eyes sparkled in the glow of the television as she nodded quickly, joyful anticipation on her face. Pizza and a movie on the couch on a Saturday night seemed to be all she wanted. That was all she needed to be happy.

He smiled back, forcing the knots in his chest and stomach to relax, indulging in soaking up the sight of her for one extra moment. Then he turned to start the film.

Early in the movie, Janie Lyn refilled her plate. Then, a few minutes later, she set the plate aside, never taking her eyes off the screen. Max finished his entire pizza and sat back against the couch. He pulled the lever to raise the recliner-end of the couch. Janie Lyn shifted closer to Max to share the footrest.

At some point during Arthur's tests and self-discovery, Janie Lyn inhaled a sharp breath, then exhaled deeply and let more of her weight melt against Max.

When Mage was threatened and Arthur's world clicked into perspective, Janie Lyn gasped, holding her breath throughout the fight scene, but releasing it on a sigh of awe when it was over and Arthur stepped in to care for Mage.

By the time the credits ran, Janie Lyn was tucked into Max's side, his arm along the back of the couch behind her and somewhat resting across her shoulders.

"I loved it," Janie Lyn admitted.

"It's a good one," Max agreed. He was reluctant to move, not wanting her to put any space between them. He clicked the mute button on the remote.

"Janie Lyn, are you embarrassed to be seen with me?" Humiliated to ask and scared to hear the answer, a school of butterflies swarmed in his stomach.

"No! Maxwell, I—" She spoke vehemently, turning to look at him, but then stopped mid protest.

She closed her eyes, obviously looking for the words to explain what was going on. Because *something* was going on.

"Maxwell," she began again, and then released a sigh, lifting her lashes to look at him. It was dark in the living room, but the light of the TV showed the pleading in her voice mirrored her eyes.

He was a patient man, but he was anxious and antsy to understand.

"Maxwell, it's not—"

"Why do you do that?" This time he cut her off.

"Why do I do *what*?" Janie Lyn asked in reply. He was relieved to see the despondency in her eyes switch to curiosity. He wanted answers, but he didn't want to see her sad. *Forlorn* described her more accurately. That defined what he'd seen: not pain, but trouble.

"You're the only one who calls me Maxwell instead of Max. At least since my momma died. Why do you do that?"

"Why do you call me Janie Lyn, instead of just Janie?" She lifted her chin and narrowed her eyes in an act of defiance that was rather short-lived.

"Because it's your name." Max watched her closely and went on high alert when her shoulders slumped and she ducked her head. He shifted to look at her, prompting her to sit up from where she'd been lounging against him while they'd watched the movie. He did the same, dropping the footrest and setting both feet flat on the ground. "Isn't it?"

Still no response.

"Ja—" He stopped with a sigh. He ran a hand through his hair, reining in his emotion to try again. "Janie—"

"It's part of my name, yes," she interrupted, rising from the couch and walking to the glass wall. It had started storming, heavy rain pouring into the pool and splattering on the new pavers. "Lizzy. Elizabeth. *That* is my name. Elizabeth Jayne." Her tone became angry, and she turned to face him with a backbone of steel. "Elizabeth Jayne Lyndale. From Athens, Georgia. Of *the* Athens, Georgia Lyndales." Her Southern accent was in full force as fury rang in her eyes.

"I've seen the headlines: Runaway heiress to a Christmas legacy," he said with a whistle. She'd been looking away, but she tossed a glare over her shoulder in response to his comment. He stood to follow her to the window, but her icy expression encouraged him to sit back down on the couch. He was flabbergasted. Had no idea what to say in response to her revelation.

"It's not that I don't want to be seen with you, Maxwell," she finally explained. "It's that I *can't*."

"You ran away? From your own family?" He couldn't comprehend how someone could walk away from their family when he would give anything to have all of his together again.

"They're not like your family," she said emphatically. His dismay must've been evident. "My father was the youngest of three boys. The two older boys weren't kind big brothers. They didn't share a loving relationship like you are used to with M'Kenzee and Maree. By the time he graduated high school, my father had been bullied into submission. His brothers were into very questionable businesses all along the Eastern Seaboard, and when they told him to marry the daughter of a business partner, he did what he was told. Ironically, in spite of their 'family business' practices, the woman he married was devoutly religious. As soon as they were married, my parents became missionaries and left the States. Their 'church' wasn't like the one you grew up in, nothing like the one Maree and

Miss Sadie attend here in Green Hills. It was dark and taught of covens and prophecies. Gram once told me that she and Pops begged them not to go back, begged my mother and father to stay in Athens, help at the bakery, and study the Bible with them. Gram never stopped praying for them, praying that their eyes would be opened to the lies they'd accepted so they could get away from that cult."

Max had a hard time processing all that Janie Lyn told him. It sounded like a movie script, a creepy and sinister one. Just wrong.

"Her prayers were never answered," Janie Lyn went on. "My father was too weak to break away even if he'd wanted to; although, from what I've studied about cults, the lure of unconditional love and acceptance that is typically displayed to recruit group members was probably exactly what my father craved. I'm sure he was easy to control once he was there. And my mother? I'm positive that she never wanted out. She wouldn't have seen leaving as an escape."

"How did you?" Max asked. Then he went on to clarify, "Escape that life, I mean."

"My parents had been married almost two years when I was born. They'd visited their 'church' and gone on a few 'missionary trips' with them—" She continued using air quotes when she said certain words, as though they'd called their activities by normal names, but Janie Lyn wouldn't allow herself to do the same. "—but I was born in Athens. My mother wasn't happy to have a child. I was a nuisance that got in the way of her 'calling,' so, thankfully, she often left me with Gram and Pops."

She never used her parents' names, only referred to them as her mother and father. Not even Mom and Dad. That alone gave him a chill and left his chest feeling empty.

"They would come home for months; a couple of times they were in Athens a full year or even longer. But in the end, they always left. Eventually, they never returned."

"Janie Lyn, I'm so sorry." Max rose from the sofa and walked to her. He wanted — needed — to offer sympathy, to hold her hand or touch her shoulder, something to provide human contact.

He reached toward her, but she shied away.

"It was for the best, really. Gram and Pops raised me, and for that I was the luckiest little girl in the world." Her valiant smile practically broke Max's heart. "Long before I was born, Pop's parents had turned the family bakery over to him and Gram. They ran it together. Gram was a magician when it came to baking, cake decorating, and culinary inventions, so the popularity of the bakery blossomed. Her legacy bloomed. Pops was a genius with the business aspects. He'd gone to college to be an accountant, which was convenient, and the marketing and advertising came easy for him. I called them the Dynamic Duo," she finished with a laugh. "They were a power couple before those were a social media trend." Her voice faded away, and she stared off into space.

Max approached her again, this time entwining his fingers in hers, not allowing her to shrug him off again. He gently tugged her back to the couch and pulled her down to sit next to him.

"Keep going," he encouraged, laying both of her hands in one of his while his other hand tucked a strand of hair behind her ear and then settled on her lower back. He hoped she felt the support he tried to lend.

"As the bakery became more successful, my uncles became more unruly. They were hateful and rude and demanding. Gram looked the other way, unable to face the conniving grown men her sweet boys had become. Not any better, Pops enabled them, always giving them money to get out of trouble in hopes they would have some miraculous epiphany and walk away from the choices they were making. Instead, a rival crime family sent a message to my uncles through my grandpa."

She took a shaky breath but didn't look at Max. He rubbed her back, again offering his support without derailing her train of thought. Reliving this couldn't be easy for her. At the same time, Max believed unburdening oneself was therapeutic, and he suspected she'd bottled all this inside for a long time.

"It started unraveling ten years ago," she said. "We didn't understand the symptoms yet, but Gram began showing signs of mild cognitive impairment. She'd forget she'd already made a pitcher of tea or complain she couldn't smell when things were done baking in the oven. She made mistakes doing tasks she'd done in the kitchen a million times. That went on for about two years, her decline steady, but slow.

"Then, one particular day, she'd been especially foggy and what she called 'muddle-headed.' I was sixteen and had just passed my driver's test. That evening, Pops told me to take her home. He asked me to heat up soup for supper and insist that she rest. I knew it would take a few hours for him to finish up once the shop closed and the employees left for the evening. I didn't think anything of it when he hadn't arrived by the time I helped Gram get ready and climb into bed. I went on to my room to do homework and must've fallen asleep around midnight. I hadn't heard Gram get up during the night, and I guess I just assumed that Pops had come home."

Janie Lyn's voice had become shaky, her words coming quickly, almost breathless. Her hands had been resting in his, but the more agitated she became, the tighter her grasp became. By that point in her story, her fingers were clenched onto his.

"The police rang the bell at the gate around six the next morning. They'd been called when the first shift of bakers arrived at four forty-five and found Pops beaten and left for dead in the parking lot behind the main building. An ambulance had been called. I'm sure the EMTs did everything they could do, but it was the coroner that drove Pops away."

"Oh, no," Max exhaled, wrapping Janie Lyn in his arms. He tucked her head under his chin. Janie Lyn's hands trembled. Tears streamed down her face.

"He died alone during the cold night." Her voice was thready. "Alone. Bloody and in pain."

Max pulled her closer. "No, he wasn't alone. I promise, honey, the Lord was with him." Then he let her cry for as long as she needed.

When she shifted to sit up from his embrace, he leaned to grab several tissues from the lamp table.

"Thank you," she whispered when he placed them in her hand, keeping one to wipe at the tears still running down her cheeks. "I'm sorry. I'm always crying on you."

"I'm not." Max made sure his voice was steady and solid. Sure. He gave her a moment to catch her breath. "Will you tell me the rest?"

"Yes," she answered, "although, it doesn't feel like there's much more to say. Losing Pops flipped a switch, served as a catalyst for Gram to enter a quick mental decline. Within a year, she could no longer help at the bakery, so I'd taken over most of the ownership duties. A large operation, we had teams of bookkeepers, bakers and shift supervisors, dining room managers, a maintenance crew, and custodial staff. Alternatively, the bakery itself remained small enough that our employees felt like family, very loyal and dedicated to the business as well as to me."

Janie Lyn took a deep breath. Her tears had dried up, so Max gathered her tissues and stood to take them to the trash in the kitchen. He returned with two glasses and a bottle of red wine.

"Thank you," she said as he handed one glass to her. Her words were more mouthed than spoken.

"Always," Max pledged with a nod. He gave her a moment to sip her wine, a minute to finish collecting herself. "What did your uncles do after Pops was killed?"

"I'm not really sure. The police ruled the homicide as a random mugging, although the assailants could have stolen thousands of dollars from the bakery but didn't even go inside after attacking my grandpa. It didn't matter — we all knew the truth. I'd guess my uncles retaliated in some way, but thankfully, I was oblivious to their lives.

"It was hard to go on without Gram and Pops in the bakery. They were the glue that held our company together. It was different at the bakery without their influence and impact, but they'd created a well-oiled, smooth-running machine. For the most part, very little changed for anyone looking in from the outside. Daily orders were filled, lunches were served, and Christmas cakes were delivered around the world just like before. My uncles didn't become an issue until I was in college."

Max refilled their glasses but set his on the coffee table. He turned to give Janie Lyn his full attention as she continued.

"I attended the University of Georgia but lived at home to help take care of Gram. Sometime during the fall semester of my sophomore year, I think it finally dawned on my uncles that someone was paying the bills, providing in-home healthcare for Gram, and controlling the finances at the bakery. I came home from a group study session one night to find the house dark and Gram gone. My stuff lay strewn on the front lawn. Boards on the windows and chains on the doors prevented anyone from getting inside the house. I rushed to the bakery to find new locks there, too. I slept in my car and waited until the morning crew arrived before sunup. We huddled in the parking lot together until one of my uncles showed up around nine o'clock, the eldest and the scariest."

Janie Lyn shuddered. She'd lived through this nightmare, and he hated that she'd been forced to do so on her own.

"There were two even scarier-looking men with him."

"Good Lord, they sound like the goons in a mobster movie," Max said, amazed this had actually happened in real life.

"Exactly," Janie Lyn conceded. "Gram had been moved to a nursing home, the beautiful antebellum home she and Pops had bought and restored throughout their marriage had been ransacked, and the bakery accounts had been emptied, completely drained."

"And you were homeless," Max interjected.

"Well, yes," she allowed with chagrin. "That too."

"How long did it take you to find Gram? My bet is less than half a day." He grinned at her as he said it, determined to illustrate how much he believed in her.

She smiled back with a sly smirk. "Just under two hours, but to be fair, there were only a dozen or so nursing homes on our side of the city, and I knew my uncles wouldn't have put much work into finding a good facility for Gram. I was also lucky in that Gram and Pops had insisted I learn to manage my own money. They'd opened accounts in my name and social security number when I was a child. I was the sole owner of the accounts once I'd reached eighteen, so no one else could touch that money. Gram and Pops had contributed to those accounts generously over the years. They claimed it was payment for the work I did at the bakery. If so, I was grossly overpaid. I'd have gladly helped run the company for the rest of my life without receiving a penny in pay."

"*So*," Max drawled out, easing the tension with comedic humor. "You are an independently wealthy woman," he teased.

"That's actually the problem," she said with a guffaw. Her words sobered him. "At least one of them," she added in a quiet voice.

"How so?"

"Gram succumbed to dementia not long after they took her away. My uncles have run the bakery into the ground. They want access to my accounts to try and keep it going."

Max gave a whistle. "Lyndale Christmas Cakes. I'm guessing the upcoming holidays are pretty lucrative for a company known across the globe for their seasonal specialty."

"Yes, very," Janie Lyn acknowledged.

"On the same level as those marshmallows at Easter?"

"Beyond," she admitted with a smirk. "Think more along the lines of French fries from the world's most recognizable burger place."

"Yikes!" Max shook his head. "How in the world did your uncles run a company worth that kind of money into bankruptcy so quickly?"

"I'm sure I don't want to know. But, Maxwell, it's more than just the money."

Her voice quivered again, and Max knew the rest was not going to be good.

"In for a penny, in for a pound, right?" He joked just enough to take the fear out of her eyes. "Janie Lyn— Elizabeth. Whatever name you want to be called…I'm here, and I'm not going anywhere. I promise," Max pledged, tracing a finger across her cheek and then below her bottom lip. *How can skin be this soft?*

"I'm not going anywhere," he promised again.

15

> ***A secret remains a secret***
> ***until you make someone promise***
> ***never to reveal it.***
> **Fausto Cercignani**

Maxwell's voice had dropped as his finger traced over her cheekbone. His words sounded husky and raw. The look in his eyes brought a flush and a tingle to the skin he touched with both his hand and his gaze.

Janie Lyn's heartbeat sped up.

Elizabeth. She could go back to using Elizabeth now. At least here in the house with Maxwell. But Elizabeth didn't sound quite right anymore. She wasn't sure it fit who she was now. No, better to stick with Janie Lyn. Besides, she couldn't take a chance on someone hearing her real name, so Janie Lyn seemed safer.

In for a penny, he'd said — one of Pops's favorite sayings, she remembered with a smile — so she squared her shoulders to tell him the rest.

"I'm the recipe they need to make the Christmas cakes. That's why I ran when Gram passed away from Alzheimer's. Without me, they can't fulfill the holiday orders. I'd rather let the Lyndale Family Bakery close for good than allow them to profit from it. I won't go back." Defiance strengthened her voice. It only made her more sure of her decision.

"Wait," Max said. "You are the recipe? You mean you *have* the recipe, right?"

"No, I *am* the recipe. Gram taught me how to make the spice syrup that goes into the cake batter, but it was never written down. Each summer, we'd boil and can enough for the next year. The bakers had access to the jars, but none of them ever helped create them. Gram and I were the only ones who ever made her 'secret sauce.' They would've run out by this time last year. I didn't try a cake last winter, but I saw reports that consumers detected a difference. The cakes didn't taste the same, didn't have the same look or feel that people expected. Sales dropped drastically. Like you said earlier, the Lyndale Christmas Cake is the proverbial golden goose; it alone can fund the entire year ahead. Even if my uncles can keep the doors open through the end of December, the company won't survive that type of backlash a second year."

"You are the recipe," Max repeated. Understanding was dawning in his eyes. "Your uncles sound like some pretty bad people. And their business associates didn't mind roughing up your grandpa to the point of murder."

"That's right," Janie Lyn confirmed. "The bakery can't live without me, and I'd rather die than go back."

She lifted her chin to make her point: she *wasn't* going back.

"Please don't say that," Max whispered. "Don't say it like that."

"I've come to terms with it, Maxwell. I will miss the home I loved with Gram and Pops, but it's already gone. They are both gone. I will miss my friends at the bakery, the music playing in the background as people chatter and visit while mixing dough, kneading bread, and frosting cakes. I will miss the smell of the icing for the cupcakes and cookies, the cinnamon buns and coffee aromas early each morning, and yeast and fruit and fresh-baked breads. But all of those are gone now, too. That life is gone, and I've made a life I love just as much here. Green Hills is my home, and although I gave up on miracles many years ago, I do feel blessed to have found it."

"Miss Sadie would say it was God's work," Maxwell said.

Janie Lyn smiled, but a big dark, thunderous cloud hung over them, and they both knew it.

"So, you're not embarrassed to be seen with a dumb jock." He nudged her with an elbow.

"Maxwell Davenport, you are far from being a dumb jock. Like worlds, light-years, and eons away! And I'm certainly not embarrassed to be seen with you. Truly, you've become one of my very favorite people in the world." She looked up at him from beneath her lashes, feeling shy after her confession. "I'd be proud to go anywhere with you. If I could," she added.

"I'm not sure how to take that," he said with a wink, and when her eyes opened wide with disbelief, he continued. "I mean, you've reduced your world to about six people, so it shouldn't take much to be one of your favorites." She grabbed a throw pillow from beside her and hit him square upside the head with it. "Seriously," he continued as he fielded her pillow punches, grabbing the cushion out of her hands and tossing it to the side as he folded her arms uselessly in front of her. "You said *one* of your favorite people. Not even The Favorite. Just another one of the group."

Now he was holding both her arms with one hand and using the other to tickle her ribs. She giggled and squirmed and tried to wrestle back with her legs. It felt so good to laugh. To joke. To feel free.

Somehow Janie Lyn ended up lying along the length of the sofa, Maxwell sitting between her hips and the edge of the cushion. He was leaning over her, smiling down at her. The weight of his upper body, the warmth of his touch, the glow of his gaze — they stopped her heart.

She loved him. Oh, dear God, she loved him.

"And you can," he said, pulling her focus from the bombshell she'd just discovered.

"I can what?"

Maxwell stopped tickling her ribs. He released the light hold he'd had on her arms. They fell onto her chest as he set a hand on either side of her head. He remained like that, hovering over her, eyes glittering and smile shining.

"You can go out with me."

"Maxwell, I can't. I—" He stopped her protest with a gentle finger to her lips.

"Hear me out," he coaxed, but he didn't remove his finger from her lips until she nodded in agreement. "I'm going to church with Maree and Miss Sadie in the morning." Janie Lyn immediately started to protest, so he put the finger back to her lips. "I'm not finished yet… I know that is too public a place for us to sit together, so I'm not asking you to go with us. But I'll come pick you up afterward to go out to Miss Sadie's for lunch. And after that, we'll go to the Majestic for the afternoon matinee. They're showing some old black-and-white film that nobody is likely to go see except the two of us. You can walk in first, and I'll come sit with you after the lights go down in the theater. It'll be dark. No one will even notice us."

He slowly removed the finger from her lips, tilting his head in a questioning gesture that reminded her of an adorable puppy batting its adorable eyes to get its adorable way.

"Max—" He must not have liked the reluctance in her voice because he immediately closed her lips again.

"If you keep it up, I'm going to find a better way to stop you from speaking nonsense." His head shifted, and one eyebrow lifted as if daring her to test him.

Janie Lyn wasn't sure if that was a threat or a promise. Either way, her pulse quickened.

"Say yes," he implored. "Go to the movies with me. We will be ridiculously careful. You'll wear that awful cap. I'll act grumpy so no one tries to talk to me. And we'll meet on the inside after the previews start. Come on, say yes."

She wanted to. She wanted to, so badly.

"For the record," she said, impishness in her tone, "my cap is for *your* football team." She couldn't stop herself from ending with a snooty humph.

His only response was to light up even more, his smile amping up in voltage to a megawatt setting.

Who was she kidding? She hadn't been able tell him no when he asked her to stay at the house yesterday. She couldn't tell him no now, either.

"Okay—" She paused when he whooped and pumped a victorious fist in the air. She raised her voice to be heard over his celebration. "On one condition."

He brought his gaze back down to her. "Anything."

"You can't tell anyone what I've told you."

He sobered instantly, shifting to sit up straight. With both feet once again firmly planted on the ground, he rested his elbows on his knees and clasped his hands under his chin.

Janie Lyn moved to kneel on the couch, facing him although he still looked down at the coffee table instead of at her.

"Maxwell, trust me. This is the only way." She hated to beg so boldly, but she believed it to be true. The only way to keep their loved ones safe was to keep them all in the dark. "If Miss Sadie or Maree or anyone else knows, they'll want to make it better. They'll want to fix it, and there is no fix. There is no solution. As I told you, I will not go back. I will not do their bidding, and I will not be their puppet."

"But maybe we *can* help you." He finally turned to look at her. "Maybe—"

"No," she insisted. "They are ruthless, violent, dangerous people. I will not help them fund a crime syndicate. I won't be the reason they ruin more lives, and I won't lead them to Green Hills."

"Okay," Maxwell relented. His hands raised in defeat. "Okay," he repeated. "We will do this your way."

Janie Lyn released the tension that had taken hold of her neck and shoulders as she gave Maxwell one grateful nod.

She rose from the couch and gathered up their paper plates, napkins, and tea glasses.

"For now," Maxwell added as she flipped the light on in the kitchen.

"For always," she insisted when she returned to gather up another load to take to the kitchen.

Their eyes met in a tug-of-war, a test of wills. Maxwell's jaw locked, his gaze direct. Janie Lyn looked away first, bending to pick up the wineglasses and half-full bottle.

This time when she walked away, she swore she heard him say, "We'll see."

16

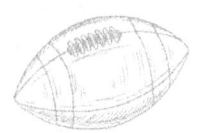

Keep the glasses on and the cap down low.
Harry Connick, Jr. as
Tripp Spence in Mickey (2004)

Max had not slept a wink.

He'd wanted to stay up all night researching the Lyndale Family Bakery, the Lyndale family, and the "runaway heiress." There had been loads of news coverage when she first disappeared two years ago, but he hadn't paid close attention. Over time, the frequency with which the story popped up had decreased. But it was still an unsolved case with a celebrity element to it, so the gossip hadn't gone away completely.

The only thing that had stopped him from logging on to his computer was the stark terror in Janie Lyn's eyes when she talked about her uncles. He didn't want to trigger anyone watching search engines, especially not while he was here in Green Hills.

Max had agreed with Janie Lyn on that one issue: it was imperative that nothing draw her family's attention to the people they loved right here in their sleepy corner of southeast Oklahoma.

So, instead of gathering intel and devising a plan to fix her predicament — because despite what Janie Lyn had accepted as truth, Max *did* believe there was a solution out there — he'd tossed and turned until he couldn't stand it any longer.

By five thirty a.m., he'd thrown on workout clothes, grabbed his keys, and headed out for a run. When that hadn't decreased his frustration by even a fraction, he jogged to the high school weight room and let himself in with the key his friend Scotty, the head football coach of the Green Hills Wolf Pack, had given him to use at his convenience. It appeared that six fifteen on a Sunday morning was the perfect time.

He worked to exorcise the demons haunting his mind as forcefully as he deemed safe in a weight room by himself, without a spotter, a cell phone, or a single soul knowing where he'd gone.

When that, too, failed to clear his head, he jogged home, showered, and dressed for church.

When he emerged from his room, Janie Lyn had already left, presumably for the memory care facility.

At least now he had a better understanding of why she was so passionate about volunteering there, so determined to bring attention and awareness to ending Alzheimer's disease. And equally determined *not* to bring attention and awareness to herself.

It had been one hell of a story.

Max tried to be the exception rather than the rule when it came to sports figures using foul language. He often reminded his teammates there was always a better word than the foul four-letter kind. He teased them, but always in truth, that cussing was a sign of laziness and they were too bright to speak that way.

In this case, even Max couldn't come up with a better word. No, Janie Lyn's story— Elizabeth Jayne Lyndale's story was one *hell* of a story!

It was going to be torture not telling his family what was going on. If the tables were turned, Max would be furious if any one of them kept such a serious matter from him. He'd already begun preparing an argument to convince Janie Lyn that they needed to at least tell Rhys so he could keep an eye open without worrying Maree or Miss Sadie.

Throughout church, his thoughts flipped between that debate, persuading Janie Lyn to come out of hiding, and keeping her safe if she ever agreed. He interjected scattered prayers of protection and guidance, and by the time services ended, he was mentally repeating Joshua 1:9... *Be strong and courageous. Do not be afraid.*

When he pulled back into his driveway, he was an absolute mess. He needed to see Janie Lyn.

He stormed through the back door to find her walking toward him. Seeing her safe and whole lifted a weight from his chest. He strode to her, tossing her baseball cap and glasses to the floor as he wrapped his arms around her.

He was probably squeezing the breath out of her, but he couldn't stop. His brain had been playing tricks on him. As staunchly as he'd tried to push out negative thoughts throughout the morning, a thread of doubt had seeped in. Would her uncles find her? Would she be home when he got there? Was she safe? Was she secure? Would she run?

"Maxwell?" He clung to her so rigidly that she could barely speak. "Are you okay?"

She probably thought he was losing his mind.

"As long as you are," he murmured.

"Did something happen?" When he didn't reply, she began to fidget, shifting her weight from foot to foot. "Maybe I shouldn't go to lunch at Miss Sadie's," she hedged.

"Nothing happened." Max finally unlocked his arms from around her. But he didn't drop his hold completely.

With his hands on both of her shoulders, he gazed down into her face. He didn't know what he was looking for specifically. Just a little more reassurance.

Her head tilted to one side to study him. One corner of her lips lifted in a half smile.

Max brought his lips to her forehead and then hugged her once more before picking up her hat and glasses.

"Sorry," he said, handing both items to her and stepping back to give her a modicum of space. "The longer the morning lasted, the more urgently I wanted to be back home. I needed to see you with my own two eyes." Once she'd put on her hat and glasses, he lifted his hand toward her.

"I'm sorry, too," she replied. She clasped the hand he'd offered, and they walked through the house and into the garage.

"Whatever for?"

"I'm sorry for saddling you with this secret. It's a lot, and it was unfair to unload it on you."

He opened her door on the passenger side of his truck. When she brushed by him to get in, he reached out to cup her cheek. She stopped midstep, one foot on the running board, the other still on the ground.

"Janie Lyn," he said, guiding her gaze to his. "I'm glad you did." He didn't want to leave any room for doubt. "You don't ever have to worry about telling me anything. I have broad shoulders; I can carry this just fine. And I will be here to help carry you through — if you'll let me — no matter the challenge."

"Thank you," she replied, her voice barely a whisper.

"Now climb up," he said as he dropped his hand from her face and stepped aside. "I'm starving, and Miss Sadie's cooking is waiting." Max gave her a wink and closed the door.

Lunch didn't disappoint: pot roast with carrots, potatoes, and onions; corn pudding; creamed spinach; homemade biscuits topped with whipped butter and more of his sister's strawberry jam.

The fellowship was even better than the food. Maree and Rhys were still aglow over their engagement. Miss Sadie was in full mother-hen mode, tending to the crowd. With the Jensen family joining them, there was no talk of the recent fires. Instead, everyone made sure to keep the conversation light and fun.

Max noticed Janie Lyn remained quiet, but she didn't shy away from the group. The smile on her face and her laughter at the stories and memories that were shared felt like gifts.

Her happiness was a gift. *To* Max. He'd never experienced such a selfless thought, but there it was. *Her* contentment and well-being were most important, suddenly his highest priority. His enjoyment was dependent upon hers. She came first. How had that happened so quickly?

Max chuckled, which caused Janie Lyn to look his way. Their eyes met, hers a pale, luminescent green. He could easily get lost in them. His chest swelled as warmth spread through it. His smile grew wider.

She squinted in question.

He winked in answer.

Janie Lyn blushed.

Max had fun with their silent conversation. He liked that the two of them seemed to exist in their own little world. But he was also ready to have her to himself.

He pushed back his chair, stood, and began stacking the plates and dishes around him.

Rhys followed his lead, whispering a word in Maree's ear when he reached for her silverware. Color infused her cheeks, but instead of diverting her eyes, she looked at Rhys with an expression of clear challenge. Rhys shook his head with a laugh and kissed her lips. Lightly, but right there in front of everyone.

Max wanted that, wished he didn't have to hide his feelings for Janie Lyn.

"Can I help?" Zachariah was the oldest of the Jensen kids and looked to be ten or twelve. When they'd been introduced, Zachariah's eyes had grown wide, as often happened when Max met football fans, both young and old. Of course, Zachariah's eyes had gotten even larger, filled with admiration and the utmost respect, when Rhys arrived. Firemen still trumped football players, exactly as they should.

"Did you cook?" Max asked the boy.

"No, sir," Zachariah answered.

"Me, neither," Rhys supplied. "So, we get to clean."

"Yes, sir," Zachariah said, nearly saluting. You'd have thought Rhys gave the kid a new toy rather than permission to do dishes. "Come on, Joel," he added to his younger brother, who was only four or five. "Grab that tub of butter. They need us."

Those still sitting around the table managed to contain their giggles until the two boys had disappeared into the kitchen.

"Thank you," Mrs. Jensen offered, her eyes shining with moisture.

"We appreciate their eagerness! Besides, Momma always said being adorable would only get one so far, so it was wise to be useful, too," Max teased.

"Yeah, but she was saying it to me!" Maree heckled Max. He responded by tugging on her hair with his free hand when he passed her chair on his way to the kitchen.

By the time the dining room table was cleared, the leftovers put away, and the kitchen clean, Max was chomping at the bit to leave. He'd had a wonderful afternoon — icing on the cake of a fabulous trip home.

Always a little greedy when it came to sweets, both literally and figuratively, now he wanted to add a few sprinkles on top… He wanted to spend the rest of the day with Janie Lyn.

"Ready?" Max asked her when he walked out onto the front porch, where the grown-ups were sitting while the kids chased and played in the yard.

"Sure," Janie Lyn replied evenly, but a skitter of nerves darkened her green eyes.

He didn't want to add to her worries or cause her anxiety. But surely they could sneak away to a show on a sleepy Sunday afternoon in small-town Oklahoma, right? Her world consisted of Miss Sadie and her boarding house, Maree and her design studio, volunteering at Memorial Care, and now Max's house. He wanted her to have more, even if that was nothing grander than a movie at the theater with a big tub of buttery popcorn and a cold soda. That wasn't asking too much, was it?

They didn't offer where they were headed, and Max was glad no one asked. He didn't want to deceive anyone, but he also didn't want them asking to tag along. No, what he wanted was simple: Janie Lyn to himself and an opportunity to prove to her they could be together.

The first and only theater in town, the Majestic had been built in 1921. Luckily, it managed to avoid demolition when her counterparts in Tulsa were torn down to make space for new structures in the '60s.

It was designed as an atmospheric movie palace with opulent elements such as plaster columns, wooden trellis work, and a night sky projected on the ceiling. The effect was that of an open-air, outdoor theater, placed in a luxurious garden under twinkling stars and billowing clouds. The seats were still cushioned in heavy red velvet. Like in the early days of moviegoing, an introduction by Mr. Warren, the theater proprietor, preceded every show. Next the audience was treated to a few minutes of entertainment such as a magic trick, a song accompanied by Mrs. Warren on a stately black lacquered baby grand piano that lived on a side stage, or even a yo-yo or hula hoop contest for the kids. After that, a short film was played, usually a cartoon, but sometimes a vintage newsreel. Then it was time for the feature; there were no previews or trailers.

Although the films shown were often classics and it took an extra fifteen minutes to get through all the "pregame" activities, no one complained. The Majestic was a treasure. And this was Green Hills. Life moved at a slower pace. Time felt less chaotic here. Moments were somehow more appreciated.

Max loved every bit of it.

"I adore this place," Janie Lyn said with awe and reverence when they turned off Main Street and drove in front of the art deco building. "Just look at the details, the lace and foliage carved into the stone. It's breathtaking."

"Breathtaking," Max agreed, looking only at Janie Lyn.

He pulled into the alley behind Maree's shop, Main Street Design, which was just around the corner from the theater. Knowing she didn't want them to be seen arriving together, he let Janie Lyn out of the truck there. Once she'd walked out of his line of sight from his rearview mirror, Max drove through to the other side of Maree's block. There wasn't any parking available on the street in front of the Majestic, so he made a show of looking for the perfect spot along the shops facing the courthouse square.

Dawsey's, everyone's favorite candy shop, was open with kids running in and out still wearing their church clothes. Maree's studio was closed, but the massive window display lit up her space like a Christmas tree. Three Bells, a sandwich shop and pub on the row of storefronts, buzzed like a hive of activity, with every patio table full and the thrum of the late lunch crowd coming from inside. Additional restaurants around the square and further down the street like Luca's and the Three-Toed Turtle looked busy as well.

Maxwell was confident no one would pay him any attention, and if someone did recognize him, they'd have no idea which business he was visiting.

He meandered his way to the theater, window-shopping along the way, careful not to draw any scrutiny.

He purchased his ticket and stopped at the concession window to buy them popcorn, a box of chocolate-covered caramels per Janie Lyn's request, and a jumbo soft drink for them to share, with two bendy straws.

Dark as the sky on a starless night, it took a few seconds for Max's eyes to acclimate when he entered the theater. A vintage reel of Betty Boop played on the screen. Max found Janie Lyn at the back of the theater and sat down in the old-fashioned plush seat next to her, confident that not even one person had taken notice of him. Not a single soul cared that they were there…together…on their first official date.

The Majestic had one screen. There was no choice as to what one watched. Mr. Warren chose the movies, and whatever struck his fancy was the next movie shown.

Max cringed a little when Mr. Warren's selection for that afternoon turned out to be *Some Like it Hot*. The classic comedy was hilarious, but the "disguise yourself to escape the mob" theme hit a little too close to home. Luckily, Janie Lyn seemed to enjoy it, laughing throughout, nudging his hand out of the way to dive into the popcorn, smiling up at him when Sugar chose Joe despite his baggage and his claims that he wasn't good enough for her.

There were fewer than a dozen people in the theater, including Max and Janie Lyn, but they sat through the credits to allow everyone else time to exit anyway. Max didn't mind waiting. He wasn't in a rush for the day to end and was happy to slow down time in any way possible.

Max and Janie Lyn walked out to find the lobby vacant and the lights dimmed. They heard Mr. and Mrs. Warren, their voices indistinct in the box office as they closed the movie house.

The sidewalk was also empty, so it didn't occur to Max to separate from Janie Lyn as they strode past storefronts.

He draped an arm over her shoulder. She nestled into his side, her head against his heart and tucked under his chin.

"Thank you," Max breathed into her hair. She'd lifted her head to reply when movement caught his eye. A man was striding toward them, a big "fan smile" on his face. To buy them a few extra seconds, Max pretended he'd not seen him. The man kept coming.

They were passing a small alcove between two shops. Acting on impulse, Max whirled Janie Lyn into that tiny space. He backed her up against the brick wall and covered her body with his own to shield her from view.

She looked up at him in surprise.

The man's footsteps continued getting closer.

Surely the fan wouldn't follow or approach them. Resisting the urge to look over his shoulder to confirm that theory, while simultaneously reminding himself that fans did just about anything they wanted if they thought it was their right, Max did the only thing he could.

He kissed Janie Lyn.

He brought both hands up to her face. His palms covered her cheeks, further hiding her identity. His fingers tangled in her braids and wrapped around the back of her neck.

His lips settled on hers. He wanted to be gentle, but what began as a knee-jerk reaction to someone spotting them, quickly became an emotional response to the woman in his arms.

Janie Lyn's hands gripped the lapels of his jacket. She tugged him closer.

He deepened the kiss.

"Oh! Well," the man said with a laugh before turning away. His receding footsteps barely registered in the haze of Max's mind.

He couldn't get close enough to her.

Max continued to frame Janie Lyn's face with his right hand but moved his left to slide under her right arm and up her back. That way he could cushion her from the brick wall while shifting his weight to close the gap between them.

A purr escaped her throat. Or maybe he imagined it. Either way, the smooth, elegant sway of her neck called out to him like a siren.

Releasing her lips, Max littered kisses from the corner of her mouth, along her jaw, to the soft spot under her ear. When her purr grew to a groan, Max almost lost his control.

She was intoxicating.

He'd never experienced inebriation, but that had to feel the same. He was literally drunk on the taste, the warmth, the feel of her.

Janie Lyn's hands crept up to cup his jaw. She held his head in place as he continued to lavish kisses across her soft skin. When he reached the notch between her collar bones and felt the scratch of her sweater, he knew he had to stop.

He was losing his mind, gladly, but he had to regain some composure. Ravishing Janie Lyn in an alley beside the Majestic was *not* his plan. And it wasn't fair to Janie Lyn.

Purposefully, he lightened his kisses. Couldn't stop them entirely, but he managed to dial down the intensity. When he reached her lips again, he indulged in one last sip. He nipped at her lips, smiling at the taste of peach lip gloss. How could she have any left?

"Come home with me." Max's voice resembled gravel, sharp and rough.

"What?"

He didn't let her go, didn't allow even a breath of air between them. Holding her close and looking down into the bottomless depths of her crystal green eyes, he prayed she would say yes. He asked again, emphatically trying not to come across as desperate as he felt.

"Come home with me, Janie Lyn. To Kansas City."

That was his plan.

17

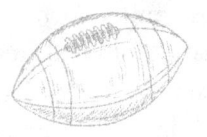

I have no words.
English idiom: to be rendered speechless
by someone or something.

*G**o to Kansas City with him?*
 The question had played in a loop in Janie Lyn's head since he'd spoken the words.

At first, she thought she'd imagined him saying them. He'd just kissed her senseless, and she'd have sworn she was hearing things.

But Maxwell had repeated them. He was serious. He truly wanted her with him.

Shell-shocked by both the kiss and the revelation, Janie Lyn functioned in a daze as Maxwell had led her through the alley, behind the downtown shops, and then hustled her into his truck.

On the way to his house, Max detoured to stop by the Fish & Spoon, leaving her in the truck while he ran in. True to their slogan of "Fifteen Fishy Favorites, Always Hot & Ready," he'd been back out within five minutes, carrying a "brookie" — Fish & Spoon's famous chocolate chip cookie sandwiched between two layers of brownie and topped with toasted almonds, caramel, and crunchy granules of coarse sea salt — along with two boxes of fish and chips. She'd still been sitting in her trance.

Go to Kansas City with him?

She didn't remember driving through Foxtail. That was significant, as Max's neighborhood was one of her favorite places in Green Hills. In the whole world, if she was being honest.

Enamored of the landscape, Janie Lyn loved driving or taking walks through it. A fascinating blend of native terrain, luscious grasses, manicured yards, and enormous mature trees created a canvas of vibrant colors and bold textures that never got old. Also a colorful array, the Craftsman-style houses included a mix of 120-year-old homes, some still in their original form, others completely remodeled, and many that were somewhere in between.

There were exactly ninety homes in the subdivision — Janie Lyn had counted the precise number of houses on each of the seven streets numerous times. Without compromising their unique design, every one of them touted several elements of distinct and skilled craftsmanship. A practically endless list of charming touches included wood trims and built-in bonuses such as hand-carved bookcases, planter boxes, boxed beams, wraparound porches, and wide window seats.

And yet, she hadn't noticed a thing as they drove through to Max's house.

She was still on autopilot when Max opened her door and extended a hand to help her out of the truck. She walked to her bedroom, closed the door, and went through the mindless motions of changing into a pair of gray knit workout shorts, her most comfortable sports bra, and an Alzheimer's event t-shirt that happened to be on the top of the stack when she opened the drawer.

Max had also changed into comfortable clothes and was leaning — arms crossed, slight grin in place — against the wall opposite her door when she emerged from her room.

She followed his gaze down to her bare feet. Huh, she'd forgotten shoes.

"You okay?" His voice was gleeful. *Gleeful!*

Janie Lyn managed to nod. Once.

Max gave a little giggle, pushed away from the wall, and clasped one of the hands hanging limp at her sides.

He led her into the kitchen. There he filled two glasses with iced tea, stacked them onto a tray with the take-out boxes, and added the ketchup bottle out of the fridge and the malted vinegar from the pantry. He tucked two napkins beneath the beverages. Then Max balanced the tray on the palm of one hand and bent his knees to reach her hand that he'd let fall.

"Can you get that?" He tipped his head toward the glass door to the back yard. Like a robot, the hand he wasn't holding lifted, unlocked the door, and opened it. Max waited for her to walk through. When she didn't budge, he shook his head with another laugh and walked outside. Still leading her like a puppet on a string, he twirled her under his arm so she faced the house and could shut the door.

Then Max tugged her over to the picnic table and deposited her into one of the chairs. He set out the food, laid a napkin in her lap, and stole a quick kiss on her lips.

Instantly, they tingled.

She looked up at him and marveled.

She'd often thought him a dream. Would she wake up to discover none of this was real? That he hadn't shielded her from the man on the sidewalk? That he hadn't kissed her within an inch of her life? That he hadn't asked her to stay with him in Kansas City?

Was the utterly clear, uncomplicated, and unrefined look of love in his eyes just a figment of her imagination?

With her face lifted to his, Max curled his fingers around her jaw and smoothed his thumb across her skin.

Her face tingled, too.

Indeed, everywhere he touched, tingled. Everywhere he looked. Everywhere he kissed.

He made it hard to breathe.

"Eat," Max commanded before dropping his hand from her face and shaking his head yet again.

He sure seemed to do that a lot.

He sat down and opened his box of fish and chips. She watched him add ketchup next to the fries and drizzle malt vinegar over the fish. Then he salted the whole thing. Just before taking a bite, he cut his eyes over to her.

"Janie Lyn, eat!" This time she followed his direction.

Surprisingly still steaming hot, the fried food comforted her. The batter had an essence of sweet corn and rich butter. The flaky fish tasted light and fresh. The French fries were homemade, the potatoes sliced long and thin and cooked until they were crispy and brown on the ends but still soft and starchy on the inside.

Max had twice as much food in his basket, but he still finished in half as much time. When he got up from the table and went inside, Janie Lyn didn't even look up from her box and simply kept eating. She was ravenous.

But hadn't she had breakfast just that morning? Yes, before leaving for the memory care facility.

Hadn't they enjoyed a huge lunch at Miss Sadie's? Yes, before leaving for the movie theater.

And hadn't they indulged on popcorn and candy at the Majestic? Yes, before the kiss.

The kiss.

Janie Lyn returned her last bite of fish to the box. She glanced up to watch Maxwell walk toward her. Her head tilted to the side to better study him.

When would she stop feeling dazed every time she looked at him?

He'd turned on music through the outdoor speakers. Janie Lyn recognized the classic country, which Maree also leaned toward. The singer was crooning about believing in babies and old folks, superstars and foreign cars. She liked it.

Max set a bowl in front of her and placed one — this time thrice as full as hers — in front of his chair as he sat in it.

"I'm not a puzzle to decipher," he said, picking up the spoon propped in the bowl. His voice had shifted from gleeful to amused.

Janie Lyn raised an eyebrow at him before looking down to see what was in the bowl.

Max had heated a significant slice of the brookie and topped it with ice cream. The scents of warm chocolate chip cookies, toasted almonds, and sweet vanilla assaulted her senses. Dessert, breads, and food in general had always been her love languages.

Her eyebrows — both this time — lifted even higher.

In for a penny, in for a pound, she reminded herself.

About seven bites in, she feared she'd be sick. It was so good, but she was *so* full. She slid her bowl next to Max's and smiled at him when his eyes met hers. She watched as he finished both bowls, and when he pushed back his chair, she did the same.

Together they loaded the tray, and again she opened the door for him. This time, however, she didn't require handholding to place one foot in front of the other.

That was progress, right?

Janie Lyn rinsed the bowls and set them in the dishwasher while Max put the food boxes in a plastic grocery bag, which he tied in a knot and took out to the trash container in the garage.

She assumed it was time to hash out this situation…the *Go to Kansas City with him?* situation. Just the thought had her heart racing again.

But Max didn't say a word. Instead, he sprayed and wiped down the countertops, turned off the light, and took her hand.

We're back to that, huh?

Janie Lyn's pulse truly sped into overtime when Max led her directly to *his* bedroom. Then into his bathroom. And stopped next to the massive claw-foot soaking tub made of refurbished and resurfaced cast iron. The back was sloped to make lounging luxurious, and there was a thin simple wooden plank resting across the sides toward the front but well clear of the faucet.

He flipped the drain and turned on the water. Steam immediately rose from the spout. He reached under the sink to grab a glass jar of bath salts. The scent of gardenias filled the space.

Janie Lyn looked at him quizzically.

"Maree's," he answered sternly, using a lighter from a drawer to light a candle sitting on the tray. The smell of gardenias doubled.

Max took three fluffy towels from the linen cabinet — a washcloth, a hand towel, and a huge bath sheet. He laid them on the vanity and then looked around as if searching for something.

Janie Lyn's brow furrowed, but she stood aside to let him do whatever it was he planned to do.

"Stay put," Max directed. "I'll be right back."

She did as she'd been told and hadn't moved even an inch when he returned with a large cup of ice water and an old-timey radio. He tested the water, shut it off, and left the cup next to the candle.

Then he plugged in the radio on the large vanity, scrolled the dial to find a golden oldies station playing songs from the '50s, and adjusted the volume down so it wasn't distracting.

Finally, he stepped close to face her. Heat instantly filled her limbs. She felt heavy, drugged.

He stood just like that for a long moment. Deliberating? Examining? Looking right through her eyes into her heart? Maybe even her soul.

"Enjoy your bath," Max said with a husky voice. Their chemistry affected him just as much as it did Janie Lyn. "Soak as long as you like. Take all the time you need."

He ran both hands down her arms. She could feel the strength in his touch through the sleeves of her thick sweater. He turned her around and slid the ponytail holders out of her braids.

With deft fingers, he undid the plaits. Her eyes closed of their own volition when he reached under the weight of her long hair and massaged her scalp. His hands felt magical when they moved to the tops of her shoulders to knead the tension she was holding there.

She melted like butter.

After a few minutes of that torturous pleasure, Max smoothed her hair over one shoulder and leaned into the other. His lips traced the edge of her ear.

Did she just whimper? Out loud?

Then Max nibbled on her earlobe and said, "When you get out, we'll talk."

Janie Lyn's eyes snapped open.

He stepped away, and she swallowed a heavy gulp as the door clicked shut.

18

> ***When you talk,***
> ***you are only repeating what you already know.***
> ***But if you listen,***
> ***you may learn something new.***
> ***The Dalai Lama***

*J*anie Lyn hadn't spoken a single word in hours.

On the way home from the theater, Max had been worried. She'd been stunned into silence. Not promising.

Once she'd disappeared into her room, the concern had turned into humor. Honestly, how often does one's kiss cause the recipient of said kiss to go mute?

And boy was it a kiss.

Max grinned just thinking about it.

She drew him to her, attracted him in a way he'd never experienced. But he hadn't expected that kiss.

Bombs could've been going off a football field away, and he wasn't sure he'd have noticed. Even bombs would have been no competition for the fireworks exploding between them.

A ping from his cell phone cleared his head.

- *Got your message. Talk tomorrow.*

Max wouldn't break his word to Janie Lyn; he wouldn't tell any of their loved ones in Green Hills about her family and their state of affairs. But he couldn't sit back and do nothing, either.

He'd reached out to Brennigan Stewart, his best friend and their best resource to get Janie Lyn out of this predicament.

Bren was a secret agent — officially for the FBI, but Max knew there was much more to it. If anyone could navigate a peaceful end to this trouble, Max had faith Bren would.

When Max had called the number he'd been given to reach Bren in case of an emergency, he'd entered a confidential five-digit code to let Bren know who was calling and the level of urgency. Max had fully expected not to hear back for several days, maybe even weeks. The fact that Bren had replied within hours meant he must be finishing up a case or between missions.

Max prayed they could clean up this mess sooner rather than later.

The phone was still in his hand, his thoughts wandering, when Janie Lyn cleared her throat.

"Maxwell?" His name was an inquiry, her voice low, possibly the sweetest sound he'd ever heard.

He stood, flipped his phone face down, and tossed it on the coffee table.

"Hi," he said in return.

"Hi," she said on an exhale. Her lips formed a sweet smile.

Oh man, was she beautiful.

"Come sit with me?"

She nodded in reply and walked into the living room. Elation poured through him when she chose the sofa where he'd been sitting rather than one of the chairs farther away.

"Maxwell, I—"

"Please don't say no before we even talk it through," he said over her words. A wave of fear rippled through his body. "Now, I know you are scared. You should be. I'm not belittling the danger you're in, I promise. I understand why you've done what you felt you needed to do these past two years."

"Maxwell—" She tried to interject, but he couldn't let her. He couldn't risk her saying no.

"That came out wrong." He winced. "What I mean is that I know you did exactly what you had to do to escape. And I'm so glad you did! I feel lucky and blessed and eternally grateful that God led you here, to Green Hills, to Miss Sadie, to our family."

He gripped her hands and caught her gaze.

"To me," he added. "I know this has been a wild weekend, a crazy three days. But they've shown me what life can be, what life *should* be. And now that I've lived it, I can't leave you here."

"Ma—" Again, Max plowed ahead, too afraid to let her reject him.

"I know you'll miss the memory care facility and your work there, but I promise, we will be back here every chance my schedule allows. The season gets hectic, but during the off-season and most of the summer, I can work out anywhere. And I know the thought of being recognized frightens you. I have a plan for that. I'm sure you're hesitant to trust me, but you can. You can count on me. I'm not your parents or your uncles. I won't let you down."

Max was talking too quickly, trying to say everything at once. He had to find the right words, the words she needed to hear to feel safe with him.

"My town house is secure; paparazzi have never gotten close. I have a private pool and deck, plenty of space, a great theater room, and a gourmet kitchen."

Her eyes went wide, and he wasn't sure if she found that illustrious, ridiculous, or both.

"It's a really unique layout, private townhomes with a central concierge building. We can have everything you need delivered to the lobby there at the clubhouse. The doormen are the only people who interact with the public. There are high fences; only one way in and one way out. The risk of being seen will be less than what you face here in Green Hills."

Her expression was still neutral, so he kept rolling right along.

"It's a four-bedroom floor plan. You can have whichever room you want. You're welcome to the master suite. With me. Or I can move into one of the other bedrooms. I would never pressure you — I hope you know that. And there is a library and a separate study. Use them all. There are four and a half bathrooms. No bathtub as big as the one here, but two that are close and equipped with jets. Oh, and there's a sauna out by the pool. And a steam room in the master bath."

Speaking of steam, Max was running out.

"Did I mention the fire pit?" Agony laced his voice, but he didn't care. He didn't care about anything except Janie Lyn being in his truck when he left for KC in the morning. He had to be at the football facility by one o'clock, which meant he needed to leave Green Hills first thing. That only left about eight hours to talk her into it.

"It's too modern and not nearly as cozy as the house and outdoor spaces here, but it's nice. Too nice, really. But good — really good. As long as you're there."

"Maxwell," Janie Lyn said. Then she stopped, pausing, presumably to see if he was actually going to let her speak. "Maxwell," she repeated. "I was going to say *yes*. I'll go."

19

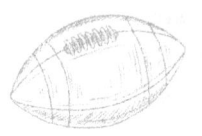

***As soon as I saw you,
I knew an adventure was going to happen.
Paraphrased from A.A. Milne***

"I thought they would be more surprised," Janie Lyn commented as she and Maxwell traveled north toward Kansas City.

"Hmm," Maxwell responded. Not really a response at all.

They'd hit the road early and were almost halfway there when they called his sister and Miss Sadie to let each know that Janie Lyn was with Maxwell. Janie Lyn had worried what they might say, but Maree had cheered, and Miss Sadie had mumbled something about a day's work.

"Do you think they suspected something?"

Maxwell turned his head to meet her gaze momentarily and then looked back at the road.

"I think they love you," he said, which Janie Lyn found to be about as cryptic as Maree and Miss Sadie had been.

She answered with her own *hmm* before looking out the window to watch the world fly by. When her eyelids drooped, she didn't fight to keep them open. When Maxwell nudged her shoulder with his balled-up sweatshirt, she took the makeshift pillow and snuggled into the corner between her seat and the passenger door.

"Janie Lyn," Maxwell said quietly. "Lay your head on the console between our seats." The truck was stopped. He reached across her to move the pillow and guide her to half sit and half lie across the front seat.

"Not safe," she mumbled.

His heavy arm rested on her shoulder and resisted her efforts to sit up.

"You're fine. We're in a drive-through to pick up lunch. Sleep until we get there; the house is just around the corner."

Janie Lyn wanted to argue with him, but she couldn't muster enough energy to exert.

The next thing she knew, Maxwell said it was time to get out of the truck.

"Where are we?"

"Home away from home." Maxwell gestured with open arms as he walked across a vast three-car garage to a very tall door.

Janie Lyn glanced around before following him.

It was pristine.

She'd never seen such an immaculate garage. Essentially empty, even the floor sparkled. Spotless, it had nothing in common with the garage in Green Hills, stuffed full of fishing gear, lake toys, a woodworking bench, and tools hanging on every available inch of wall space.

Janie Lyn followed Maxwell through the door made for giants to find a sterile mudroom that had obviously never seen a clump of mud. She continued into a kitchen that nearly matched the pristine garage. Very contemporary, the cabinets had been painted dark charcoal gray, the ceiling — at least sixteen feet high — reflected prisms of light off diamond-stamped tiles made of shiny gray tin, traditional pale gray subway tiles formed the backsplash, and ash gray concrete countertops lent a sturdy heaviness that grounded the room. The appliances were all stainless steel, void of a single fingerprint. The hardwood floors had been stained a pale shade of gray, making the grain of the wood visible and pronounced.

Janie Lyn turned circles between the enormous eight-burner stove and the gargantuan island. She tried to take it all in, but she felt like Alice falling through the looking glass.

She couldn't comprehend it.

The space was certainly elegant and stylish and striking, but it was a million miles away from the warm and welcoming home Maxwell had created in Oklahoma.

"Let's eat," Maxwell announced. "Then you can explore the house while I'm at work."

She was enduring an out-of-body experience, and he was hungry. Go figure.

Maxwell ran through a quick list of helpful information while they ate: the security code, the Wi-Fi password, and how to turn on the media system. His other house had state-of-the-art electronics and built-in speakers, but a *media system?* Her mind was blown.

She tidied up the lunch mess, scared to death to leave a trace of life in the form of a streak on anything gray.

"I'm not being presumptuous," he pledged as he walked through carrying their bags. "I'm just in a bit of a rush, so I'm going to set everything in my bedroom. I mean, the master suite," he corrected over his shoulder as he disappeared up the stairs.

If the bottom floor was this tall, how many stairs did it take to get to the second floor?

"You should move anything to anywhere." He wiggled his eyebrows as he said it, coming to stand in front of her with his legs spread wide enough that his eyes were nearly level with hers. He lifted her arms onto his shoulders and rested his hands on either side of her ribs. "We have a team meeting, practice, lift, and then position meetings, so it'll be a while before I get back. There are some meals in the freezer if you get hungry. Don't wait for me to eat, okay?"

"Okay," she agreed, stepping close enough to wrap her arms tighter around his neck. His hands twitched as they looked into one another's eyes. His closed smile widened.

"I'm so happy you are here." Maxwell's words swelled with sincerity.

He didn't have a pretentious bone in his body. Despite being a professional athlete, when it came to emotions, he would never be considered a player. Upfront about his affections for Janie Lyn, he didn't shy away from them, didn't downplay them. Just the opposite, he laid them bare for her to see, to feel, to trust.

Perhaps that was why Maree and Miss Sadie hadn't been surprised that morning?

"Call my cell if you need me." Maxwell's hands had found their way around her back. He hugged her waist, holding her close to him. Close enough for a kiss, but he waited for her to confirm she would indeed call him if needed.

"Yes, I will," she promised. "Now kiss me and go."

Like the very coachable and skilled athlete he was, Maxwell did exactly as he'd been told, and at a very high level.

Janie Lyn spent the next several hours poking around the house.

On one hand, she didn't want to invade Maxwell's privacy. On the other, he'd told her over and over to look around without limitations.

She discovered the same stark, impersonal vibe in every room of the house that she'd seen in the kitchen and garage.

The living room had artwork on the walls, but not a single piece she believed Maxwell had chosen for himself. The library shelves overflowed with books, but they were too perfect, the spines uncreased, whereas the books lying around the Green Hills house were either left facedown and wide open or dog-eared to mark his spot.

In his rambling filibuster, he'd completely forgotten to mention the game room that shared a moveable wall with the home theater. There, Janie Lyn found a billiard table with the pool balls arranged and ready to break, two cross-stacked cue sticks, and the cue ball placed ostentatiously on a cut-crystal chalk holder.

In a far corner of the room sat a felt-covered game table with eight gray — imagine that — leather chairs on casters. Each chair was pushed under an edge of the octagonal table with eight matching sets of poker chips precisely ordered in acrylic trays. A card shuffler, a divided discard tray, and four decks of cards were neatly poised in the middle of the table.

In the other far corner stood a polished bar, complete with a full kitchenette, a drink dispenser, an ice machine, a wine-only refrigerator, a second refrigerator, and a dishwasher — all spotless stainless steel, of course. Janie Lyn hadn't known Maxwell to drink alcohol very often, and when he did, she'd only seen him with a beer or a glass of wine, but the wall behind the bar was an elaborate liquor display with every fathomable type of cocktail spirits in decanters that looked very posh and very expensive.

Between the two corners, a tremendous slate fireplace dwarfed the wall. In front of the hearth sat a living room configuration that included two long sofas and four stately chairs surrounding a custom-made coffee table, designed specifically for that space.

What in the world?

Janie Lyn couldn't wrap her head around it. Tempted for a moment to call Maree for answers, she decided to wait until Maxwell got home. She wanted to hear his explanation. She knew one thing for sure: this town house did *not* reflect the man she'd come to know.

And love.

20

> *Well, if you're true to yourself,
> you're going to be true to everyone else.*
> **John Wooden**

When Max got home from the practice facility, something smelled delicious.

His mouth watered by the time he'd set his keys and bag in the mudroom. He followed his nose straight to the kitchen, where Janie Lyn had just taken a baking pan out of the oven.

"Wow," he declared. A man could get used to this!

"I'm not wow-worthy. This is one of the entrées I found in your freezer. Everything is from a place called Josephine's downtown. I'm guessing it's your favorite?" Janie Lyn did her gather-twist-flip-in-front-of-her-shoulder hair thing. Then she immediately moved it to hang behind her.

"First of all," he said, sidling up behind her and sweeping her hair back over one shoulder to expose the other, "you are *always* wow-worthy." He nipped at her neck to make his point. The cold chills that puckered along her skin reward enough.

"Secondly," he continued, "I missed you." He wrapped both

arms around her and pulled her against him. When she set down the hot mitts and stacked her arms over his, he felt something click into place.

"And last but not least," he said as he turned her in his arms to lavish some long-desired attention on her lips, "Josephine's is a long story." He attempted to look apologetic, remorseful, contrite — all of the above — when she pulled back from the kiss and considered his words with a speculative gaze.

"*That* sounds loaded." At least she was smiling — kind of — when she said it.

"Let's save it for after dinner." He said a quick prayer for her grace and understanding.

"Good plan." She gave him a full smile, and he felt much better. "There was quite a variety in the freezer, and the description on every label sounded incredible. I chose 'Olive & Chicken Cacciatore.' I hope that's one you like." She had created two place settings at the island and moved the baking dish onto a hot plate between them.

"It'll be great. Would you like a glass of wine, ice water, tea?"

"Maybe a small glass of white wine? Despite my rather long nap in the truck this morning, I'm still exhausted. If I have more than a little wine, I'll be falling asleep on this barstool."

"It's been a pretty—" he paused to find the right word, "fantastical few days, followed by an extra-long one traveling here. I'd say you've earned your fatigue."

"*Fantastical*, eh?" She lifted her eyes but not her head; her sage green eyes twinkled from beneath her long, thick eyelashes.

"I think it's been pretty fantastic." His voice dropped. Without even trying to flirt, she could get his blood boiling in the best meaning of the phrase.

"Hmm." She sat taller on the barstool, then rested her elbow on the island and her chin in her hand. Wonderfully inquisitive, she must have a few dozen expressions of curiosity and vigilance. Each one of them alluring, each one beguiling. "Yes, I would agree with *fantastic*."

She dropped her hand into her lap and went back to eating.

Max watched her a few seconds longer. How had he ever looked past her? How had he not noticed her enchanting beauty the very moment he met her? That mistake would have him questioning his sanity for the rest of his life.

As if in answer, Psalms 27:14 popped into his mind: *Wait for the Lord; be strong, and let your heart take courage; wait for the Lord!*

All in God's timing, Miss Sadie would say.

"Maxwell?" With a mouthful of pasta, he raised an eyebrow in answer. "What *is* this place?"

He choked on his food. She handed Maxwell his wineglass. When that didn't help, she moved to the fridge to fill a glass of water. Eventually, he got his coughing under control.

"You don't like it?" He was careful to keep his tone and expression neutral. He wanted to hear her own thoughts; he didn't want to influence her opinion.

"Oh, it's splendid. Absolutely gorgeous. Every single room could be featured in a magazine. But the magazine would be an issue of *Luxe* or *Haute Living*. There's nothing wrong with those magazines, nothing wrong with the products they advertise — they are sleek and striking, slick and svelte. There is a tremendous market for this style. But, is this your style? It's such a contrast from what you've worked so hard to create in Green Hills."

Max heard concern in her tone. Was she doubting who he was, who she'd agree to spend time with, who she was starting a relationship with?

There was no need to worry. She knew *him*, the truest parts of him. She knew his heart.

Feeling pure joy, Max stood and pulled her from her stool.

His smile was uncontainable, splitting his face from ear to ear.

He wrapped her in a boisterous bear hug, rocking them back and forth.

"Maxwell?" Her voice was muffled by his chest as he swayed them in circles. "Maxwell, what is wrong with you?"

"I hate this house," he confessed. Then he began dancing her around the kitchen.

"What?"

Max set Janie Lyn back on the ground and stepped back to scan the rooms around them.

"I. Hate. This. House." He emphasized each word individually with his arms out wide.

"Maxwell, I don't understand," she said, confused by his erratic behavior. Roaring and flitting and flailing about were undeniably out of character for Max. He saved those outbursts for the football field, and even then, only after an exceptionally good or infuriatingly bad play.

He pulled his barstool out and leaned against it with his back facing the island. He tugged her hands until she was standing between his outstretched legs.

"With the exception of my sisters, everyone who's ever seen this place has oohed and ahhed over it. *The fixtures are soooo dramatic. The colors are soooo strong and masculine. The space is soooo amazing.* Not one person has questioned that it looks nothing like *me*. Either they were afraid to hurt my feelings, or they were spellbound by the price tag. The point is, you are the only one who saw through all that. You recognized that I don't fit here."

He soaked in the sight of her, caring and strong. He'd always been struck by her quiet ability to get things accomplished. He'd known she was smart. And patient — time and again he'd marveled at her calm reserve when dealing with contractors, workers, and roadblocks around the remodeling and landscape projects in Green Hills. Brilliant, she had a knack for logistics and planning. She led with her heart, honest and real.

As a survival method, she'd trained herself to fade into the background. She'd been hesitant to speak out for fear it would draw attention to her. In doing so, she'd made her words more valuable. If she was saying something, then it was important. *She* was important. Her opinions, her thoughts, her feelings… They'd become of the utmost importance to Max.

He smiled at her. It was difficult to put into words, but somehow, Max just knew: she was the one. Janie Lyn was *his* one.

"Then why do you have it? If you hate it, why did you buy it?"

"Hate is a strong word." He scoffed when her eyebrows lifted in dismay. "I know, I said I hate it—"

"Passionately," she remarked.

"I'll give you that," Max said, ducking his head for a second before looking back at her. "Really, it's indifference." He watched her eyes narrow, but true to herself, she listened and observed.

"When I was drafted to the Chiefs, I received a nice signing bonus. I'd gone from stretching my scholarship stipend far enough to feed, shelter, and clothe three people to having what felt like unlimited funds. Thankfully, Bren's parents were there to guide me." Max looked down again. He'd been holding Janie Lyn's hands in his, and now he was running his fingers through hers, twisting and entwining them. Nerves, he knew. Remembering that time in his life, how much he'd needed and missed his own parents, made it hard to sit still. He wrapped his hands around her fingers and brought them to his lips before continuing.

"Mr. Stewart put me in touch with good people who helped me structure a financial plan that would guarantee I could take care of the girls regardless of how long football lasted. The 'splurge' the financial team encouraged was real estate. *Max, me boy,* I can still hear Bren's dad and his crazy, mixed-up accent. *Cars devalue when you drive them off the lot, vacation memories blur. But, son, property will always be a prime commodity.*"

Bren's parents had flown back to Oklahoma from their home in Scotland to be with Max during that time; he shuddered to think of the ways the world might've taken advantage of him if they hadn't.

"When I started looking for a place to live here in Kansas City, I told the real estate agent I needed at least four bedrooms, enough for Maree, M'Kenzee, Bren, and myself — the only people I could ever imagine wanting to stay overnight. I told her I like to watch movies. Bren added that a game room would be nice. The girls requested a pool, if possible. The team referred the agent, so I'm sure she was used to working with players and their families. This was the first place she brought us, and when I saw it, I just figured this was what professional football players bought. It was fully furnished — looked exactly as it does today. The shiny surfaces, the bells and whistles, and the ridiculously difficult-to-work media system were a world apart from the run-down, two-bedroom apartment we were living in while I played college ball. Seeing the looks in the girls' eyes as we walked from room to room, I was sold. Literally. The agent wrote the contract, and I bought it on the spot."

"Without seeing anything else?"

"One and done," Max answered. "I was so out of my element, it wouldn't have mattered how many she showed us. Whenever she said, *This is what you want,* I'd have said, *Okay.*"

"I can't believe Maree and M'Kenzee liked it."

"Like I said, it's a far cry from the conditions we'd been living in since our parents died. I wasn't twenty-five yet, so the money Momma and Dad left us was still being controlled by a trust. That had covered the utilities and most expenses. My scholarship provided the apartment, and my per diem went to groceries for the girls. I ate on my meal plan at school and wore whatever clothes the equipment manager handed out to the team. The girls and I, we didn't have a style. To be honest, we didn't care about colors or decor. We walked through here and saw all this space, huge rooms and ultra-high ceilings. A bedroom for each person was more than we'd ever had. We couldn't imagine anything better. The fact that I didn't have to shop for furniture, dishes, towels, or anything else seemed like a Godsend."

"And you never wanted to change anything? Add a color, maybe?"

Max laughed at her gentle teasing.

"Nah," he answered. "M'Kenzee was nineteen and going to Oklahoma State University. The trust paid for her tuition, books, room, and board. She had a part-time job working in a dart and billiard bar close to campus. I wanted her to have a normal college experience, so I made her live in the dorms instead of driving back and forth. She still managed to be home every weekend and any weeknights I was on the road with the team."

"A bar just for throwing darts and shooting pool? Driving home when you told her to stay at school? That sounds like M'Kenzee.

Ever the headstrong one." Janie Lyn said it kindly, with a compassionate grin.

"That's an understatement if ever there was one," Max agreed. "Maree was only seventeen, but she was determined to graduate early and was finishing her senior year of high school. She had already decided to stay in Tulsa and had earned an academic scholarship to attend the University of Tulsa in the fall."

"Maxwell." Janie Lyn halted his story. "You did a wonderful job."

He sobered. He blinked a few times to push back the emotion threatening to run over. "They went without a lot of things," he said, hearing the regret in his voice. Feeling it in his chest.

"But never you, Maxwell. They never went without your attention, without your love."

He gave a slight shrug to acknowledge Janie Lyn's compliment, still reluctant to give it much credence. "Anyway, Mrs. Stewart helped Maree find a cute bungalow close to the university, and I bought it for her sight unseen. That little cottage became our home base, never this place."

"How long have you lived here?"

"This is my ninth year in the league," he answered. "Wow, I'm getting old." It was hard to believe it had been that long. "Seven years is the goal when starting a career in the NFL," Max explained. "Three means you're vested in the pension program, four adds an extra annuity program, but seven means your monthly retirement income is a healthy amount. It's heartbreaking to see how many guys walk away from the game after only a year or two, basically broke. They blow through their guaranteed money thinking those checks last forever. Then, either they've suffered injuries or they were simply a miss in the league. They've lived and lost their dream by the age of twenty-eight. Life from there on out is a struggle. I was determined *not* to be that guy."

Janie Lyn lifted her arms to rest on his shoulders and stepped closer into the frame of his body. Max sat taller on the stool and moved his hands to her hips.

"Well, Mr. Rookie of the Year, Pro Bowl MVP, eight-year

veteran, I'd say you've hit it out of the ballpark." Her voice was sultry, hypnotic. She was so often guarded that Max was a goner when she relaxed enough to reveal her flirty side.

"That's baseball," Max corrected as he wrapped his arms around her lower back to ease her lips toward his. "In football we say, *He out-kicked his coverage.*"

She closed the minuscule gap between them. He tried to hold still, wanting her to feel in control. His gut clenched when her lips took his. When she deepened the kiss, he lost the battle.

He'd absolutely out-kicked his coverage!

Sliding his hands up her back, he urged her even closer. He felt her heart pounding, or maybe that was his.

The pounding grew louder and louder.

"Maxwell." Janie Lyn breathed his name onto his lips. His nerves thrummed. "Maxwell," she tried again, "I think someone is at the door."

"What?" He tried to crawl out of the web of desire she'd spun around him.

"The knocking," she said. "Someone is at the door."

21

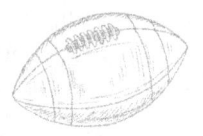

Expect nothing.
Live frugally on surprise.
Alice Walker

Max's glare shot daggers at the door. It had to be one of the doormen from the clubhouse, so Janie Lyn offered to answer it, giving him time to breathe. She could only imagine how she looked…hair a mess and lips swollen.

She pulled a big sweatshirt over her t-shirt and jeans, tucked her wild flyaways under her ball cap, and slid on the fake eyeglasses for good measure.

The costume hadn't been necessary.

Janie Lyn opened the door to find the most beautiful woman she'd ever seen, but the woman looked right past her.

"Max! You're home!" The woman was vivacious with enthusiasm as she strode in, only noticing Janie Lyn enough to push her blazer and handbag into Janie Lyn's hands on her way through.

Their visitor breezed right over to Maxwell, who had opened the dishwasher and begun rinsing their plates. Without hesitation, she placed her hands on his shoulders and leaned in to give him a light kiss. Janie Lyn was happy to see him turn his head so the kiss landed platonically on his cheek. The look on his face declared he was as dumbstruck as Janie Lyn.

Who was this woman?

She was magnificent. Her deep brown eyes lifted like a doe's; her flawless mocha skin glowed with a soft, velvety tone that looked as though it had been retouched with a photography filter. But it couldn't be, as she was certainly three-dimensional.

And all three dimensions were spectacular. Janie Lyn wasn't short, per se, but this woman was tall, at least five-ten if not closer to six-foot. Her sleeveless silk blouse showed off arms that could only be described as buff. She managed to be both lean and voluptuous, in all the right places. Her curves were to die for.

Stiletto heels clicked as she walked to the cabinet, took out a wineglass, and helped herself to their open bottle.

"Mmm, that's nice," she purred. "And goes perfectly with the cacciatore. Did you enjoy it?"

"Yes, thank you." Maxwell shook off his bewilderment enough to answer, but he hadn't done a good job keeping up. "Mary Beth, what brings you by?" His voice was polite, but Janie Lyn detected an underlying strain.

The woman — *Mary Beth* — didn't seem to notice.

Janie Lyn stepped to the sink, using one hand to push Maxwell out of the way. He did as prompted and walked toward the living room. His guest followed, wineglass in hand. She perched on the arm of the sofa when he sat in a wing-backed chair.

"I saw you on my social media feed and knew you were back in town—"

Janie Lyn dropped the handful of silverware she'd been washing. The clanking halted Mary Beth momentarily, but she didn't look away from her drink, thus missing Maxwell's alarmed look at Janie Lyn.

"On social media?" he asked before Mary Beth could keep going. Was there thinly veiled panic in his voice? Was Maxwell holding his breath in anticipation as Janie Lyn herself was?

"Yes, in a video from practice. You did have practice today, didn't you?" Mary Beth set her wineglass on the table, suddenly interested in his response.

Janie Lyn exhaled with relief and refocused on returning the kitchen to its squeaky-clean condition. She needed to ask Maxwell how he managed to maintain that when he was so casual and relaxed at home. In Green Hills, she meant. Janie Lyn still wasn't sure where he considered *home*.

"Yes," Max exclaimed with a little too much zest. Janie Lyn flashed him a look. He needed to dial it down a notch. "Yes, we did." His voice was back to normal.

"How was your weekend? Your family and that tiny, little town you like to go on and on about?" Mary Beth didn't sound judgmental as much as she simply sounded — and looked — every inch the vibrant city girl.

"It was marvelous," he answered, all three words dripping with richness and warmth. Janie Lyn's hands stilled. She snuck a glance in his direction.

"Wow!" Mary Beth sounded impressed. "That good, huh?"

"Absolutely beyond compare." His words were heavy with hidden meaning that only Janie Lyn could comprehend. They sent chills over her arms, through her torso, and all the way down to her toes, which curled.

"Well, I'm glad you're back." Mary Beth walked to the kitchen island to refill her glass and then sat on the sofa cushion closest to Maxwell rather than the arm where she'd roosted before.

It was as if Janie Lyn wasn't even in the room. She strove for that, normally. But, she sensed Maxwell was conflicted. Kind and thoughtful always, this moment would certainly create an internal tug of war for Maxwell. He'd want to introduce Janie Lyn to his friend. But this was better. Retreating into the background unnoticed was better. This was a win.

"You missed a fabulous weekend here, too." Mary Beth began to expound in great detail, something about VIP treatment at the tennis championships and a Parisian *mascarade carnaval*. Janie Lyn managed to drown out the chatter by allowing her own thoughts to run amuck.

What was she doing here?

It had been less than nine hours and already someone had seen her, seen new photos of Maxwell on the internet. She was being irresponsible. This was crazy.

Even worse, it was dangerous.

Janie Lyn couldn't stand the idea of putting Maxwell in the line of fire. Her uncles and their associates were not the kind of people one got mixed up with. They were brutal, heartless, and cold.

They'd already cost her Gram and Pops. She couldn't — wouldn't — risk losing anyone else she loved. Janie Lyn would do whatever it took to keep Maxwell, Maree, their family, and her friends in Green Hills safe.

"They're really rolling out the red carpet. Max, we simply have to be there," Mary Beth was saying dramatically when Janie Lyn slunk up the stairs.

Throughout the day, she'd been eternally optimistic. Maxwell had said he had a plan to alleviate Janie Lyn of her family predicament, a plan for her to flourish in this new life she'd begun to create.

His friend, Bren, was a covert operative or something equally bizarre. They'd spoken briefly while Maxwell drove and Janie Lyn slept on the way to Kansas City. She had been in and out, not entirely following their phone conversation, but her hopes had been buoyed by what she'd heard.

Apparently, Brennigan was headed to watch Maxwell's game here at Arrowhead Stadium on Sunday. He promised to gather some intel before he arrived, and he'd reassured Maxwell that her troubles would be eradicated. *Eradicated?* That sounded both scary and promising.

She'd been so encouraged by Bren's certainty — and so trusting of the devotion that Maxwell didn't bother to veil when he looked at her — that she'd spent a chunk of the afternoon unpacking her things. In Maxwell's room, no less.

That was where he found her, presumably after showing Mary Beth to the door.

"That was torture," Maxwell said, falling backward onto his humongous bed and letting a forearm fall across his eyes.

Janie Lyn didn't respond. She was darting around the room, swooping up folded items she'd arranged in the dresser drawers.

Maxwell rolled to one side and propped his head on his hand.

Janie Lyn flew into the closet, came back with an armload of clothes, and began removing their hangers.

"Wait!" Maxwell gasped. "What are you doing?" He hopped up, grabbing the items draped over her arm.

"This is a mistake," she said, turning toward the bathroom.

"No, it's not," he refuted, putting her clothes right back on the hangers she'd set on the bed. "I'm sorry about Mary Beth — she was the long story I wanted to tell you. She won me at an auction. We went out a few times, to dinner and lunch, but only as friends. At least on my end. I promise. Mary Beth is great, but she's not for me."

He sounded chagrined, worried Janie Lyn was upset about another woman.

"Maxwell, I don't doubt your faithfulness." He let out a sigh of relief. "I doubt our intelligence."

"Janie Lyn," Max groaned. "Nothing has changed. The town house is safe, you are secure, and Bren will be here in a few days. We *will* find a path forward. Together!"

She picked up her toothbrush and toothpaste. He took the items out of her hands.

She grabbed her brush and comb and mirror set. He took those out of her hands.

She opened the shower to retrieve the shampoo and conditioner she'd placed on the tiled shelf. He took them out of her hands, too.

Their back and forth tussle persisted, with Janie Lyn trying to gather her belongings and Maxwell taking them away until his arms were completely overloaded with toiletries and Janie Lyn was glaring at him.

She *humph*ed and spun on her heel to resume her mission of unhanging her hang-ups.

Maxwell dropped her things in the sink with a clatter. Then his arms locked around her from behind. She tried to continue her task, but he hadn't left her arms any space to move. She dropped what was in her hands with a defeated sigh.

He adjusted his hold until she was leaning back, letting his body support her. Tired of resisting what her heart wanted, she rested the back of her head on his shoulder.

He provided such comfort, an incredible sense of safety. He'd become the foundation she wanted to build her new life upon. But was it truly possible or only a mystical wish?

Maxwell and Janie Lyn stayed like that for several minutes — until his lips kissed the top of her head. They moved to her temple. Traveled over her cheekbone. Then hovered over her ear.

"You unpacked your things in my room." She detected a victorious smile in his low, raspy voice.

Janie Lyn tried to elbow him in the ribs, but he only twirled her in his arms.

She'd been right. He was grinning like a fool.

"Don't get ahead of yourself," she warned, trying to sound light and playful but also needing to be definitive and clear. "I've made it this long with my 'virtue' intact. I don't intend to change that until I'm married."

Maxwell raised her chin so she couldn't look away.

"I told you yesterday, I'll never pressure you, never ask for more than you want to give. Just promise me you won't run away."

"Maxwell, we didn't make it a single day. How in the world will we keep my presence here a secret long-term? You are so well-known around here. Not just here — around the entire country! People are fascinated with you. They stalk you, good-naturedly, I hope, but fans follow your life, nonetheless. It'll only be a matter of time before we slip up, before someone realizes I exist. Then that *someone* will make it their prerogative to identify me."

"Then I'll take a break from football."

"Absolutely not!" she yelled, flabbergasted. He'd said it as if it was no big deal, as if he was clocking out a few minutes early on a Friday afternoon. "You will not walk away from your career because of me," Janie Lyn insisted. "Nor will I allow you, or anyone else, to be in jeopardy. Me leaving is the best option."

She was breathing heavy and raising her voice — something she rarely, if ever, did.

"No." He was utterly calm.

"I won't be gone forever." She tried to sound convincing. "If what you say about Bren is right, it might only be for a short while."

"No."

"Maxwell, be reasonable."

"No."

"Would you please say something besides *no*?" She inched toward exasperation. She gave a *grrrr* and turned away from him to gather more clothes from the dresser.

Maxwell took hold of her wrist and brought her back around to face him.

"I love you."

"What?" It came out desolate, wounded. "You don't want to love me," she said, shaking her head as tears began to sting her eyes.

"I do." Still so damned reasonable.

She stepped back, trying to establish some space between them, but Maxwell stepped forward. Janie Lyn shook her head more vigorously as desperation threatened to overwhelm her.

"I do," he repeated, countering her negative gesture with a definitive nod. His steps forward consumed more space than her efforts to retreat. Her last shuffled step resulted in a thud as her body met the wall. She'd run out of space to flee.

Maxwell flattened his palms against the smooth wall, one on either side of her head. He smiled.

She was falling apart, shattering into a million razor-edged pieces, and he was smiling.

Janie Lyn tried to duck under his arm. She couldn't breathe, needed air.

Maxwell simply leaned into her to halt her progress.

He lowered his chin to look into her eyes and waited patiently until she relented and allowed her gaze to connect with his.

Fine. She could be just as stubborn and bullheaded as necessary.

She intentionally glowered up at him, lips pursed to form a hard line. Her jaw could not have clenched any tighter.

Her attempted display of temper only caused him to smile wider.

"I love you," he said again.

"Maxwell!" She hated the way her voice resembled a whiny plea.

"I refuse to apologize for loving you." He laughed. "You make me want to say I'm sorry, but I'm not. I love you."

Giving up the fight, she deflated on a sigh. Her forehead fell forward until it met his chest. He chuckled as she accepted defeat.

Maxwell's hands fell to Janie Lyn's hips. He pulled her with him as he took a step away from the wall. Then he lifted her arms around his neck and folded his own arms against her back.

"Come on, it's not *that* bad, is it?" His guilty grin relaxed into a very sexy smile.

"It will be." Her words were mournful, dejected. "If something happens to you, it will be."

A single tear fell.

"Can't you tell?" He engulfed her in a hug, stroked her back, and played with her hair. His touch soothed, his presence a balm. "I'm not easy to get rid of."

As if she were no heavier than the armload of clothes she'd held earlier, Maxwell lifted her into his arms and carried her to his bed. He set her in the middle. She crossed her legs, and Maxwell tossed those clothes into her lap.

"Hang those up," he ordered, handing her the empty hangers. "Please," he added with a wink to soften the command.

Then he set everything she'd put in her suitcase back into the dresser drawers, systematically undoing her tantrum.

She wasn't a tantrum type of girl. She'd felt abandonment; she'd felt heartbreak. She'd even felt life-threatening fear. But she'd never felt like this.

With the room back to normal, Maxwell took hold of one of Janie Lyn's ankles, straightening her leg to remove her tennis shoe. Then he did the same with the other. He took her shoes to the closet and came back holding a t-shirt. He extended a hand palm up for her to grasp, and when she did, he gave her a guiding tug to climb off the bed.

Maxwell handed Janie Lyn the t-shirt as he prodded her toward the bathroom.

"Wash up," he told her. "I'm going downstairs to check the doors and turn off the lights." With that, he kissed her forehead and gave her a gentle push. "And *don't* think while I'm gone."

Janie Lyn reorganized the abundance of stuff he'd dumped into the sink, putting everything back in the empty drawers she'd found and claimed that afternoon.

She brushed her teeth and washed her face. She swiped her lips with hydrating serum and dabbed on some eye cream and moisturizer — Gram had insisted that one was never too young to put off getting old.

She changed into the t-shirt Maxwell had given her. It read, *Tulsa Football 2009 Alzheimer's Awareness Game* — a decade-old shirt from college. Very soft and very big, it swallowed her and made her feel like a little kid. Earlier in the day she'd discovered his drawer of boxer shorts; she borrowed a pair to wear with the tee.

Not sure what to do with her neatly folded stack of dirty clothes, she set them in the bottom of the closet next to where he'd stored her suitcase. *Something to figure out tomorrow.* For the moment, she'd reached the end of her rope. Too much emotion in one day was exhausting.

Janie Lyn sat in the middle of the bed again when Max walked in. This time, she'd pulled back the quilt and set the decorative shams on a chair. The covers were pulled up over her hips, her hair brushed out.

Maxwell's baby blue eyes darkened to the deep shade of the Mediterranean Sea.

Her heart skipped a beat. She had to concentrate to swallow.

"Take either side," he said as he walked to the bathroom. His voice sounded darker, too.

Janie Lyn flopped under the covers. She'd chosen the side of the bed farthest from the bathroom, leaving the bedside table with the lamp and phone charger for Maxwell. She faced the wall and scooted as close to the edge as possible without falling off her tiny sliver of mattress remaining.

What had she been thinking?

She heard Maxwell open the door and click off the bathroom light. She wanted to sneak a peek at him but was afraid of what she'd see. Instead, she held perfectly still. She wasn't trying to feign sleep, but she wasn't *not* trying to, either.

Max laughed when he saw her. He set his phone alarm, plugged it into the charging station, and turned off the lamp.

The mattress dipped beneath his large body. Her nerves were a frazzled mess.

He rolled toward her. She squeezed her eyes shut.

His arm draped over her side, his hand wrapping under her ribs.

He lifted and dragged her back to the center of the mattress until she was cuddled up against him. Her eyes flew open. Wide. His body was like a furnace, emanating so much heat.

Again, she concentrated to swallow. She hoped only she could hear her throat croak.

No such luck…Maxwell chuckled under his breath.

He adjusted his hand, which was still nestled under her ribs. With his other hand, he smoothed her hair up and over to lie on the pillow. Then he kissed the side of her face and laid his head on the pillow beside hers.

She felt the tension in his legs loosen, felt his weight melt into the bed. She couldn't help but do the same.

She was safe. In Maxwell's arms, she was home.

"Maxwell?" She whispered his name.

"Hmmm," he halfway replied.

"I love you, too."

22

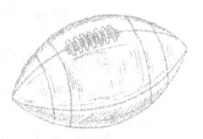

> ***Commitment***
> ***is what transforms a promise***
> ***into reality.***
> ***Abraham Lincoln***

Her words were manna from Heaven.

Max curled even closer, nestling Janie Lyn into his chest, and drifted to sleep.

The next morning, Max awoke feeling refreshed, happy, at peace. And smelling bacon.

He stretched in bed, grinning like a fool. He couldn't help it. He simply could not stop smiling.

Max wasn't naive. Outsiders might look at his life and assume it had been an easy road to success and celebrity. In truth, it had been a painful, jagged, rocky road. He'd lived through tragedy. How could anyone think that being orphaned at the age of ten made for an "easy" life?

He'd dedicated his life to his sport, given copious amounts of his blood, his sweat, his tears, and almost all of his time to honing his craft. He knew natural talent played a part; he was grateful, thanked

God every single day for the athletic skills he'd been gifted with. But even the most incredible athletes — true physical phenoms — fizzled out of the game if they didn't progress, improve, and prove their value week in and week out.

Max and Janie Lyn still had hurdles to clear; life would always present challenges. And her family presented much worse of an issue than mere hurdles and challenges. No, he wasn't looking through rose-colored glasses.

But Max did believe in looking forward. He'd committed his heart to her, to the love he felt for her. He'd committed himself to *them*. Every vision of the future now included Janie Lyn. He imagined their life together as he made up the bed, flew through the shower, stepped into joggers, and grabbed a t-shirt. He scurried down the stairs with quick feet.

He stopped short when he reached the bottom step, his eyes falling upon her as his head popped through the neck of his shirt.

She had on his grilling apron. It had been a gift from Maree, handmade and embroidered to read *Kiss the Cook*. Under that, she wore her sleep clothes. His boxers looked good. Real good.

She'd turned on some music. He relished the way she half sang along and half hummed to the tune while folding a massive omelet in a skillet. The bacon sizzled in a small frying pan. Coffee waited in the pot, and she'd placed a pitcher of orange juice on the table. Color ignited from a jelly jar of flowers that must've come from the planters and pots decorating the pool area on his rooftop balcony, the final holdouts to fall.

This was the vision. The dream. This was what he wanted.

Janie Lyn looked up with a smile as Max approached her.

"Hi," she said, blushing when he didn't stop walking until they were nose to nose.

"Good morning." He barely got the words out before he was tasting and devouring her lips. He wrapped an arm around her waist to hold her to him when her knees buckled.

"Oh my," she exhaled.

"Just following the apron's orders." He winked at her and made sure she had regained her balance before moving to steal a piece of bacon. "You don't have to cook for me."

"I want to cook for you."

"But you don't *have to*, Janie Lyn." Max filled a mug of coffee and leaned his hips against the kitchen counter. "That's not why you're here."

"Why am I here?" Intent on that omelet, she resisted looking at him.

"Because you stole my heart, and now I don't want it back." He set the coffee cup down and stepped behind her. His hands came to her shoulders. He kissed the top of her head. "You're here because I can no longer imagine being anywhere without you."

She finally turned from the cooktop, although she still had the spatula in hand.

"We'll take care of each other," she pledged, lifting onto her tiptoes to plant a chaste kiss on his lips. "Which means I get to cook for you."

Then she laid her empty palm against his chest and pushed him away from her workspace.

"I'm not complaining — this smells amazing. I just wanted you to know I don't expect that." Max sipped his coffee. "Can I at least help?"

"Nope. It's ready. Let's eat," she said with a smile.

Max retrieved something from the mudroom and then met her at the table.

"Here," he said, offering a set of keys. "There's no reason for you to be a prisoner while I'm gone to work."

"Maxwell," she started. "I'm fine here by myself during the days. I brought my laptop to keep working on a project I've started. I'm writing out all the recipes Gram taught me. Maree includes recipes in her quilt books and asked me to collaborate on one. M'Kenzee offered to take all the food photos once I'm ready to start baking. I have plenty to do to keep busy while you're gone."

She fit perfectly. His sisters adored her. He loved her.

"That's great! I'm willing to sacrifice myself to be your taste-tester," Max said, wiggling his eyebrows to reveal his ulterior motive.

"But seriously, I'll take my truck; you use the car. It's in the garage, and there's also a house key on the fob. Without me tagging along, no one will recognize you. You should go check it out. Kansas City is a fun place." The thought that she was better off exploring on her own than in his company bristled, but even without the threat of his local fame casting a gloomy cloud over them, he spent long hours at the football facility. For her to be happy here long-term, she needed to create a life — a community — to enjoy.

She looked down at the key chain he'd handed her. The light blue plastic appeared to be vintage, from a motel room a long time ago. In shiny gold letters, the words *The Lodge at Daisy Lake, Green Hills, Oklahoma* were printed below three trees. One side of her mouth lifted when she turned it over to find fancy lettering on the back. *Thank you for visiting!* She looked at him with her head cocked.

"I used to stay at the lodge when I'd visit Maree. Before I bought the house," he explained. "It's gorgeous out there, so green and peaceful. I still love going out on the lake, but I wanted a house in town. I thought Maree might share it with me, but she was dead set on that tiny apartment above her studio. Now I guess she stays at Rhys's place most of the time. And if they ever set a date for this wedding, she'll move the rest of her stuff to his house. But the lodge is special. It was a step toward belonging somewhere, all three of us."

"You think M'Kenzee will settle in Green Hills?" There was a thread of doubt, or maybe uncertainty, in her voice.

"M'Kenzee's been mad for a long time. When Momma and Dad died, I was lost. Maree was sad. M'Kenzee was angry. She's always been the feistiest, and their accident put a chip on her shoulder that she hasn't been able to shake. I pray that she finds a way to set it aside. I pray she will hand over the pain and frustration she carries around. It's a heavy burden. If she can ever manage that, then I think she'll finally be open to the concept of home. Maybe she'll open her eyes to falling in love and find someone to share her life with. I hope she does…there's nothing like it."

She smiled up at his last words, shyly, but with understanding in her gaze.

"I feel bad for leaving you with the dishes after you cooked such a feast, but I've got to head out or I'll get fined for being late to work."

"Fined?" she asked with disbelief as he leaned in to give her a quick kiss.

"Yep," he answered as he walked toward the door. "Commitment is a big deal and a requirement if a team's going to be any good. Anything that adds value to the organization comes with a price tag." He stopped at the door to look back at her. "I'll see you tonight."

"I'll see you tonight," she repeated with a nod.

23

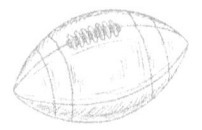

> ***Man produces evil***
> ***as a bee produces honey.***
> ***William Golding***

Athens, Georgia

"Turn that crap off," Stanton Lyndale sneered from the kitchen. His current live-in girlfriend loved trashy gossip television. Stanton hated the drivel.

He was starting to hate her as well.

Felicity was nice to look at and fun in the sack, but the more time Stanton spent with her, the less he could stand to have her around. Her voice, which he'd once described as an angel's song, had turned to fingernails on a chalkboard. Axel liked to call her F'loozity. Unequivocally ignorant and daft, Stanton's younger brother appeared to have gotten it in this case.

Neither of the men believed in the value of a day's hard work or a job done well, but even they had marveled at Felicity's ability to stare at the TV screen for hours on end. From talk shows and reality shows to competition shows and celebrity news shows, she spent the bulk of her days and nights spellbound and enthralled by the lives of strangers.

"Come watch with me," Felicity hollered back. "It's all about famous football players. Come on, Suga' — you love football."

Axel raised an eyebrow at Stanton. Stanton responded to both nitwits in his life by simply closing his eyes. No wonder his head hurt... No one should be expected to put up with *this* every day.

"Can't she cook for us?" Axel whined.

"No, she can't cook," Stanton growled back. "Look at her." He pointed the end of the knife in his hand toward the living room. "She subsists on cigarettes and cheap wine. She's not touching these steaks. Now finish peeling those potatoes and stop complaining."

"I wish we had Mom's bread to go with dinner," Axel said longingly. "And her green bean bundles." His voice had gone all soft and dreamy. "Remember them? How she wrapped each bundle in bacon and baked them just perfectly?"

Stanton was tempted to poke him with the blade.

"Well, find Eliza—"

"Oh my Gawd," Felicity's voice shrilled, interrupting Stanton's snide remark.

Stanton slammed the knife into the cutting board. Ready to bellow a command for her to leave, her next words stopped him in his tracks.

"Why, that looks just like Lizzy!"

Stanton rushed to stand behind the couch and look over Felicity's head.

"Where?" he demanded without an ounce of patience.

"Oh, you missed it, darlin' — this is a Cleveland Brown who's been courtin' Savannah on the *Sands of Time*. It's my favorite soap opera. Aren't they gorgeous together? Can you imagine all these pretty girls landing themselves a big, strong, and rich football player? I swear, they've figured it out!"

"Where's the girl who looked like Elizabeth?"

"I told you, honey," she crooned at him, as though he was the imbecile in the room. "That was the story before this one."

"Well, rewind it."

"I'm sorry, baby. I'm using the DVR to record *The Real Housewives of Atlanta* right now, so I can't back up this show." Her eyes were big, scarily innocent.

"Will this show air again?" He made an effort to talk slow and be patient, but Felicity was trying his last nerve.

"Mmmm? I doubt it," she said, shaking her teased blond hair with an apologetic shrug. "But you haven't missed much. Here, sit right down, and we'll watch together." She patted the couch cushion next to her, looking up at him with such hope.

Stanton might have felt sorry for Felicity if she wasn't so incredibly vapid. And if he wasn't already busy feeling so sorry for himself. But he did walk around to plop down on the couch.

He flopped to slouch against the back cushion. He had to know if the girl Felicity had seen really did look like Elizabeth, if it could *be* Elizabeth.

"Ax," Stanton roared as he sat up to think through his quandary. "Get in here!"

Axel arrived, potato and peeler in hand.

"What's up?"

Stanton cringed. How could everyone around him be so oblivious?

"Felicity saw someone who looked like Elizabeth," he explained.

"Oh, yeah," Axel said congenially. "Where?"

"On the television," Stanton snarled through gritted teeth.

"On the television? Well, that's cool!" Axel replied, genuinely impressed.

"It would be a lot cooler if we could find her in person," Stanton added dryly. "We need to scour the tabloids, see if we can find that picture again. I have to know if it's her. Damn, I wish I'd seen it."

Stanton felt physical pain.

The bakery was essentially dead. He hadn't made payroll in months. Most of the employees had walked out after Elizabeth disappeared. The people he'd replaced them with had been as clueless as his current companions. The bank accounts were empty, and he owed a lot of money to a lot of bad dudes.

The only way out of this mess was to find Elizabeth, force her home, and deliver on this year's Christmas cake orders. He was fed up with her games. When he got his hands on her, she'd never try something stupid like this again.

"If only I knew which football player they were talking about," Stanton thought aloud.

"What do you mean?" Felicity's program had ended, so his monologue must've finally broken through her stupor.

"I mean that if I knew the football player in the photo with the girl who looked like Elizabeth, then maybe I could find Elizabeth." Jeez, talk about beating your head against a brick wall.

"Sweetie," Felicity drawled while shaking her head. "Why didn't you just ask?" She scooted to face him, hands fisted under her chin. She resembled an excited puppy, eager to please her master. "Boo Bear, you're so silly… I know all the eligible bachelors on TV!"

24

***To be deeply loved by someone gives you strength,
but to love someone deeply gives you courage.
Esther Huertas***

Back in Kansas City

Janie Lyn was both shocked and amazed at how seamlessly she and Maxwell settled into a new routine. Maybe the ever-elusive yet wise "they" were right... Maybe life *was* easy when you found the home you were meant to have. And maybe that home was a person rather than a place.

Each morning, she slid out from under the delightful cocoon of the soft sheets, the beautiful quilt that covered his bed — the only nod to color in the room — and the weight of Maxwell's strong arm draped protectively over her with a smile on her face. She felt cheerful, at peace. She was happy.

Then she cooked.

Maxwell had told her he could grab breakfast in the cafeteria at the football facility — the training table, he called it. But the kitchen really was her favorite place to be, and cooking for Maxwell brought her a joy she'd never imagined. Their breakfasts together felt like an indulgence, the perfect way to begin the day.

After they ate, Janie Lyn shooed Maxwell out the door, cleaned up the kitchen, and further indulged in a luxurious shower. Two showerheads and eight body sprayers seemed a bit excessive, but since they were there, she figured she might as well enjoy them.

Next, she'd tidy up the bathroom, gather the used towels, and get dressed for the day. Nothing needed her attention upstairs since Maxwell made up the bed as soon as he got out of it — a fact that endeared him to her even more... Pops always said that a tightly made bed set the tone for a well-run day — so she'd head back to the kitchen.

Her recipe project was going well.

She'd found an online software application that turned out to be exactly what she needed. It was intended for food blogs, which she couldn't do right now. But maybe someday. Looking through the company's demo pages and clicking around on websites that used the software got the wheels turning in Janie Lyn's mind. She had a blast fantasizing about what could be.

By Thursday afternoon, she'd filled a spiral with notes of how she would organize her own pages, thought through brand elements, and selected colors, styles, and fonts. She imagined an online shop to build on Gram and Pops's vision for the bakery. She'd call it the Christmas Kitchen. It would be a unique and charming boutique that enveloped all the best parts of the holiday season: cookies and candies and cakes, candles and spice pouches and wintery potpourri, Christmas hymns and all the best carols.

Perhaps Maree could put her in touch with quilt manufacturers to sell patterns with trees and toys and teddy bears. And M'Kenzee might allow her to sell framed photographs depicting marvelous holiday traditions. Oh, and one-of-a-kind ornaments and home decor. Flower arrangements with candy canes and twinkling lights. Christmas tree skirts and pinecone baskets. Wreaths...big and small, classy and flashy, indoor and outdoor...lots and lots of wreaths.

The possibilities are endless!

Laughing at herself and how quickly she'd gotten caught up in her fantasy, Janie Lyn refocused on the chicken casserole she planned to make for their dinner. A simple recipe Gram had made on a regular basis when Janie Lyn was growing up, she didn't need Maxwell to test the flavors — she knew it was fail-safe — but she'd developed a hankering for it when she'd typed it up that morning. They had all the ingredients to make it except one: nacho-cheese-flavored tortilla chips.

Make it without the chips or run to the store?

Run to the store?

A quiver snaked through Janie Lyn's stomach. A chill ran down her spine.

She'd been there for four days and had not yet left the building.

Each day, Maxwell placed the car keys into her hands as he pressed a kiss to the top of her head on his way to the garage to leave for work. He'd urged her to get out, to look around town. He'd mentioned the 18th & Vine Jazz District, the Crossroads Arts District, and Country Club Plaza. He'd told her about museums and exhibits that sounded fascinating, landmarks and sculptures she needed to see, and an unbelievable music scene. He'd told her he wasn't knowledgeable enough to do justice to the food vendors and restaurants, so they'd have to work their way through those in person. Together, he'd pledged.

Maxwell had described a vibrant city, different from the pace and amenities of Green Hills to be sure, but also a fun and flourishing place to live. *Bloom where you're planted*, Gram would say. Janie Lyn was pretty certain she'd heard Miss Sadie give the same advice. Maxwell seemed very adept at that, at embracing the here and now and choosing to be joyful in that moment.

She could do that. She decided then and there, she *would* do that.

Janie Lyn switched out of her cutoff shorts and into a pair of ankle-length light khaki slacks. She traded her oversized sweatshirt for a jade green crewneck sweater with pleated, poofy sleeves that gathered at her wrists in wide buttoned cuffs. She slipped on a pair of colorful tweed pumps with short block heels.

She'd sold most of her jewelry to have cash when she was on the run, but she hadn't been able to part with the pearl necklace and earrings Gram and Pops had given her. She remembered the gleam in Gram's eyes when she'd unwrapped the gift to find the iconic blue boxes. Her heart had clamored, and she whipped her gaze up to Gram. Every Southern girl recognized that powder blue satin ribbon.

"No need to get goofy about it," Pops had grumbled, his voice thick with emotion he was trying to cover up. "Let's put 'em on and see if you even like them."

Janie Lyn loved them! They were the first pieces of high-quality jewelry she'd ever worn, much less owned. Exquisite, timeless, and lovely. But what made them truly special was the joy she'd seen in Gram and Pops's eyes when she wore them.

Standing before the full-length mirror in Maxwell's bedroom, she caught a tear before it fell and messed up the makeup she'd just applied.

For the first time in two years, she'd put on *her* clothes.

Since the day she'd run away from Athens, she'd worn only what she could buy at thrift shops and garage sales. The overalls, ball caps, and solid cotton tops weren't blah or boring by themselves, but Janie Lyn had learned how to make them — how to make herself — utterly unremarkable. She'd mastered the art of blending in and being completely forgettable.

She stared in the mirror wide-eyed, astonished to see herself looking like herself.

You can do this. You will *do this.*

Maxwell had said his town house was in the Brookside neighborhood, and Janie Lyn didn't want to take the car. She did a quick internet search for a grocery store within walking distance. The search results were an eclectic variety of galleries, spas, boutiques, accessory shops, and delicatessens. She didn't see a traditional grocery store, but she was sure she'd find her chips somewhere in the array of businesses.

Janie Lyn grabbed a light jacket from the closet upstairs and walked out before she could chicken out. She experienced a moment of anxiety as she descended the stairs on the front stoop, but she talked herself through it and kept moving forward.

Imaging herself wearing the emperor's new clothes as she walked out of the clubhouse lobby and onto the busy sidewalk, she really missed her ball cap and frumpy, oversized overalls.

She did have her sunglasses, though. She slid them on, took a deep breath to gather her grit, and stepped into the flow of pedestrians.

It was amazing. Not one person paid her an ounce of attention. In fact, almost all of them focused solely on their cell phones. Some people held their phones up to their ears, looking but not seeing where they were going. Others looked at the screen, talking over a video call, and also *not* seeing where they were going. And still some pedestrians did both, wearing earbuds and looking at their phones while not watching where they were going. No one noticed the world around them.

Other than frowning at her when she stopped suddenly to admire a window display, no one seemed to care that she was there. No one said *good afternoon*. No one smiled. No one made eye contact. It was mind-boggling. And sad. Perhaps she'd spent two years being worried and cautious for no reason.

The stores were *not* sad.

They were amazing. One shop sold handmade soaps; another sold candles scented with essential oils. Several stores displayed unique clothing for customers of all ages. She also found a pharmacy, a dry-cleaner's, and three day spas nestled among the dazzling finery.

There were several pet shops and dog parks. Kansas City was obviously very pet-friendly. No wonder Maxwell had so much fun with Hank, his one-year-old red cane corso.

One week into Hank's training program, Janie Lyn could only hope Hank was handling their separation better than Maxwell was. He'd taped computer printouts together to create a three-month calendar and attached it to the refrigerator. There was a huge blue star drawn on Hank's graduation day, and the other boxes were numbered, ending with a *1* on the day before the star and working backward through the weeks. Before Maxwell went upstairs each night, he used a permanent marker to cross off another day. He was literally counting down the days until Hank was home.

Janie Lyn chuckled at the thought as she went into the Pet Palace to browse. The shop stocked a splendid array of products: hand-braided leashes in bold colors, magnificent beds and blankets, and an entire wall of organic dog foods and treats. After scouring every shelf, Janie Lyn couldn't resist a three-pack of football toys and a cookbook titled, *Doggie Donuts for Dido*. She couldn't wait to surprise Maxwell with the goodies.

From there, Janie Lyn purchased a cone of cinnamon-glazed pecans from one food truck and a cup of hot tea from another. She continued to meander through the throng of people. She took time to savor her snack, finally relaxing into her outing, yet still staggered by the number of shoppers in the middle of a weekday afternoon.

Just as Janie Lyn reached for her phone to put the town house address into the map application, a spice shop caught her eye. She had to go in. Like every store she'd seen in Brookside, it was housed in a unique building at least a hundred years old and had been restored with care and dedication to the original architecture and style of the neighborhood. Inside the shop were shelves, rows, and multilevel displays of spices, herbs, and seasonings. Mystified by the amazing assortment, Janie Lyn perused spices ranging from ordinary, everyday basics to exotic, difficult-to-find ingredients.

"Ma'am," the young woman behind the cash register said to get her attention, "it's five till six. We'll be closing soon."

"I'm so sorry," Janie Lyn exclaimed. "I was completely caught up in your products and lost track of the time. I came to Brookside looking for tortilla chips for a recipe. That was just after lunch. I've been window-shopping for almost five hours." She couldn't believe it.

"I totally understand," the kind young lady empathized as Janie Lyn took the jars of spices and seasonings she'd been carrying up to the counter. "It's easy to get sidetracked around here."

Janie Lyn paid cash for her purchases and declined the employee's invitation to join the shop's email list. Again, maybe someday, she mused.

"The deli across the street and down on the corner has a full market in the back of the dining room. They'll have your chips," the woman said with a smile.

"Thank you — you have a lovely shop! I will definitely be seeing you again soon."

Now in a hurry, Janie Lyn rushed through the deli, buying what she needed without allowing herself to study the shelves this time. She walked briskly back to the town house.

Luckily, the casserole didn't take long to toss together. Nor did it take long to bake.

She was just taking it out of the oven when Maxwell got home.

"Janie Lyn," he called from the mudroom. "Hey—" He stopped short when he caught sight of her. "*Heyyy*," he repeated with undisguised appreciation. "Talk about wow-worthy!"

With a sparkle in his eyes, he took one of her hands and, lifting it above her head, twirled her under their arms to take in her appearance.

"You're beautiful," he said. The reverence in his voice set off a hum in Janie Lyn's heart. "Exquisite."

She blushed under his scrutiny.

"Are we celebrating something?" Maxwell asked as he took her other hand in his, giving her arm a slight tug until she stood directly in front of him.

"Hmmm." She deliberated for a moment. "Yes, I guess we are."

His head tilted, and his eyes narrowed. His playful nature made her grin. It also made her cheeks heat even more, but he always seemed to have that effect on her.

She pulled her hands from his and turned to walk into the living room, where she picked up a bag from the coffee table.

"I went shopping today."

"In town?" His eyebrows knitted.

Janie Lyn nodded a quick affirmation, nibbling her bottom lip to hide her nerves and to hold back the smile trying to emerge. She handed him the bag from the pet store.

"For me?"

"Really more for Hank, but since he's not here, you can open it."

Maxwell pulled out the cookbook first and laughed when he saw the title. He flipped it over to read the description. His smile deepened.

"Doggie donuts." He laughed. "Hank's gonna devour those!"

Janie Lyn felt silly for feeling nervous. She knew he'd like the footballs, too. Still, a wave of relief and pride washed over her at his delight when he pulled the toys from the bag.

"Oh, yeah! Hank can play fetch all day long; these will be perfect for the yard in Green Hills." Setting the bag on the kitchen island, Maxwell tucked the balls under the arm holding the cookbook and wrapped his free arm around Janie Lyn. "Thank you."

His intent expression made Janie Lyn squirm under his crystal blue gaze. Her fidgeting prompted him to pull her closer to his chest.

"Thank you," he said again. "Hank and I will have fun with those. It was nice of you to think of us while you were out."

Didn't he know she thought about him all day, all night, every waking moment?

She braved another look into his face, starting with his chiseled jaw and chin, moving slowly over the supple softness of his lips, over his strong cheekbones, and finally meeting his eyes again. In them she saw a reflection of the same passion and attraction she fought to tamp down.

Yes, *entirely* too many feelings. She was drowning in them, drowning in him.

She forced a swallow and moistened her lips.

"Dinner's ready," she whispered, trying to break the trance he held her in. Her voice came out wobbly and weak.

Maxwell's eyes drop to her mouth, and his chest expanded.

"Then we better eat," he finally said. He smiled and winked, but his voice was a little hoarse, too.

They were skating on thin ice. Janie Lyn knew they both realized it. She was thankful Maxwell possessed more control and self-discipline than she seemed able to muster.

Because if it had been up to her, dinner just might have been delayed.

The meal was wonderful.

Afterward, Maxwell studied the tape from the week's practices. Sunday's game would be a tough one — the Cowboys were a staunch opponent — so Maxwell was going over blocking assignments and the new plays they'd put on for the week.

Janie Lyn applauded the patience and tenacity of Maxwell's approach. She'd been working on her computer and long since lost count of the number of times he reviewed each play. When he showed no signs of being finished anytime soon, she quietly went upstairs to get ready for bed.

As she was washing her face, brushing her teeth, and going through her routine of eye cream and moisturizers, Janie Lyn retraced her day and their evening together.

Maxwell's pride in her courage to venture out in the neighborhood buoyed her confidence. He'd said several times how glad he was that she'd enjoyed her afternoon.

He desperately wanted her to like Kansas City.

And she did. She liked it very much. It had a rich personality, and she could understand why he'd been happy to spend his entire playing career in one place and with one team. She'd only ever lived in Athens and Green Hills. Kansas City was unlike either of them. It had its own vibe, and she could already tell it was a fun one.

That afternoon had gone well — really well. He was right; she *had* been courageous.

Nothing bad had happened. No one had bothered her or even noticed her.

She wouldn't hesitate to go shopping in Brookside again. She was even looking forward to it.

With a smug smile and a deep sense of satisfaction, Janie Lyn changed into the t-shirt and boxer shorts she'd borrowed from Maxwell. There was something blissfully intimate about wearing them; they made her feel like he was hers.

Maxwell would say he *was* hers. And that he wanted nothing more than for her to be his.

Janie Lyn had no doubt about that. The chemistry between them could blow an electrical power grid. Heat sizzled between them. No, she didn't doubt that he wanted her in every sense of the word.

But true to his pledge, he hadn't pressured her. Their kisses intoxicated them both, but that was as far as their intimacies had progressed. Again, his patience impressed her. She knew that he would never fully grasp how much that meant to her, how much she respected *him* for respecting her.

She was sound asleep when he finally lowered onto bed, but she stirred enough to smile when his arm wrapped around her, dragged her to the spot where she was sheltered in the frame of his chest, and stayed draped over her with his hand tucked under her ribs. He'd done that same thing each night she'd been there. Every time, she'd smiled at his gesture, at his need to keep her close.

They had a routine. They were establishing habits, the little things that couples did naturally.

They were getting to know one another, and everything Janie Lyn learned about Maxwell made her love him — and admire him — more and more.

25

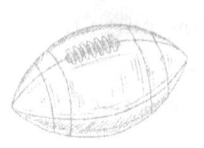

> *Keep smiling, because life is a beautiful thing*
> *and there's so much to smile about.*
> *Marilyn Monroe*

Saturday morning, Janie Lyn awoke to an empty bed.

She expected Maxwell to be downstairs, but it was empty, too. She checked the small courtyard that served as the backyard. No luck.

He must be on the rooftop, but she needed a hot cup of tea to take up there with her. She leaned against the kitchen counter, thinking about what a wild and crazy eight days it had been since Maxwell appeared at his house in Green Hills. She waited for her tea to steep and got caught smiling off into space when Maxwell came in from the garage. He carried two plastic tubs stacked on top of one another and made quite a ruckus.

"What in the world?" She pushed away from the cabinet to help him.

"If you don't want to stand out at the game tomorrow, you'll be needing some of these." A mischievous gleam shone in his eyes as he said it.

Maree and Rhys, M'Kenzee, their friends Landry and Davis, and Brennigan Stewart were all driving in to watch Maxwell play. Janie Lyn intended to go. Her foray into the city had convinced her, she could — and should — have a full life. One couldn't do that if they never left the confines of a house.

She'd moved about in Green Hills, interacting with the community there. Nothing bad had ever happened. Granted, she'd been very careful and done her best not to draw attention. She could do that here in Kansas City, too. She would still keep a low profile, but she *would* allow herself to have a life. A life with Maxwell.

That was the trick: *with* Maxwell.

She hadn't yet figured out a way to be out and about *with* him.

Maxwell was still a high-profile, celebrity-status professional athlete. He was mentioned almost every morning in the *Kansas City Star* and almost every night during the sports segments of the news. The Chiefs posted daily on social media, and Maxwell was prominent in those pictures and videos. He was in a number of commercials for everything ranging from the dealership where he'd bought his truck to the veterinarian he'd chosen for Hank. For Janie Lyn, Maxwell served as a spokesperson for the Alzheimer's Association both here and in Oklahoma. He'd been named one of KC's "10 Hottest Bachelors" by a local gossip tabloid.

And Janie Lyn was still running — hiding — from her uncles.

She wished they would just give up on her, that they would let the bakery go. But she wasn't holding her breath. The Lyndale Christmas Cake was their cash cow. Stanton would never let *that* go.

Axel was less vicious — still awful, but less cruel. But he, too, wanted the benefits that would come with Janie Lyn's return to Athens and her following their orders. Axel wouldn't disobey Stanton, and Stanton wouldn't stop until he got his way.

Janie Lyn recalled what she had told Maxwell a few days ago: the bakery couldn't live without her, and she'd die before going back.

Maxwell had faith that Bren would arrive with a plan — they'd spoken on the phone a few more times, and it seemed that Bren's research into her family had been eye-opening and valuable to the

FBI. Maxwell believed that she'd soon be free of this noose, that they'd be free to build a normal life together. Janie Lyn wasn't so sure.

"You're gonna love these," Maxwell said, waking Janie Lyn from her thoughts, as he pulled the most obnoxious-looking pants from one of the tubs. He shook them out and held up the waistband to show them off.

"What *are* those?" she asked, stupefied. They were hideous... red, yellow, and white zebra — maybe? — stripes that appeared to have been slashed and overlapped to create the absolute ugliest fabric she'd ever seen. They looked like parachute pants from the '80s with ultra-baggy legs and elastic at the waist and ankles.

She reached out to touch them, but thought better of it and retracted her arm. Her hand lifted to cover her mouth as one does when trying not to be sick. All she could do was shake her head.

"There's more." Maxwell's eyebrows wiggled, his eyes alight with a devilish glint. "Madam?" He gestured for her to sit on the couch. Once she had, he proceeded with a display of the loudest, brightest, most horrendous fashions she'd ever seen.

There were slacks and blazers made from materials printed with the logos, helmets, and graphics. There were two zoot suits and four styles of cheap feathered fedoras. There were bodysuits of all red and all yellow that made Janie Lyn think of a green clay character from Saturday morning cartoons when she was a little girl. There were temporary tattoos, face paint, and tubes of hair coloring. Maxwell pulled out handfuls of plastic beads and fake gold chains. He owned a rope necklace attached to a sizable medallion of Maxwell's face!

Janie Lyn could only be defined as dumbstruck. She had no words and could only watch the show the same way one can't look away from a disaster. She didn't want to see the appalled expression on her face when Maxwell set the first tub — now empty — to the side and took the lid off the second.

It was crazy.

He continued to unpack boas and scarves, t-shirts and sweatshirts, clown suits and wigs. There were ball caps, red and yellow cowboy hats, and a handful of headbands…all bedazzled to the hilt. There were sweatbands and jerseys and a set of wearable signs that spelled out "Go Chiefs!" and created a ten-seat-wide human billboard. The *pièce de résistance* was a sandwich board and matching headset that advertised, "I love you, Max" on one side and "You can score with me!" on the other, complete with a three-dimensional goal post and foam hearts.

Janie Lyn pressed her lips together to keep from laughing, both hands now covering her nose and mouth.

"Well, what'll it be?" His smile beamed upon her. It resembled the smile of a god — a god of the sun — and would have easily rivaled Apollo's radiance.

She feared the tears of mirth threatening to overflow might give her away.

"Maxwell," she said with the patience of a preschool teacher once she could speak without laughing out loud. "Why do you have these…things?"

"They were gifts. From fans." Janie Lyn had no idea how he could answer with a straight face.

"Gifts? From fans? Who like you?"

"These are just my favorite presents," he answered. "I can't keep everything they send. We have donation boxes at the practice facility where we regift the things we don't have room for."

"But you made room for *these*?"

"And aren't you glad I did?" He teased her, yet he maintained a look of complete seriousness.

"You want me to pick something from this collection to wear to your game tomorrow?"

"If you wear anything else, you'll stick out like a sore thumb," he said with a huge grin.

She sat stunned.

"Maybe the red-and-yellow wedding dress with the 'Marry Me, Max' veil? It looks like it's just your size."

"Well, yes, it *is* appealing," she allowed. "The two footballs on a bandeau of red, white, and yellow roses across the chest make it truly special." Determined not to crack, Janie Lyn shored up her self-control. "Just out of curiosity, Maxwell, what will Maree and M'Kenzee be wearing?"

"Something boring, no doubt. Probably just jeans and a jersey."

"Every-day blue jeans and a normal football jersey?"

"Yep." He feigned disappointment.

"Your jersey?" The humor had dropped from her eyes and her voice. She couldn't wear his jersey. Couldn't wear the atrocious wedding dress or any sign that said she loved him. She couldn't wear anything that said Max, or Davenport, or linked her to him. She had to pretend she was a random fan who just happened to be sitting in the seat beside his guests.

"You will, too," he promised, tossing aside the silly accessories still in his hand. He sat beside her and lifted Janie Lyn onto his lap. He raised her chin to look into her eyes. "Maybe not tomorrow, but soon. You will."

Then he wrapped his arms around her, hugging her in his embrace and tucking her head under his chin. They stayed there for a few minutes. Janie Lyn forced herself to imagine their future as he did, rather than as she feared it might be.

Dwelling on what might or might not be down the road only wasted their precious time together.

Brushing off her melancholy, she sat up, smiled into his beautiful blue eyes, set her hands on his incredibly muscled chest, and said, "I think I'll go with the circa-1970s sequined sweater." She jumped up and dug through the discarded pile of clothes until she found the vintage piece. "The boatneck is *très chic*, and the diamond pattern will cause the sunlight to shimmer off the gold, yellow, red, and white sequins to perfection." She held it up to her shoulders with one hand while her other hand propped one sleeve out to the side. She shifted side to side and twisted at the waist to illustrate the glittery effect. "What do you think... Maybe some red polyester bell-bottoms to go with it? Or maybe a skater skirt with tall white pleather go-go boots?" She waggled her own eyebrows as he had done earlier.

Laughing, he reached out a hand and snatched her arm. She dropped the sweater as Maxwell pulled her toward him. She tumbled onto the couch, stretching out beneath him. The vibration of his laughter, the rich timbre of his voice reverberated through her, warming her nerves as it filled her senses. This had happened so quickly, yet it felt so real. So right.

Maxwell rested his weight on his forearms to keep from crushing her. He really was a very large man, strong and lean, and undeniably beautiful.

"You'd be beautiful in a paper bag." He spoke with certainty just before lowering his lips to hers. They kissed and nuzzled and cuddled. Then Maxwell paused, leaning back to look down at her in earnest. "But maybe the gold Gumby suit instead?"

Janie Lyn gently punched him. He tickled her. And their affectionate wrestling match resumed.

---

*I*n the end, Janie Lyn went with the sequin sweater, a pair of old blue jeans, and her usual faded Chiefs cap. She braided her hair and put on the fake eyeglasses. She hoped it was gaudy enough to blend in, but not spectacular enough to stand out.

Rhys offered to swing by to pick her up, but she'd graciously declined. She was more comfortable calling a rideshare service and meeting them there. Maxwell had given her a ticket and a lanyard that provided family-pass credentials, so she could get in anywhere the rest of the group wanted to go. She was good with that, but strolling in with the Davenport family could attract photographers. That felt like too much of an unnecessary risk.

Janie Lyn walked to the pharmacy a block down from Maxwell's town house complex to order a ride from the app on her phone; she didn't want to be seen climbing into a car wearing her "fan outfit" right outside his address. She meandered around the store while she waited and even bought a huge pair of Jackie O sunglasses with oversized square frames that perfectly matched the era of her colorful sweater.

She traded them with the clear-lens glasses and was glad for the disguise that covered her eyes when the car pulled into the drop-off lane at the stadium.

Arriving by herself meant she could take her time to relish it all.

What a sight! Unreal, and she hadn't even begun to make her way through the tailgates. The sights, the smells, the cacophony of sounds overwhelmed the senses. No wonder they were called fans — they were unquestionably fantastic.

And fanatical.

Maxwell hadn't exaggerated when he said the insane *gifts* he'd shown her at home were the norm on game day. The wild prints and colors were exuberant. The costumes were crazy. Football logos and graphics had been plastered on every available surface including cars, trucks, campers, trailers, motorcycles, and scooters… flags, banners, pennants, and posters…giant helmets, miniature football fields, and portable goal posts…couches, recliners, cocktail tables, and barstools…televisions…plates, cups, napkins, and plasticware…and grills. Everywhere. She saw more grills, griddles, and smokers than she could have possibly imagined.

Food covered every flat surface. Burgers, chips, and dips. Sausage on a stick, walking tacos, and copious amounts of barbecue. Hot dogs, corn dogs, and six-foot subs that required every inch of the long tables they sat upon. Wings and beans and vats of potato salad. Together, all the scents should have smelled awful, yet somehow her mouth watered.

When a raucous group of tailgaters offered her a plate and invited her to eat, she only hesitated for a moment, glancing down to double-check that her family credentials were hidden beneath her top. Then she piled the extra-large paper plate with pigs in blankets, gooey mac and cheese, curly fries, cold broccoli and bacon salad, and grilled peaches topped with goat cheese and honey drizzle. At their insistence, she added a football-shaped bowl of banana pudding.

She couldn't believe she was sitting in their mock living room — complete with red leather couches, helmet area rug, and theater-sized big screen — enjoying an early dinner and watching a pregame broadcast talk about Maxwell and the way the Kansas City offense was firing on all cylinders.

She didn't say much as they ate, content to simply absorb the atmosphere. It was unlike anything she'd ever seen.

What a world.

Once she'd finished, Janie Lyn thanked her hosts and made her way to the entry gates of the stadium.

She took a moment to look back across the parking lots, scan the tailgates, and marvel at the day.

She was *here*. And she had to smile.

26

***When people watch football,
they're looking for fun things.
John Madden***

*J*anie Lyn found Maree, Rhys, M'Kenzee, Landry, and Davis already in their seats when she got there.

The guys watched and argued over the warm-up and pregame activities, which had just begun. Maree and Landry discussed wedding ideas with excitement and animation while M'Kenzee sat like a sardine sandwiched between the two.

Janie Lyn slid into her seat. She gave the group a quick hello but assumed her most *un*assuming persona. To the casual observer, she intended to look like any other random, unknown, and unimportant spectator attending the game.

It took her less than a minute to locate Maxwell on the field.

He looked like a warrior. Resplendent in his shoulder pads and football pants, he exuded strength. His muscles rippled with harnessed energy. Her cheeks heated, but still, she couldn't take her eyes off him. Again, she was thankful for the jumbo sunglasses that hopefully hid her obsession with number eighty-seven.

When they stood for the national anthem, Maree reached across both M'Kenzee and Landry to squeeze Janie Lyn's hand. The two exchanged a small smile and then covered their hearts with their right hands.

At the end of the song, when all eighty thousand fans in attendance roared *home of the Chiefs* in place of *home of the brave*, Janie Lyn jumped and accidentally let out a squeal of surprise. She did better when they began chanting as one unit. They were ferocious, and Janie Lyn understood the importance of a home field advantage. It was quite intimidating; she couldn't imagine what it felt like to be the visiting team.

As a team captain, Maxwell walked to the center of the field for the coin toss.

Janie Lyn saw his eyes scanning the family section as he walked back to his sideline.

When his gaze found her, he patted his chest twice, a gesture meant just for her. Hand signs were vital to the game. The coaches, players, and referees used them to communicate the plays that were called, personnel and sets, their many different formations, penalties, and timeouts. Many of his teammates had secret signs for their families; Maxwell had decided that two taps over his heart would be their sign for *love you*.

The Chiefs won the toss and deferred their option to receive until the second half, so they were on defense first.

Janie Lyn watched him stretch. He walked to various players to pat them on the helmet, shoulder, or rear end. He shook hands with the coaches. Maxwell was very methodical; going through his ritual flipped a switch in his mind and in his body.

The Chiefs' defense forced a three-and-out, and Maxwell's unit took the field.

He pointed out intricacies and shifts to his teammates, encouraged the guys, and rallied his troops. He was magnificent. He'd told her the game was won in the trenches, and she saw that he was perfectly in his element amidst that battle.

Janie Lyn couldn't bear to sit down — she was too nervous for Maxwell. Maree and M'Kenzee were equally spellbound by the game, cheering and hollering with the crowd. Landry seemed more interested in flirting with Davis, who seemed happy to oblige her by teasing back in his usual jovial manner. They were all having a fabulous time.

Of course, it was easy to relax and have fun when your team was winning.

The first quarter was a tight tug-of-war. Campbell, who Janie Lyn remembered from the practice film Maxwell had been studying at home, busted loose after a dicey one-handed catch along the sideline to score the first touchdown. The Cowboys answered by charging down the field, but they had to settle for a three-point field goal when a penalty backed them up to fourth-and-nine from the thirty-yard line.

Evenly matched, the two teams put on quite a show. Each offense took one step forward, only to be pushed two steps back by the other defense. Janie Lyn's nerves were wound as tight as a bow just watching them. She could only imagine what it felt like to be out there playing.

On the final play of the first half, the Chiefs' quarterback faked a handoff and looked downfield. Maxwell made a double move, running down the sideline. He stopped to come back.

"The corner and safety both bit," Rhys exclaimed.

Instead of the comeback route, Maxwell bolted up the field.

"Max is open," Davis yelled.

"Throw it!" M'Kenzee screamed.

Janie Lyn flashed a quick glance at them and then looked back at Maxwell.

The quarterback slung the ball. Maxwell extended his hands low, almost to the ground, and caught it in-stride. He stayed on his feet, managed to stay in-bounds, and tucked the football under his arm and into his ribs, just as he had the dog toys in the town house. He turned to run toward the end zone.

He evaded one tackle by stutter-stepping just as the defender launched himself toward Maxwell. He held off another one with a stiff arm to the guy's chest. There was one last player between Maxwell and a touchdown.

Maxwell took an imperceptible glance back — or perhaps he simply knew where his teammate was — and pulled up slightly to slow his speed. That gave Campbell the fraction of a second needed to get in front of Maxwell and block the defender. Maxwell had a clear path for the last ten yards. He crossed the goal line as time expired.

"He scored, he scored!" The crowd went wild.

Fireworks went off. A cannon boomed. The stands shook like an earthquake rattling the earth.

Maree, M'Kenzee, and Landry were hugging and jumping up and down. Rhys and Davis were high-fiving every fan within arm's reach. Janie Lyn was light-headed.

And she was exhausted. It had only been one half of one game, but she was completely and utterly worn out.

How many games were in a season? How did the players do it? *How did their wives and girlfriends survive?*

The point-after attempt was good; the teams jogged into their locker rooms for halftime, and Janie Lyn collapsed into her chair.

Bursting with pride, she couldn't stop smiling. Her heart threatened to explode. Any chance it could be over now? With the score fourteen to three in Maxwell's favor?

She barely noticed the halftime show and was just coming out of her stupor when M'Kenzee announced she wanted to go to the concession stand for a drink and a funnel cake before the second half began.

Oh dear… Another half.

"I'd take a pretzel," Maree said. "And a bottle of water, please."

"Mmm, me too," Landry added.

By the time the guys chimed in, M'Kenzee had a long list and would have an armful of food to bring back.

"I'll go with you," Janie Lyn offered. Adding sugar to her already frazzled nerves might be a bad idea, but the walk and a drink were bound to help.

27

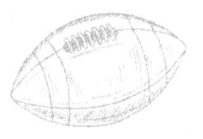

*Bad things can happen, and often do—
but they only take up a few pages of your story;
and anyone can survive a few pages.*
**The Barbizon Diaries:
A Meditation on Will, Purpose,
and the Value of Stories
by James A. Owen**

Making their way to the concession stand at the end of halftime was like swimming upstream. They were fighting the crowds trying to get back to their seats before kickoff.

In the melee, Janie Lyn got ahead of M'Kenzee, and the two were separated.

M'Kenzee was desperately trying to see where Janie Lyn had gone when the space between them — perhaps fifteen yards — opened up for a split second to reveal a brute of a man grabbing at Janie Lyn.

"Hey!" M'Kenzee yelled, running toward them and pushing people out of her way.

Instinctively, she put a hand on her camera. As a professional photographer, her camera always hung around her neck, and Max's football games were a great source for incredible pictures and social media content.

M'Kenzee continued yelling and running after Janie Lyn and the man. In an act of second nature, her thumb slid over and flipped the power button on. She raised her arm to hold the camera high and began clicking the button, letting the shutter go continuously as she aimed it toward the assailant.

Janie Lyn kicked and screamed, doing everything she could to get away.

The man was a giant, easily as big as Max. But ugly as sin. Pocked skin and a bulbous, red nose rounded out his puffy face. A mean scar split one eyebrow and ran across his oily forehead.

What is happening?

"Somebody help her!" M'Kenzee screamed as people stood gaping at the scene unfolding around them. "Do something!" How could they freeze like idiots?

Janie Lyn raised a ruckus, fighting tooth and nail. She'd lost her cap and sunglasses. Her braids were a tangled mess. She'd almost worked loose of his hold until he used his other hand to grab her by the hair.

He dragged her barbarically. Janie Lyn scrambled to keep her footing, swinging at him and clawing at the hand in her hair.

He noticed M'Kenzee gaining on them and moved to thwart her inevitable attempt to attack him and free Janie Lyn. In doing so, he shoved Janie Lyn into a tiled concrete column.

Janie Lyn cried out as her face hit the structure with a horrible crack.

"Janie Lyn!" M'Kenzee yelled, worried about the force with which Janie Lyn's head had met the post.

The blow didn't slow either girl's frenzy to free Janie Lyn from the man's clutches.

M'Kenzee called for the police at the top of her lungs and used all her strength to pull the man's hands off Janie Lyn. She, too, clawed at his face, scraping her nails down his neck and arms.

At the same time Janie Lyn kicked at his legs and torso, her hands wrapped around the fist and wrist still entangled in her hair. Her nails cut into his flesh as blood ran down her face.

"Help us!" M'Kenzee shrieked again as security officers ran toward them.

When they were mere steps away, the would-be abductor released Janie Lyn, giving her one last shove to the ground as he pushed people toward the officers and ran.

M'Kenzee didn't wait to see which way he went; she dropped to Janie Lyn who slumped into a heap on the floor.

Within a minute, the EMTs arrived, put Janie Lyn on a medical cart, and said they were taking her to the team's medical facilities under the stadium.

M'Kenzee tried to reassure Janie Lyn. She tried to calm her down, but Janie Lyn frantically begged them not to tell Max. As they drove her away, Janie Lyn pleaded, "You can't tell him."

Stunned and bewildered, M'Kenzee hurried back to their seats to get everyone and Janie Lyn's bag. She didn't have a clue how to explain what had happened.

"Come on," she told them.

"What?" Maree asked without taking her eyes off the game.

"Come on. We've got to go." M'Kenzee's angry tone got their attention.

"Go where?" Rhys countered, ever the cool-headed one. M'Kenzee scowled at him.

"Something's happened," she answered.

"What's happened?" Maree was getting scared, M'Kenzee could hear it in her voice.

"An accident." M'Kenzee wasn't sure how to answer because she wasn't sure herself.

"What kind of an accident?" Maree asked.

Rhys caught on. "M'Kenzee, where's Janie Lyn?" She ignored her sister's fiancé. They had a turbulent relationship, one she'd come to terms with since he seemed to be Maree's perfect soulmate, but when chaos erupted, M'Kenzee reverted back to her knee-jerk distrust of most people.

"M'Kenzee, *where is Janie Lyn?*" Rhys was a brave soul; not many people questioned her with such command once, much less twice.

"Let's go," she fired back. "I'll explain when we get downstairs."

"Downstairs?" Davis chimed in. M'Kenzee cut her eyes to answer him.

"Yes, under the stadium. We need to get to the training room."

Even with their family credentials, it took thirty minutes to talk their way into the secure team area to find Janie Lyn. She'd been set up in a "quiet room" at the back of the medical facility in the bowels of the stadium. It was a secure location intended for players who might suffer a possible concussion during the game. The medical facility itself functioned as a small hospital underneath the behemoth venue. A small group of medical personnel milled about in the room with Janie Lyn, and things appeared to have calmed down.

M'Kenzee sighed with relief. Janie Lyn was safe.

Several times M'Kenzee tried to go into the exam room, but each time someone denied her entrance. She gave the lackey assigned gatekeeping duty her iciest glare, but no matter how she tried to explain the situation, he refused to let her in.

As firemen, Rhys and Davis were allowed a little more access and were able to briefly check in on Janie Lyn.

"Must be nice to carry a shiny badge around everywhere you go," M'Kenzee sneered.

Maree saw right through her gruff demeanor and wrapped M'Kenzee in a hug. Maree was the *only* person who could get away with that. "Janie Lyn's in good hands," Maree assured her. "Rhys and Davis will find out all they can and see what we can do."

M'Kenzee hugged her back and then stepped away to pace while they waited. Maree and Landry huddled together in a corner.

What in the world is going on?

"Janie Lyn will be okay. She's in a little shock," Rhys announced when he and Davis rejoined the girls. "All she's said is that no one can tell Max what happened."

"What *did* happen?" Maree asked.

As one, the group turned to M'Kenzee for answers she didn't have.

28

No one ever told me that grief felt so like fear.
C.S. Lewis

"Great game, Max!" The tight end coach beat a hand on Max's shoulder pads and then wrapped a hand around Max's sweaty neck to give him a hug. "You're done for the day."

"Coach, we might get another possession," Max pointed out.

"We're up thirty-five to three; the defense has completely shut them out in the second half, and you've got three touchdowns on the day. You're done," Coach said with a pointed look.

"Yes, sir," Max relented.

"Congratulations on a big day!"

"Thanks, Coach," Max said with a grin. "You too."

"Mr. Davenport?"

Max turned to see a policeman approaching him.

"Yes, sir?" Max had seen the officer standing by the bench throughout the second half, but a lot of security stood on the sidelines, so Max hadn't thought much of it. Now his heart stopped, and his stomach dropped.

"Could you come with me, please?"

Max broke out in a different kind of sweat, one caused by instant nausea. His heart rate jumped from still to staccato. He clenched his fists to stop his hands from shaking.

"Where is she?" A million horrible images flashed through his mind. "*Where is she?*" Max demanded a second time, in a tone that left no question.

"In the quiet room, sir."

Max took off at a sprint. He stopped outside the doors to the training wing to pull off his shoulder pads. An equipment manager was walking by and stepped up to help him.

"Put this in my locker," Max commanded. "Please?" he added, trying to sound kind when he knew his voice was flat and angry.

He was terrified to open those doors, terrified to see her hurt.

He inhaled a deep breath, gripped the door handle, and faced his fear.

Max surveyed the scene: police gathered, doctors consulting, and his family huddled across the room. He strode their way but simply made eye contact with Rhys to establish that his sisters and their friends were all okay.

When Rhys gave a single nod of affirmation, Max walked past without stopping or even pausing. From the corner of his eye, he saw M'Kenzee step toward him, but he couldn't talk right now. He had to get to Janie Lyn.

An armed guard — a guy wearing an FBI jacket — turned to stop him. Another man looked up from a set of stadium maps spread out over a treatment table.

"Let him in," Bren told the watchman at the double doors. Then he walked around the table to halt Max's progress across the room, to stop Max from making his way to Janie Lyn.

Max met Bren's eyes, but he couldn't find his voice to ask what he needed to know.

"She's okay, Max. She's going to be okay," Bren promised him. "There was a lot of blood, so don't panic. They've already sewn her up, and they gave her something to help her relax. You freaking out won't help her. She was distraught, adamant that no one tell you during the game."

"What in hell happened?" Max was trying to control his temper, his volume, and his fear, but it wasn't easy.

"We're working on that."

Max bit the corner of his bottom lip to keep from raging at his best friend.

"I won't wake her up, but I have to see her," he said coolly.

Bren stepped aside. Max found it difficult to breathe as he walked to the bed where she lay.

He grabbed a doctor's stool and wheeled it under him to straddle so he wasn't looming over her. His hands came to rest on her arm which lay along her side.

His touch startled her, which broke his heart a little more.

"It's me," he whispered. "I'm here."

Janie Lyn opened her eyes and turned her head to face him. "Oh, Maxwell, I'm so sorry."

She tried to sit up.

"No, please." His voice wavered. "Please don't say you're sorry, and don't try to move right now." One hand slid down to hold hers, and the other moved to cradle her head, safely clear of her wounds. "I wish you'd sent for me earlier. I hate that you were alone."

"I met Bren. He's been here," she said, trying to assuage his guilt. "I didn't want to mess up your game. Did we win?" Her words were slurring, her eyelids drooping.

"Yeah, beautiful, we won." And yet he felt like he'd run a marathon and lost miserably.

"Oh good." She tried to smile up at him. "I like watching you play." Her thready voice faded away as her eyes closed.

Max studied her as she settled into sleep. Then he laid his forehead on the blue cushion of the training table they'd used for her bed.

His thumbs ran over the soft skin of her hand, over the silkiness of her hair. He wanted to scoop her up in his arms and take her home where he could hold her close and never let her go.

His shoulders shook. His chest burned.

Overcome with emotions, he let his tears fall. Just for a moment, while no one was watching.

29

> ***There are three things all wise men fear:***
> ***the sea in storm,***
> ***a night with no moon,***
> ***and the anger of a gentle man.***
> ***The Wise Man's Fear by Patrick Rothfuss***

A strong hand rested on Max's shoulder. Bren.

"How did this happen? How did they find her?" He lifted his head and wiped his cheeks with each shoulder so he didn't have to release his contact with Janie Lyn.

"We're working on it. It's going to take—"

"Work faster," Max snarled through clenched teeth.

"Let's go." Bren didn't take the bait to snap back. "You need a shower. We can talk on the way to the locker room."

"I'm not leaving her."

"She's resting — which is what she needs — and you stink."

Max glowered at Bren.

Then he stood from the stool and leaned over to place a soft kiss on her lips.

"Do you trust these guys? Are you sure she's safe in here if you go with me?"

"They kept M'Kenzee out. At least for a while."

Max reluctantly agreed with an affirmative tilt of his head.

"Ten minutes. You better talk fast."

"Janie Lyn can't go home with you," Bren said as they entered the team locker room. Luckily, enough time had passed since the end of the game that the players had already come through and cleared out.

Max stopped to stare at him. "Come again?" Bren was the closest thing Max had ever known to a brother; they'd grown up together, experienced lots of life together. It had been ages since he and Bren had gotten into a good fight. Seemed to Max like today would be the day.

"Whoever did this will want to use your connection to try again."

"We know who—" Max tried to point out the obvious, but Bren cut him off.

"Or your family, and their connection to Janie Lyn. You don't want that, and Janie Lyn won't allow it."

"*Won't allow it?*" Max turned on Bren and stepped up to face him, chest to chest. "Janie Lyn is lying in the training room, knocked out from a botched kidnapping — best-case scenario — or an attempt on her life. Her clothes are ripped to shreds. Her face is swollen, bloody, and stitched up — to use your own brilliant words. I don't think she's in a position to make major decisions right now." His tone grew in frustration and anger with every point he made.

"You know her better than I do," Bren began, and wasn't the least bit concerned with the hateful look Max tossed at him. "Do you think she'd want to put Maree and M'Kenzee in danger? What about Miss Sadie?"

Max walked away from Bren. He paced in a tight circle as he ran his hands through his hair. Then with a moving start, he punched the heel of his hand into a locker with a feral growl.

He rarely lost his cool. Fun-loving and a big ol' teddy bear, Max made it a point to be a patient friend to all. It took *a lot* to push him past his composure. But at that moment, his frustration was compounded by fear, his fear compounded by anger, and his anger compounded by his inability to fix what had gone wrong. Terribly, terribly wrong.

"They've shown their hand," Bren said reasonably. "Her uncles made a critical mistake today. Trying to snatch her in the middle of a massive crowd, at a venue that posts armed security at every entrance? That reeks of desperation. We'll figure out how they knew she'd be here. We'll back-trace their movements. We *will* find them."

Max didn't answer. He rested his arms on the locker door he'd just dented and would need to have replaced. His head hung between his arms while his breathing evened out and his heartbeat settled back to normal.

"She's everything," Max said quietly.

"I know."

"I can't lose her," he added.

"I know," Bren said again.

"Keep her safe."

"I will."

30

*Not only that, but we rejoice in our sufferings,
knowing that suffering produces endurance,
and endurance produces character,
and character produces hope,
and hope does not put us to shame,
because God's love has been poured into our hearts
through the Holy Spirit who has been given to us.
Romans 5:3–5*

"I just need a few things from Maxwell's house." Janie Lyn tried to sound rational and unruffled, although she felt anything but. "I'll run by there and then be on my way. It won't take bu—"

"Janie Lyn," Maxwell said from across the room, halting her rambling. Her head lifted to meet his gaze.

His red and glassy eyes spoke for him. He looked exhausted. Miserable.

"I'm so sorry, Maxwell." Her breathing was shallow. Her head felt faint again. It wasn't the trauma of the attack. It wasn't the head wound.

Walking away from Maxwell was torture.

Someone had brought her a change of clothes: a pair of soft gray sweats and a string bag to put her other things in. She made a big production of folding her clothes just to have something to do with her hands. She kept fidgeting with the remains of the sequined sweater until Maxwell stilled her hands.

He held them gently and turned her to face him.

She forced a flimsy smile and launched into another monologue before he could speak.

"I regret bringing this ugliness into your life. I should never—"

"Don't say that," he said, pleading with his eyes. "Please don't regret these past ten days."

His voice broke, which shattered her feeble strength. She crumpled into his arms, turning her head to bury her face in his chest.

Sobs shuddered through her body. Max's hands moved over her back to soothe; one cradled the back of her head and neck to shelter her.

"This is temporary. We'll talk every day," he promised.

"Maxwell, we can't." She pulled away to look up at him. "I can't point them in your direction."

Bren cleared his throat before walking over to them.

"This is my burner phone," he said, handing an old-style flip phone to Janie Lyn. "There's no way your uncles are running with anyone smart enough to break our cybersecurity, but if they find a way to trace it, it'll take them straight to the FBI."

She took the phone and felt a tiny surge of hope.

"We're going to make our exit very public. We'll plant footage of Max, his family, and other players with their families watching the ambulance as it leaves the stadium, sirens blaring, the whole nine yards," Bren explained. "The football team's PR team will hold a press conference to release a statement saying a deranged homeless man wandered into the stadium and attacked a spectator in line at the concession stand. They'll keep your identity out of it, make it sound random for now."

Head spinning — and pounding — she concentrated to keep up with their plan.

"The only people who know it was you will see you leave for the hospital while I stay here. I'll look like any other player looking on," Maxwell told her.

"That's good," she said. "But it's not enough."

"What do you mean?" Bren asked, but Maxwell closed his eyes in agony. He knew where she was headed.

"Maxwell, you need to be seen out on the town."

"No, there's no reason for that," he argued, his voice despondent.

"Yes, there is," she insisted while Maxwell shook his head. "Ask Mary Beth to dinner, attend a concert, go do something fun with friends. If the paparazzi post photos of you enjoying life, my uncles will realize I wasn't anything important."

"Then I'll be living a lie," Maxwell said deadpan.

"Max, it's not a bad idea," Bren said cautiously. Maxwell flashed a murderous look at his friend.

"I'm supposed to *convincingly* behave as if I'm a single playboy, hopping from party to party and date to date? Meanwhile, Janie Lyn will be forced to live by herself, sequestered from everything she enjoys? Great plan, Bren."

"It's just the first phase. And I'm not saying you have to play the part of a wild bachelor. Just do what you would've done before you and Janie Lyn—" Bren's voice died out, alluding to the fact that Maxwell and Janie Lyn's whirlwind romance had only been a thing for less than two weeks.

"That life ended for me," Max said. "I don't want to go back to an existence that doesn't include you." He spoke directly to Janie Lyn. He didn't bother to hide the love in his eyes.

"I love you, too." She mouthed the words.

"Bren, we're ready," a female agent said from the doorway. Bren walked over to speak with her.

Janie Lyn went back to stuffing her jeans into the bag. She held up the sequined top and looked between it and Maxwell. "I ruined it," she said ruefully.

"I bet you looked amazing," he said.

"We have a gurney for you, Janie Lyn." Bren reached out to hit the button on the automatic double doors.

"Okay," she said. "I'll be right there."

She added the sweater to the bag and cinched it tight.

"I lost my favorite cap. The camo one," she told Maxwell.

"I know a guy who can get you another one." He cradled her jaw in his hands, caressing his thumbs over her cheeks, sliding one over her lips. "God, I love you."

Maxwell lowered to kiss her. It was a kiss to curl her toes, one she'd never forget.

"I had such fun," she said, her lips still touching his. Tears streamed down her cheeks again. "It might not have lasted long, but it was wonderful. I loved every minute."

She didn't look back as she walked away.

31

> *It is done...*
> *the precious portrait*
> *placed in the hands of the gentlemen...*
> *for safe keeping.*
> Dolley Madison

"How is she?"

"Max, it's been two hours."

"So?"

"So, she's exactly the same as the last time you called," Bren told him.

"Still asleep? She's in concussion protocol after—" He had a hard time saying the words *she was attacked*. He'd seen the video footage, and it amazed him she'd not been much worse off than she was.

"No, she's awake," Bren filled in when Max failed to finish his sentence. "Would you like to speak to her?" Bren mocked him, speaking as if it were a run-of-the-mill question. Max didn't bother answering.

"Hi." He loved the way Janie Lyn's accent gave the simple two-letter word an extra syllable. *Hai-yhhh.*

"Hi, yourself," he said with a smile. Just hearing her voice made the night more bearable. "How was your nap?"

"Lonely."

"Well, let's keep it that way until we're under the same roof," he teased.

"Deal," she promised.

"I saw the video. Janie Lyn, you were so strong, so brave." He would spare her the details of what watching the attack had done to him. No man wanted the woman he loved and cherished to envision him rushing to a toilet to throw his guts up.

"I was a bawling mess. M'Kenzee was the brave one. She came at that man with all she had, slashing at his face and ordering people to find the police."

Her voice trembled; he hated to hear her upset.

"You both were incredible, both managed to scrape his skin. The FBI got DNA from under your nails. And M'Kenzee got photos on her camera. Paired with the security footage, Bren said they already know exactly who they're looking for."

"That's good." Her words were optimistic, but she sounded defeated. He changed the subject.

"I packed some things for you. Bren said an agent will come get them tomorrow morning and deliver everything tomorrow afternoon." From that timeline, Max assumed that the safe house where they'd hidden her wasn't in Kansas City.

"Thank you, Maxwell." He never tired of hearing the way she said his name.

"Tell me about the game, the good parts," he urged.

She went through everything from the moment she stepped out of the car to the moment he scored that first touchdown. Max was pleased when she told him about the awe she felt walking amongst the fans, feeling their spirit, and sharing their appreciation for the game he loved to play. He was full-out laughing when she told him about a family of nine in red-and-yellow plaid overalls, every member matching head to toe, from the elderly grandparents to the pudgy twin toddlers. He was grateful when she told him about the tailgaters who'd offered her lunch and included her in their celebration. She described their setup in such vivid detail that he felt sure he could find them again. He planned to do just that at the next home game, personally, to tell them thank you, and see if he could upgrade their seats or do something nice in return.

Max enjoyed hearing that she'd been really into the game. He felt a little guilty when she explained how nervous it made her. He tried to assure her she'd get used to it in time.

Time, both their friend and their foe.

Weariness tinged her voice; he needed to let her go for the night.

Max promised he'd call again in the morning to check in on his drive to work and again tomorrow night when he got home from practice. He promised to call every day until they were together again.

And he did.

Each morning they talked about the upcoming day, and each night they went back through the day together.

Max could've stayed on the phone for hours and hours, but she needed rest to recuperate, so he'd end the call when her energy started to fade.

He also called Bren for updates on the investigation, ending each of those calls with the same question: how much longer?

By the end of the first week, Max thought he'd crawl out of his own skin. He was going crazy without her.

As he'd done since he was ten years old, he channeled those emotions to the football field.

On Monday night, he played the game of his career. He couldn't be slowed, much less stopped. Every block was a pancake, every route was precise, and every catch was a touchdown because the defense simply could not drag him down.

They'd played the second game of the night, so it ended well past midnight. Max called while they waited on the tarmac for their plane home to take off, but by that time, he'd missed Janie Lyn. Bren answered, said she'd watched every play, elated for his success.

She'd tried valiantly to stay awake until he called, but she'd fallen asleep on the couch.

"I can wake her," Bren offered.

"No, she needs rest," Max said, feeling sad and lonely.

"Should I leave her there to sleep on the couch?" Max heard what Bren didn't say: did Max want Bren to carry her to her room? His heart hurt. He wanted to be there for Janie Lyn. He wanted to be the one taking care of her. Instead, he was the worst thing for her, forced to keep his distance to ensure her safety.

"No, she'll sleep better in her bed." There was no need to sound so gruff. Bren was the most trustworthy man he'd ever known. Max would trust him with his life, even his sisters' lives. And Max knew that Janie Lyn loved Max just as he loved her: completely. It wasn't insecurity that had him bristling. It was agony. He was absolutely miserable without her.

"We have a plan, Max, to catch Stanton and Axel Lyndale, as well as the hired muscle who attacked Janie Lyn. It'll take a little time to get everything planted and in place, but there's light at the end of the tunnel, buddy."

The flight attendant made the preflight announcements and asked them to turn off their cell phones.

"I'll tell you everything tomorrow," Bren vowed. "And Max?"

"Yeah?"

"That was one hell of a game tonight." Bren's voice brimmed with pride. Max cracked a small smile as he hung up the phone.

If you had to give your soulmate to someone else for safekeeping, his best friend was your guy.

32

*The most effective way to do it,
is to do it.*
Amelia Earhart

"**Y**ou want to do *what?*" Max bellowed at Bren.

"It's not as bad as it sounds." Bren tried to cajole him, but Max wasn't having it.

"How do you figure?"

"Maybe I should talk to him," Janie Lyn said hesitantly in the background.

Max closed his eyes to pray for patience and strength. And for his so-called best friend to pull his head out of— No, he wouldn't go there with his prayers.

"Hi, Maxwell." Janie Lyn's voice was soft, reserved.

"Please don't do this," Max begged.

"It's the only way," she said, trying to persuade him.

"There's got to be another way, a way that doesn't involve a second attempt to kidnap or kill you." There was an edge to his voice. He hated that she would hear it, but he couldn't help it. This plan risked too much.

"Let's not talk about it now," she urged. "It could take weeks, even months, for them to try something. If ever." *Ef eh-vah.* Her sweet Georgia drawl did wonders to calm his nerves. "I watched your game last night. You were amazing." *Ah-mayyzin.*

He could do this, right? He could sit back and let the love of his life be used as live bait.

Max shook his head to clear his thoughts. He wouldn't let himself fall into a pit of worry and despair. He wouldn't waste the little time he had to hear her voice.

"Thank you. I'm glad I played okay with you watching."

"Okay? I'd say you played much better than okay."

Bren commented on the other end.

"Whatever he just said, ignore it," he told her. She laughed. Hearing that was God's healing power in action.

"We were both very proud. The announcers went on and on about you. It was really something."

"I'm just glad we won," he said with an exhale.

"Y'all play back at home this week?" She was luring him into a conversation he could handle, one that didn't involve dangerous crime-fighting stings or the unrealistic expectations that came with sports success. He let himself be led, and they talked and talked.

As he'd noticed in Green Hills, their discussions just flowed. She was an interested listener, so it was easy to share anything — and everything — with her.

If asked, he would've said he was an awful phone talker. Notoriously terrible about calling to check on people, once on the phone, his mind often wandered. Then he'd feel guilty for not hearing what the person on the other end of the line had been saying.

But not with Janie Lyn. He enjoyed whatever time he could get with her, so he was perfectly content to talk on the phone for hours.

Max could ignore the ominous cloud floating overhead. He could pretend to overlook the storm waiting to rage, if they stuck to safe topics. And Max was happy to do *that* for as long as they lasted.

33

A real friend is someone who walks in when the rest of the world walks out.
Adage popularized by Walter Winchell

They lasted until Friday.

"KCTV Channel 5 News interrupts your regularly scheduled programming with a breaking story. We want to warn you, the video you are about to see is graphic and not appropriate for all ages," the lead anchor said as the golf tournament Max had on was preempted. He'd only been half watching as he folded laundry in his bedroom, but that got his attention.

"The Kansas City Chiefs released this security footage with a request for help to identify the man seen here attacking a woman in the concourse during the September 22 game against the Dallas Cowboys," a second anchor reported. "Team officials are working closely with local law enforcement and the FBI since the altercation could have been a kidnapping attempt. The female victim is still in the hospital recovering from head trauma; further details on her condition have not yet been released. If you have any..."

Max muted the television and took his phone out of his back pocket. A little forewarning would have been nice.

"Hello, Maxwell," Bren said, answering on the first ring.

"Don't call me that."

"It's your name… Trust me, I hear it all day long. Maxwell this, Maxwell that, Maxwell is wonderful, Maxwell is amazing, blah, blah, blah."

Okay, that took a little of the blustering wind out of his sails. She talked about him. And made Bren listen. Very nice.

"I just saw the news; why didn't you tell me?"

"Because you are supposed to be disconnected from the victim, just a concerned citizen like every other member of the Chiefs organization."

"But I'm not," Max emphasized.

"No, you're not," Bren conceded with a sigh. "That's why I need to let you know we are moving Janie Lyn into Saint Luke's. We've arranged a private room on the postsurgical floor and prepared a story that she required a procedure to decrease pressure on her brain from damage sustained when her head hit the concrete column. She's healing well and expected to make a full recovery, but she will need to remain under medical supervision for another week or two. If her uncles don't bite in that amount of time, she will move to a rehab facility. We will keep her in the news until they do bite."

"You're moving forward with this, even though you know it's a terrible idea."

"You *think* it's a terrible idea. The rest of us think it's our best option."

"Tell me the details. How will you make sure she's safe the entire time she's there?"

By the time they hung up, Max felt marginally better. He wanted this to be over for Janie Lyn — they both needed this to be over so they could move forward.

When he spoke with Janie Lyn later that night, he asked about her recipe project. He told her a few embarrassing stories about

Bren and did everything he could to keep her mind off her imminent move to the hospital.

On his way to the airport to leave for his game, he took the colorful quilt Maree had made for his bed in the town house to Saint Luke's with a card that simply said, "I miss you." He left it at the nurses' station on the floor where Bren had said she was going to be. Then he texted Bren to let him know it was there and that Max would like for it to be on her bed when she arrived. He'd considered delivering her family quilt, but knowing how much it meant and that it was an irreplaceable heirloom, he opted for the other one instead.

On the way out of the hospital, he stopped by the gift shop and ordered their biggest, brightest bouquet to be sent to her room. That card simply said, "I love you."

Max hated social media and refused to engage in the time-wasting habit of constant scrolling. He made an exception to devour every snippet of information he could follow about the "mysterious girl who was attacked at a recent NFL game."

It was startling and creepy how the FBI used media and hashtags to leak the story that they wanted to share. It was exactly how Bren had laid it out to Max earlier in the week, and every single "truth" was reposted and exaggerated to epic proportions. A meme of M'Kenzee screaming at the onlookers who'd watched Janie Lyn being dragged by her hair had #HelpHer trending.

No one knew it was a plot to trap murderous thugs. No one cared if it was fact or fiction. Everyone demanded justice for the poor woman in the video who was now fighting for her life in a Kansas City hospital bed.

The whole ordeal made Max queasy. The video he'd seen too many times, the crack of Janie Lyn's head hitting the pillar, the lies purposefully being spread, the danger she was in, and most of all, the miles between them — all of it made him sick.

When the Chiefs kicked off at noon on Sunday, Max was worked up to the point of erupting. Once again, he channeled that energy into the game. And again, he played lights-out.

He brooded the entire trip, throughout the flight home, and all the next day.

"There's a bee in Davenport's bonnet," one clever broadcaster joked on the *Monday Morning Quarterback*. "And we like it!"

"It's true; Max Davenport is putting up video game–type numbers," another host of the show swore. "Can anyone compete?"

"I think not," a retired NFL player and the day's special guest chimed in. "We've never seen this type of production from that position. Whatever is pushing number eighty-seven this season is pushing him straight toward the Hall of Fame."

Max switched off the television and tossed the remote at the couch cushion.

What tripe. Total trash. If he let up, had one bad outing, they'd be saying he was a washed-up has-been. Didn't they understand? The final score, success, fame, legacy…life — they were all fleeting. None of this mattered.

But it did.

When Max calmed down — when his mind and his muscles relaxed — he admitted it mattered.

He loved the game, loved everything about it.

He just couldn't enjoy it anymore without Janie Lyn.

He was still sitting on the couch, head in his hands, when someone knocked.

He contemplated pretending he wasn't home, but the doormen would know better. Besides, at the end of the day, he wasn't a coward who ran from his troubles.

"Wow. You look rough."

"Mary Beth? What are you doing here?"

She lifted an eyebrow to ask *Excuse Me?!* without having to say a word.

"I'm sorry," he backtracked, remembering his manners. "Come on in." He dragged a hand through his hair as he held the door open for her.

"Thankfully, Janie Lyn looks to be handling all of this better than you."

"*What??*"

"I went by to see her." Mary Beth said it as if that was normal, even to be expected. Max froze on the spot.

"Josephine's is appalled that a guest in our fair city — nicknamed the Heart of America, no less — was treated so horrendously. We provided dinner for the staff on her floor at Saint Luke's. As the owner of such a kind and concerned establishment, I just *had* to make the catering delivery myself. Great photo op, you know." Mary Beth flashed a guilty grin his way, and Max engulfed her in a hug.

"Stop that," she said, swatting at his shoulder. "I hate to cry."

"Thank you, Mary Beth." It was all he could say with emotion choking his throat.

"Well, any idiot could see the way you two looked at each other when I dropped by unexpectedly. Surely y'all didn't think I bought that 'personal assistant' routine." She turned her big exotic eyes on him with a look of skepticism.

Mary Beth was stunning, unbelievably gorgeous. She just wasn't the right woman for Max.

He looked down and rocked back on his heels.

"I told her exactly that, too." Max looked back at Mary Beth. He was starved for information about Janie Lyn, like a thirsty man in a desert. "I apologized for being so rude, for not paying attention to what was clearly in front of me. I said that every girl dreams of an honorable man looking at her just the way you look at Janie Lyn."

His eyes burned. Mary Beth swiped a tear from her own cheek.

"Furthermore, I told her that y'all were the lucky ones, the blessed ones, and that this hurdle is just a brief moment in a lifetime you two will have together. And then I sat on the edge of her bed and let her cry on my shoulder for as long as she wanted."

Max watched, still struggling for words, as Mary Beth set a large paper bag on his kitchen counter and began extracting to-go boxes from the restaurant. She flipped the oven on, found two wineglasses in his cupboard, and rifled through drawers until she found a corkscrew.

"You know, not just anyone is allowed to get salty tears on my very favorite Brunello Cucinelli silk blouse." She pointed the wine opener at him.

"I'll buy you ten more," he vowed.

"Yeah, yeah." She waved him off. "I know she's important."

"How is she? Honestly. Janie Lyn tries to sound upbeat and chipper when I call. So valiant. But I'm worried about her. Really worried," Max said as he pulled out a barstool and sat down.

"Honestly?" Mary Beth filled their wineglasses and handed one to Max before sliding the foil pans into the oven. "Honestly, you picked a great one, Max."

She turned back to him, picked up her glass, and touched it to his in cheers.

"She's incredibly strong, tried to turn her Southern charm and hostessing skills on me when I first got there. Once we got past all that nonsense — and I convinced her I'm a good sport and not a sore loser over you — she let me see the brilliant, kind, giving woman you've obviously fallen in love with. We talked, we dished stories about you, we cried, and we promised to build our own relationship, outside of my friendship with you. I truly look forward to spending more time with Janie Lyn. Like I said, you picked well, my friend."

The visit was just what Max had needed.

After Mary Beth left, Max locked up the house and turned off all the lights. He went upstairs and washed up for bed. Once he'd crawled in and muted the sports show on the TV, he called Janie Lyn.

"Hello?" Her voice was groggy. He'd waited too late to call.

"I understand you had a visitor today."

"Mmm, yes, I like your girlfriend very much." He heard the smile in her voice.

"She said much the same."

Janie Lyn gave a small laugh.

"I want to marry you, Janie Lyn. I want to spend the rest of my life loving you." He paused for a heartbeat. "Don't say a word, just sleep on it," he added before hanging up.

34

***I guess a man is the only kind of varmint
sets his own trap, baits it, and then steps in it.
Sweet Thursday by John Steinbeck***

"Agent Stewart, we think Stanton Lyndale is in the hospital."

"You *think*?" Bren tried to control his voice, but the question still came out a bit hateful over the earpiece. He and Janie Lyn were watching the end of Max's game on the television in her room.

For the third week in a row, Max was punishing anyone who dared to get too close, so the Chiefs were way ahead.

"Yes, sir. We didn't get a clean look at his face on camera, but we feel certain it's him."

"All agents, be ready to move." Bren spoke slowly and clearly as he crossed Janie Lyn's room. He put the Taser into her hand, moved her thumb to the safety switch as they'd practiced, and helped her scoot down to appear more feeble than she actually was. He hated to see the color drain from her face but figured her pale, sallow complexion helped sell the act, so it was okay.

"Just be yourself," he instructed her. "I'm right here, hidden in the shower. Liú is posing as a doctor coming in to check your vitals, and there are additional agents all throughout the hospital. You are *not* alone."

Janie Lyn swallowed hard, bit her lips, and gave a quick nod. She rolled onto her side and opened a book lying on the bed beside her. He slipped out of sight but left the bathroom door open.

With her back to the door, Bren imagined that Janie Lyn jumped in earnest when her uncle's voice boomed into the room.

"Elizabeth, it's time to go home."

"Stanton," she said in a frightened voice. "How did you find me?"

Bren knew about the mob groupie living with Stanton. The FBI had traced her satellite usage and filtered through it to connect her gossip obsession with the paparazzi television program that had run the photo of Max and Janie Lyn at the movie theater in Green Hills. They'd even located the photographer.

It had not been the man Max had evaded by kissing Janie Lyn — Max swore he'd not had any other course of action. Likely story.

Instead, it had been a high school girl, just a boy-crazy teenager who'd known Max was a local celebrity and recognized him. With no parking in front of the historic theater, she was sitting in her car, taking selfies, and waiting to pick up her brother, who worked at the theater. When Max walked out of the building, she'd immediately flipped the camera out of selfie mode and started taking photos on her phone.

Within seconds, she'd posted the photo online.

#MaxSighting #ilove87 #WhosTheLuckyGirl

Didn't happen if it wasn't posted, right?

Within hours, the tabloids had it. Within days, Felicity Banks was pointing it out to her loser boyfriend and his vagrant brother.

Bren couldn't wait to haul them in.

"That doesn't matter none." Stanton's footsteps got closer to Janie Lyn's bed. "What matters is that now you can set things right. Fix what you ruined by trying to run away. That's no way to treat fam—"

"Bren!" Janie Lyn yelled.

He leaped from the bathroom just as she pushed the Taser into Stanton's chest.

The voltage vibrated Janie Lyn's arm, but she didn't let go.

Stanton dropped to the ground.

Agent Jia Liú was through the door in an instant, aiming her gun at Stanton while rolling his limp form over with her foot. Janie Lyn was sitting straight up in bed, looking wide-eyed at the fiery and vibrant young woman standing over her uncle. He was a lump on the floor, unthreatening and weak.

Janie Lyn still had a death grip on the Taser so Bren eased his hands over hers.

"Janie Lyn," he summoned. "Look at me. Janie Lyn."

She looked confused when she turned her head in his direction.

"Let go, hon. It's okay." Bren slowly loosened her hold and took the weapon away.

"Did I ki—" She stuttered over the question. "Is he dead?"

"No. No," Bren reassured her. "He will wake up soon, madder than a hornet's nest. You did great."

"That you did." Agent Liú beamed a smile at Janie Lyn. She settled a heeled boot on the small of Stanton's back while another agent fastened handcuffs to his wrists.

"Someone get a couple of warm blankets, please," Bren commanded to no one specific, but with confidence his request would be granted posthaste. He took out his phone and snapped a photo of Janie Lyn.

She blinked in surprise.

Max would drool over her soft smile and the dreamy, surreal look in her eyes. Bren sent it to him with a text that read, *Come get your girl — room 1221.*

Just as Bren slid his phone back into his jacket, the radio in his earpiece came to life again.

Agents working undercover as landscapers outside the hospital had spotted a suspicious vehicle.

It had circled the hospital numerous times and loitered around an unmarked entrance partially blocked by a cinderblock wall and an overgrown shrub. They'd cornered the car between the building and the parking lot. They'd identified the driver as the man who'd attacked Janie Lyn at the game.

He was singing like a canary before they'd even arrested him. He laid out Stanton's plan to trap Janie Lyn in her room. Her uncle had thought he could force Janie Lyn to go with him by threatening her life. With nowhere for Janie Lyn to run, and with her being in what he believed to be a frail condition, Stanton had figured to give Janie Lyn an ultimatum: either do what you're told or die.

It never ceased to amaze Bren how pathetic bullies and bad guys became when they were no longer in control.

Two down, one to go.

When Max flew through the elevator doors, Bren was walking toward him, alongside the wheelchair carting Stanton Lyndale to the patrol car that would take him to central booking at the county jail. Taking in the look on Max's face, Bren stepped between Max and the still-groggy man in custody.

Max snarled. Bren grinned.

"She's waiting for you," he taunted.

That was all it took. Max stormed down the hall in a flash.

Bren shook his head with a chuckle.

Ah, young love.

35

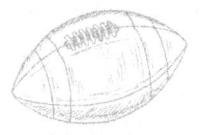

> *In the long run,*
> *the sharpest weapon of all*
> *is a kind and gentle spirit.*
> **Anne Frank**

"I'm sure there are several passages of scripture that say to forgive those who harm you. Maybe a few verses that talk about loving thy enemy," Janie Lyn pointed out from the kitchen as Maxwell carried a platter of burgers hot off the grill into his house in Green Hills.

"Humph," he grunted.

"You are exactly right," Miss Sadie agreed with a sweet smile. She, Maree, Landry, especially Maxwell, and even M'Kenzee were hovering around Janie Lyn.

They were still in a stupor over what they'd learned about her past, her identity, and her family. As Maxwell had once said, it was a wild and crazy story.

Boy, wasn't it true that truth *is* stranger than fiction?

The only person not hovering was Bren, which was good, as he would be the one to accompany Janie Lyn back to Georgia for Stanton's arraignment. While there, Janie Lyn also planned to close the bakery for good.

Maxwell was grumpy because he couldn't go with her.

After they'd left the hospital, she'd asked to go to Green Hills. They'd stopped by the town house for a few things, driven straight to Oklahoma, and arrived in the wee hours of Monday morning.

When Maxwell had called to say he wouldn't be able to be there for film, meetings, and treatment, his coach had told him to take whatever time his family needed. Janie Lyn wouldn't hear of it. They'd enjoy this one night together, and then she was sending him back to Kansas City. The Chiefs were undefeated, and no matter how much he denied it, Maxwell was a huge part of that success. He would *not* abandon the team for her.

Maxwell was also irritable because Janie Lyn wasn't more invested in making sure her uncles paid for their crimes. His perspective was out of character for Maxwell, and Janie Lyn felt sure that fear was overriding his normal tendency to give grace and love.

Her uncle Axel was still unaccounted for, and Janie Lyn knew that made Maxwell nervous, too.

She'd agreed to testify, if necessary, but she didn't want to be dragged into the drama that was bound to scuttle around their trials and sentencing. They'd made their choices over the years, and now they would be charged with many counts of charges for various crimes. They would face whatever justice a judge and jury meted out.

Not normally as spiritual as Maxwell, Janie Lyn felt at peace with whatever happened to them. Maxwell was the one having a hard time finding faith in the system. He couldn't seem to release his anger.

"He'll get there," Miss Sadie promised with a wink, as if she'd been reading Janie Lyn's thoughts. She accepted Miss Sadie's bear hug and smiled in agreement.

Even though they weren't on shift, Rhys and Davis had been called out to help with another fire. Janie Lyn hated that their conversation centered around the ongoing mystery of who was lighting the random fires disrupting life in Green Hills. At the same time, she was grateful they were talking about something besides her own situation. She also marveled at how her friends had accepted her so readily, how they'd forgiven the massive lies of omission she'd subjected them to — all without an ounce of hesitation.

Maree caught Janie Lyn closing her eyes for a quick prayer of thanksgiving. Maree's comforting smile and collaborative wink halted the split second of awkwardness and insecurity attempting to creep into Janie Lyn's mind. Maree understood her need to pause for a moment of praise. And she *was* feeling very grateful. For the first time in a long time, she felt the Lord's presence and the many blessings He'd bestowed upon her.

"When do you and Bren leave?" M'Kenzee asked from where she sat at the dining room table.

"Wednesday," Janie Lyn answered. "I need a day or so to take care of business at the bank and meet with the few employees left at the bakery. The arraignment is Friday. We'll fly back to Kansas City Saturday, and Maxwell plays on Sunday."

"What about your other uncle? Do you feel safe staying here and then doing all that traveling?" M'Kenzee knew how to get right to the point.

"I won't leave her," Bren said from the doorway. There was a flatness to his voice that Janie Lyn had never heard. M'Kenzee met his gaze for a moment and then dropped her eyes to the pickles and raw veggies she'd been playing with but not eating. Rather than reply, she picked up another carrot stick to draw more circles in the sour cream dip on her plate.

Truth be told, Janie Lyn was a little uneasy. Stanton had always been the leader, Axel the follower. But that didn't mean he wasn't dangerous. Desperate people often took drastic measures when they didn't know what else to do.

Bren had assured her that with Stanton in jail, there was little Axel could do without putting himself in their hands. He also promised they'd have protection at all times.

If it was enough to appease Maxwell, it was more than enough for Janie Lyn.

Dinner with the group had been very fun, with lots of laughter to lift the weight of the past few weeks.

Sleeping curled up next to Maxwell felt very good. Snuggled into the warmth of his body next to hers and under the protectiveness of his arm around her, she'd slept like a baby.

Sharing breakfast with him the next morning was very nice. They'd both been rather quiet, sipping coffee and picking at fruit and muffins. Needing to feel one another's presence more than anything, they'd simply sat close to one another, holding hands.

Telling him goodbye — again — was very hard.

Usually so motivated, Janie Lyn found it difficult to stay on task through the day. Getting through a few loads of laundry seemed to be all she could handle. By the time she'd packed her clothes and organized the documents and paperwork she'd printed off the internet, she was ready for bed.

On Wednesday, Janie Lyn had a quiet morning around the house and a quick lunch with Bren before heading to the airstrip in Green Hills. By dinnertime, they were in Athens.

It felt strange to be back. Everything looked the same, yet Janie Lyn felt different.

She and Bren ate at one of her favorite restaurants. The couple who owned it had been close friends with Gram and Pops; it thrilled her to see them. When she explained she intended to close the bakery Friday morning, they asked to stop by to see it one last time.

After dinner, Janie Lyn took Bren to see her grandparents' house.

They stood at the grand entry gates, looking down the drive with the sun setting on the house. It broke her heart to see the upstairs window broken and the shutters in disarray. The downstairs was completely boarded up. It probably looked terrible to Bren, but Janie Lyn still saw its magnificence peeking through.

"I know it was a lovely place to grow up," he said. Maxwell had spoken of Bren's dad and his blended Scottish brogue. For the first time, Janie Lyn heard it clearly in Bren's words. She looked over to see yearning in his expression. He kept things close to the vest, but over the past three weeks Janie Lyn had learned there were many layers to the secret agent.

"You're a good man, Brennigan Stewart, a faithful friend. I see why Maxwell loves you so much." Janie Lyn looped her arm through his, turning to walk toward the car the FBI had given him upon their arrival.

"*Yer off yer heid*, don't be spreadin' lies," he said dismissively.

"Listen to you!" Janie Lyn exclaimed with a gaping laugh. "What does that mean?"

"It means you're crazy. Come on, let's go."

Bren *was* a good man and a good friend. He went above and beyond to help Janie Lyn. He helped to make the painful process of turning the page and closing the book on her old life as bearable as possible.

Thursday morning, he sat with Janie Lyn at the bank, never letting shock or surprise show in his neutral expression. Meanwhile, her mind was blown.

Gram and Pops had created more than her personal accounts when she was young.

They'd paid their workers generously, kept the bakery in magnificent working order with the most up-to-date improvements throughout the years, and they'd deposited copious amounts of money in a hidden account owned by Elizabeth Jayne Lyndale.

An estate attorney also met with them to go over the details of Gram's will, which had been probated after Janie Lyn had run. In addition to the secret investment account and the ridiculous balance in it, Janie Lyn also owned the antebellum home she'd grown up in and a property thirty minutes south of Athens. That property was over three thousand acres, and it included multiple houses, barns, a private lake, cabins, and a working horse farm. The management team, which included the attorney, a financial planner, an accountant, a ranch foreman, a farm manager, and the property supervisor, had been taking care of everything in Janie Lyn's absence. Every member of that team had been dear friends to Gram and Pops, and Janie Lyn had never heard of a single one of them.

It was as if she'd just learned that the two people she'd known best in all the world were strangers. They'd lived a secret life. She was completely flummoxed.

"What would you like to do with it all?" The banker's question sounded like a garble of words that made no sense.

"I have no idea," she answered in awe.

"Gentlemen," Bren said, thankfully taking charge on her behalf, "you've been most helpful. Perhaps we can reconvene tomorrow morning before we head to Atlanta?"

"No," Janie Lyn interjected. "Today. I want to talk again today."

"There you have it, lads. We will break for lunch and meet back here at say three thirty?" He looked at Janie Lyn for confirmation.

"That will work." Janie Lyn managed a smile but walked out of the bank like a robot, stiff and moving her entire head from side to side to take in the world around her.

"Where to?" Bren asked once they were in the car.

"The Whispering Pines Cemetery, please." Bless his heart, Bren just kept rolling with the punches that seemed to pummel Janie Lyn at every turn.

"What is all of this?" Janie Lyn sat on the grass between her grandparents' graves. Bren had stayed behind to sit on a bench under a beautiful magnolia tree, probably calling Maxwell to warn him away from Janie Lyn's insane life. "I don't understand. Why didn't you tell me your plans? Why didn't I meet your friends, the people you trusted the most? And why didn't we visit the horse farm? Or go on vacations? Or find my parents? If those *things* weren't important, then why did you have them? Why did you leave them for me? And if they were important, why didn't we enjoy them? Together? I loved the bakery. I thought you both did, too. Was it only a job? Was I wrong about everything? Was my entire life a lie?" She closed her eyes, trying to hear answers in the breeze, trying to sense her grandparents' presence so she wouldn't feel so lost.

"You okay?" Bren asked from behind her. She wiped the tears from her face before twisting to look up at him. He extended a hand, and she grabbed it to pull herself to her feet.

"I'm desperate for clarity and afraid it will never come."

"That was a doozy of a meeting, but one thing I learned from it…" He paused until she stopped walking to look at him again. "Your grandparents loved you mightily."

"I want to do what they would have done…what I think they would want me to do now."

"Okay," he agreed. "Do you know what that is?"

"Yes, I think I do," she said with a new determination.

Bren took Janie Lyn back to town. They got lunch at a Greek sandwich shop and made notes on napkins while they ate. Janie Lyn called the bakery and told the shift manager to halt baking, sell what was in the displays, and arrange a full staff meeting at 8 a.m. the next morning. She requested that former staff members be called and invited, too. Then they walked back into the bank and made all Janie Lyn's plans a reality.

The next forty-eight hours were a whirlwind, but they were good.

She'd worked late into Wednesday night, but Janie Lyn had arranged to do all the things she felt were right for the bakery, the staff and employees, the house, and even the horse farm.

Thursday's meeting at the bakery had gone better than Janie Lyn could've hoped. It had been a gift to see and hug and visit with the people who'd been so much a part of her life. She'd always care for them because they, too, loved Gram and Pops; that was a connection that would withstand any distance.

Standing tall with her shoulders back, she'd faced the onslaught of curiosity at the courthouse on Friday. It had been another long day, but looking upon her uncle and her attacker, Janie Lyn had felt…nothing. She was proud of herself, confident that Gram and Pops were proud of her, too.

Saturday morning, she was happy to board the plane for home.

Janie Lyn watched out the window as they flew over the Georgia terrain.

"Bren?" He'd just closed his eyes, but she knew he wasn't asleep.

"Yes?"

"You used the word *mightily*," she said.

"Yes…" he said again.

"You said that Gram and Pops loved me mightily. What did you mean?"

He opened his eyes and turned his head to look at her. Then he laid a hand over hers. With a kind smile he said, "They protected you by giving you a home — not just a house — when your parents abandoned you, but a *home* full of love and happiness. Then they provided a community and a place for you to belong at the bakery, which ensured you felt loved and cherished. They equipped you with an education and the means to live whatever life you choose. They protected you, provided for you, and equipped you with everything you need to have a mighty fine life. If that's not loving you mightily, I don't know what is."

She smiled, really liking his answer. She laid her head against his shoulder.

"Bren?"

"Yes?"

"Take me home to Maxwell?"

"Yes, ma'am, without a moment's delay."

36

*Love can only be found
through the act of loving.
By the River Piedra I Sat Down and Wept
by Paulo Coelho*

"Were you nervous about the game?" Max asked.

Another good one, Max had scored one touchdown and picked up two crucial first downs. The offense had been clicking, moving up and down the field at a great tempo and finishing their drives with points. Coach said that made it their best win so far for the season, but Max had his own reason for it being the best win: Janie Lyn was there to share it with him.

After the game, the entire crew — Janie Lyn and Max, Maree and Rhys, M'Kenzee, Bren, Campbell and his wife Gloria, and a couple of other players with their girlfriends — filled a private dining room at Josephine's for a fantastic meal. Mary Beth had sent dish after dish to their table, starting with fried cauliflower and a zippy dipping sauce, followed by brown sugar bacon and blue cheese crumbles drizzled over wedge salad the size of a baseball glove, only to be bested by entreés of pastas, vegetables, and meats so tender they fell off his fork. Max hadn't left an inch of space for dessert…nor had he declined their server's offer to box up a full carrot cake to take home. It would've been rude to refuse, and besides, Mary Beth's pastry chef used plenty of juicy raisins in the batter and lavished all three layers of cake with tangy and rich cream cheese frosting, just the way Max liked it.

Then, the perfect end to an ideal day, Max relaxed on the couch with Janie Lyn. He'd pulled her onto his lap and was feeling, as the saying went, "fat and happy."

Max wondered if she'd drifted to sleep on his shoulder when she didn't answer his question. She'd been a trooper, claiming she wasn't afraid to go back to the stadium, but she must've experienced at least some trepidation after all she'd been through at the first game she attended. Those emotions coupled with a stressful, nail-biting type of game would tire anyone out. Add to that a night out with friends, and she must have been completely spent.

He snuggled her closer, and the jostling woke her.

"Hmm?" she asked. "Sorry. Did you ask me something?" The groggy sleepiness in her voice brought him joy. *Silly, really, that a brief nap on the couch, a few minutes of her closing her eyes while resting in my arms, feels so good.*

"It's okay. You sleep."

"I didn't mean to doze off. What was it?" She nudged her shoulder against him, "Ask me again."

"Were you nervous about the game?" he repeated.

"A little," she said. "Bren and Rhys were unwavering bodyguards glued to either side of me all day. It was a good thing I never needed to visit the ladies' room." She laughed and paused for a breath. Then she turned toward him with an endearing smile and continued. "But I was more nervous when the Patriots kept negating our touchdowns. We worked so hard to score, and then they'd march right down the field to match it."

"Their quarterback is pretty good," Max said begrudgingly.

"Yes, I think I heard that somewhere," Janie Lyn teased.

"You and Mary Beth seemed thick as thieves at dinner," he commented.

"She's brilliant! And we have big plans."

"Do I get to hear them?" Max asked.

"Soon," she told him.

"Do they have anything to do with the burnt-out warehouse you were talking to Rhys about? Or the shipment of kitchen appliances Bren said should arrive in Green Hills in a few weeks?"

"Maybe." *Mayh-bay.* His girl could flirt in two languages.

"I've been thinking," Max said, smoothing a hand over her temple to tuck a strand of hair behind her ear. He ran the lock between his fingers and thumb. His eyes followed his hand.

"Mm-hmm," she said playfully.

"About your name," he announced.

Janie Lyn straightened, but she didn't leave her perch on his knees.

"What about it?"

Max moved his hands to rest on either side of her waist. She might try to move to sit beside him on the couch, and he wasn't willing to let her go even that far.

"Well, what do you want to be called? Elizabeth doesn't sound quite right, but it's your choice. You get to be whoever you want to be."

"Elizabeth doesn't *feel* right either," she confessed. "Gram called me Janie when I was a little girl. At night, she'd tuck me into bed and say, *Oh, how I love you, Elizabeth Jayne, my sweet Janie Lyn.* Then she'd kiss my nose and pack my covers around me like a burrito." She smiled at the fond memory. "When I was running from Athens after she died, I'd close my eyes and listen to that memory in my head over and over. It kept me going when I didn't think I could take another step. When we were sitting in the diner in Tulsa and Rachel and Suzanne asked my name, that's what tumbled out. That's what felt right."

"I love that diner." He winked at Janie Lyn and enjoyed the color that immediately blushed her cheeks.

"I'm not Lizzy anymore. And Elizabeth feels like a stranger," she mused as she turned to put her shoulder against him, curling into his hug.

Max liked her cheek pressing into his heart. He snuggled her deeper into the sheltering cage of his arms.

He inched his hips forward on the cushion, and Janie Lyn straightened her legs along the length of the sofa. Max leaned them back to recline against the couch.

He was content to sit right there, holding her against his chest for hours.

"Janie Lyn still feels right. I think I've grown into her."

"She *is* pretty darn amazing," Max conceded. He felt her cheek shift into a smile. "So, I should call you Janie Lyn Lyndale?"

"No, that sounds silly."

"Then what will you do for a last name?" Max's heart skipped a beat. He was hopeful and fishing for the answer he wanted above all else.

Janie Lyn sat up, forcing Max to drop his arms. She scooted back onto his legs, moving one of hers to the other side to plant her feet on either side of his hips. Then she gathered and flipped her hair, just as she had standing beside his pool, dripping water on the deck that first day, the day he finally saw her.

She tilted her chin and studied him in that way she often did.

This was it. This was the rest of his life. Cherishing her, holding her, supporting her. Loving her. *This was it.*

She traced a finger down his jawline and slid her thumb across his bottom lip. Then she smoothed her palm down the side of his face and neck, petting him while admiration gleamed in her gaze.

His heart ceased beating altogether. He waited with bated breath.

"Why," she said, drawing it out until it dripped with Southern charm as she lifted her eyes to his. "I thought I'd take yours."

Love is not written on paper,
for paper can be erased.

***Nor is it etched on stone,
for stone can be broken.
But it is inscribed on a heart
and there it shall remain forever.
Rumi***

―――

The End.

But not for long. Please enjoy this sneak peek into Book 3…

THREE TIMES TO MAKE SURE

*I'll try anything once,
twice if I like it,
three times to make sure.
Mae West*

Three Months Ago — Kansas City, Missouri

"Max, I—" M'Kenzee Davenport didn't get a chance to finish what she wanted to say as her big brother stormed through the room. He gave their sister's fiancé a tight nod, and disappeared into the training room where doctors and trainers buzzed around their friend Janie Lyn after she'd been brutally attacked on their way to the concession stand during Max's football game.

OHHH!

M'Kenzee stomped her foot, enraged at his dismissal. She needed to tell him something, and she would not be ignored.

"Ma'am, I'm sorry, but you're still not allowed in here." The agent guarding the door grated on M'Kenzee's last nerve. She'd already tried to reason with him multiple times, and he refused to pay attention. To make matters worse, Max couldn't be bothered to even acknowledge her. How ridiculous.

"But I have to talk to someone about what's happened," she said. *Again.*

"Officers will get around to your statement when they can. Until then, you need to stay out here." He didn't even look at her as he brushed her off.

"You just let my brother—"

"Ma'am, don't make me tell you again," he threatened, looking up at her from where he sat in a chair just outside the door she needed to enter. His eye contact lasted for only an instant before his gaze went back to his phone.

The little twerp didn't look old enough to shave. M'Kenzee could take him…even with his shiny FBI windbreaker, his fancy badge hanging on a lanyard around his neck, and the compact sidepiece strapped in the holster on his belt. *If this guy illustrates the future of law enforcement in America, our country is in grave peril.*

"If you could just—"

He scooted his chair sideways to ignore her.

She'd had enough.

M'Kenzee looked over her shoulder. The rest of their group huddled in the far corner, seemingly fine together. She inhaled to shore up her resolve and shoved the door open behind the agent.

In his scrambling alarm, she sidestepped the agent and entered the training room to see Max sitting beside Janie Lyn's physical therapy table. Her eyes were closed, her face and arms already turning black and blue, and her hair and clothes were crusted in dried blood. Max held her hand. He leaned forward, his forehead resting on the cushion next to her arm.

M'Kenzee stopped short.

If a picture spoke a thousand words, the scene before her narrated an epic novel of despair.

Ohhh.

She'd had no idea. Their little sister, Maree, had hinted that she thought something might be going on between Janie Lyn and their big brother, Max, but Maree, a hopeless romantic, liked to imagine the whole world was falling in love at any given moment. M'Kenzee usually allowed Maree's ramblings to go in one ear and out the other without giving them too much credence.

M'Kenzee knew Janie Lyn had spent a few days in Kansas City. M'Kenzee assumed Janie Lyn needed to help Max with a few house projects he couldn't make time for during the football season. Clearly, there was more to it.

"Ma'am, you cannot go in there!"

The agent reached forward to grab M'Kenzee. Her natural instinct to protect herself kicked in. In a defensive move, she turned to twist the man's arm behind his back when a strong, deep voice behind her took control without even rising in volume.

"She's fine, Agent Nadir."

Oh.

M'Kenzee knew that voice.

She released the agent and lifted her hands in compliance. Agent Nadir snarled at her, clearly embarrassed that he'd been about to be bested by a civilian, and a girl at that. She raised an eyebrow and pursed her lips, a silent challenge. His features twisted. She hoped he didn't spit on her...for his sake.

"That'll be all, Agent Nadir," the man across the room said, clearly still in charge and dismissing the weasel.

M'Kenzee closed her eyes, dreading this moment.

"Hello, M—" Brennigan Stewart's Scottish brogue had a distinctive, mocking tone about it.

M'Kenzee whirled to face him before he could finish the greeting. Shooting daggers his way, the look in her eyes threatened his death if he said the wrong thing.

"—Kenzee." He chose wisely. "Max is spending a moment with Janie Lyn. The team doctor sutured a pretty nasty cut, and she's going to be terribly bruised. Otherwise, she seems to be okay, all things considered."

A family outing to cheer on her older brother, Max, who played tight end for the Kansas City Chiefs, had somehow turned into a crazy, chaotic afternoon.

Wanting to grab drinks and a pretzel before the second half

started, M'Kenzee and Janie Lyn had been making their way to the concession stand, fighting their way upstream through the crowd, when they'd gotten separated in the melee.

Next thing M'Kenzee knew, a fierce-looking brute of a man just a few steps ahead of her grabbed Janie Lyn, pulling her away by her hair while Janie Lyn kicked and screamed with all her might.

M'Kenzee began pushing people out of her way, rushing to catch up. Years of working all over the world as a photojournalist had her grabbing the camera hanging around her neck. At the same time, she fought to get closer to Janie Lyn. As second nature, she flicked the power on, aimed the lens toward the action, and clicked photos on the run.

Just as M'Kenzee got close enough to lunge for Janie Lyn, the hulk noticed M'Kenzee. He shoved Janie Lyn into a tiled concrete column in the concourse of the stadium. M'Kenzee heard Janie Lyn cry out as her face cracked against the structure.

"Help us!" M'Kenzee shrieked as security officers ran toward them.

When they were mere steps away, the would-be abductor finally released Janie Lyn, giving her one last shove to the ground as he pushed people toward them and ran.

M'Kenzee didn't wait to see which way he went; she dropped to Janie Lyn, a huddled heap on the floor.

Within a minute, the EMTs arrived, put Janie Lyn on a medical cart, and drove her down the ramps to the team facilities under the stadium. Since then, M'Kenzee had been desperate to figure out what had happened, get a detailed update on Janie Lyn, and find someone official to share what little she did know. The entire ordeal felt surreal. Unbelievable!

To make matters worse — *infinitely* worse — she stood face to face with Bren.

Well over six feet tall with disheveled auburn hair, a thick day-old beard, and startling green eyes, he looked exactly as she remembered. Perfect.

Every bit the confident FBI agent, he reeked of power and superiority.

"Why are you here?" she asked without preamble.

"I'm sure Max will fill you in when he can," he said instead of answering.

"I need to talk to someone, and no one will hear me out. I was with Janie Lyn when that man—," M'Kenzee started saying.

"Are you okay?" he interrupted. His voice didn't change, but the alertness in his eyes reached a new level.

"I'm fine. But I need to talk to someone. I saw him and tried to stop him. I scraped my nails down his disgusting face and arm. Maybe there's enough DNA to help find him. Also, I have to give this memory card to someone. They're not my best work, to say the least, but I got photos of the guy attacking Janie Lyn."

Bren just stood there, looking at her. His eyes darted over her features, down her body, and back up to her face. He studied her dark blond hair. What did he think of the pixie style, so different from the last time he'd seen it? His thoughts were unreadable as his gaze lingered on her mouth. She felt the caress across her lips, although he still stood several feet away and had not even touched her.

It made her uneasy. And when her hackles went up, her temper went with them. She lifted her chin, determined not to let her nerves show.

"I'm very glad you're not hurt." His voice rasped. His words were for her ears only.

M'Kenzee's heart rate sped up. He walked forward until they were so close that she could smell the heady, spicy scent of his cologne. Still, she refused to back down.

"Who should I see about the DNA? And who wants the memory card?"

"I'll take the card," Bren said, holding out his hand. M'Kenzee hated that her own hand trembled when she removed the card from her camera and set it in his open palm.

Bren clasped her shaking hand with his other one, immediately running his thumb over the back of her knuckles. Was he trying to calm and soothe her? Or was he testing the softness of her skin for himself?

Book 3, Chapter 1

She tried to pull away, but he held on.

"We need to get that DNA," Bren murmured. He didn't release her hand, but he did call a forensic tech over to scrape her nails and collect a sample. Once done, Bren walked M'Kenzee to a sink, turned the faucet on, and lifted her hands under the stream of warm water.

"I can wash my own hands," she grumbled when Bren lathered soap in his own hands and started massaging the suds into her fingers.

But she didn't stop him.

His touch felt too good.

Once he'd rinsed their hands, turned off the water, and pulled a few paper towels from the dispenser, she'd gathered her wits enough to yank away one of the towels.

"Always so prickly," Bren mused.

M'Kenzee finished drying her hands with jerky motions, wadded up the towel, and chucked it in the trash can. Finished with this little encounter, she moved to leave. Bren reached out once more and took hold of her arm when she walked past him.

She felt the warmth of his firm, yet gentle grasp all the way to the pit of her stomach. She kept her eyes glued to the floor.

"You're as gorgeous as ever," Bren said in a low, husky voice, his Scottish brogue deep and pronounced, a sure sign that he'd lifted the veil of his cool veneer.

"You shouldn't talk like that," M'Kenzee replied. She tried to sound indifferent, but her own voice betrayed her.

"Why not?" Bren countered, pulling her arm toward him until she finally met his gaze. M'Kenzee took in the gleam in his emerald green eyes, the flecks of white diamonds that made them glisten. She indulged in one last sniff of his scent, so masculine and clean. She even enjoyed their test of wills for a split second before he spoke again. "Can't a man compliment his wife?"

ABOUT THE AUTHOR

Ashli Montgomery is a wife, a momma, and an author whose passion is sharing love stories, books, quilts, yoga, recipes, and all of her favorite things in life. She is quilting to mend the mind by spearheading a community of quilters through Quilt 2 End ALZ, Inc., a 501(c)(3) nonprofit she launched to use her quilting hobby as a platform to advocate for an end to Alzheimer's disease.

Ashli writes wholesome and heartfelt, small-town romance under the pen name Virginia'dele Smith to honor Syble Virginia Tidwell, Adele Gertrude Baylin, and Etta Jean Smith. These three cherished grandmothers were beautiful role models, teaching Ashli to love without judgment and always put family first. Through Grandma Syble's journals and appetite for books, through Momadele's priceless cards and handwritten letters, and through many, many hours of visiting over fabric at Mema's kitchen island, Ashli also learned to treasure words.

You are invited to join Ashli in Green Hills, check out *Book 0: My Manifesto*, a behind-the-scenes biography from Virginia'dele Smith, and learn more about the author by subscribing to Ashli's newsletter, *The Gazette*, at www.AshliMontgomery.com

CPSIA information can be obtained
at www.ICGtesting.com
Printed in the USA
BVHW040304240822
645327BV00005B/9/J

9 781957 036083